Methodological Thinking

Methodological Thinking

Basic Principles of Social Research Design

DONILEEN R. LOSEKE

University of South Florida

Los Angeles | London | New Delhi
Singapore | Washington DC

Los Angeles | London | New Delhi
Singapore | Washington DC

FOR INFORMATION:

SAGE Publications, Inc.
2455 Teller Road
Thousand Oaks, California 91320
E-mail: order@sagepub.com

SAGE Publications Ltd.
1 Oliver's Yard
55 City Road
London EC1Y 1SP
United Kingdom

SAGE Publications India Pvt. Ltd.
B 1/I 1 Mohan Cooperative Industrial Area
Mathura Road, New Delhi 110 044
India

SAGE Publications Asia-Pacific Pte. Ltd.
3 Church Street
#10-04 Samsung Hub
Singapore 049483

Acquisitions Editor: Jerry Westby
Editorial Assistant: Laura Cheung
Production Editor: Laureen Gleason
Copy Editor: Erin Livingston
Typesetter: C&M Digitals (P) Ltd.
Proofreader: Kate Peterson
Indexer: Michael Ferreira
Cover Designer: Anupama Krishnan
Marketing Manager: Terra Schultz
Permissions Editor: Karen Ehrmann

Printed in the United States of America

Library of Congress Cataloging-in-Publication Data

Loseke, Donileen R., 1947-

Methodological thinking : basic principles of social research design / Donileen R. Loseke.

p. cm.
Includes bibliographical references and index.

ISBN 978-1-4129-9720-1 (pbk.)

1. Social sciences—Methodology.
2. Social sciences—Research—Methodology.
I. Title.

H61.L587 2013
300.72—dc23   2011040900

This book is printed on acid-free paper.

Certified Chain of Custody
Promoting Sustainable Forestry
www.sfiprogram.org
SFI-01268

SFI label applies to text stock

12 13 14 15 16 10 9 8 7 6 5 4 3 2 1

BRIEF CONTENTS

DETAILED CONTENTS

LIST OF EXHIBITS

PREFACE

-·-◆-·-

As I started writing this, a new SAGE Publications catalog containing 87 pages of books about methods and statistics appeared in my mailbox. I paused to ask myself the obvious question: Is another book really necessary? I need to justify why I hope what I offer here will be helpful to those who teach social research methods and to those who study them. I will begin by describing what I see as common problems in the outcomes of methods courses, because these are what I am responding to in the following pages.

For several years, I taught methods courses to undergraduates and more recently to first-year graduate students. I also currently teach senior seminar and a range of substantive sociology courses that require undergraduates to design and conduct small-scale research projects, and I sponsor thesis research projects of MA students. These experiences have led me to three observations: First, while textbooks tend to focus on training students how to *do* research, most undergraduates do not plan to become researchers. They are in these courses because they are a requirement; they are something to suffer through in order to complete a social science major. Emphasizing the *how to* aspects of research is a disservice to undergraduates who have no practical need for this knowledge. More important is what these students—what all students—need to learn is how research methods are ways of *thinking* about the world.

My second observation is related: Research methods classes tend not to give students the knowledge and skills necessary to evaluate research done by others. This is troublesome because while very few undergraduates go on to become social researchers, all students are consumers of research. Knowing how to evaluate truth claims is an increasingly important skill in our mass-mediated world.

My third observation comes from working with advanced undergraduate students in their senior seminars and with graduate students designing thesis research: Methods courses often do not prepare those students who *do* go on to design research. Students tend to retain miscellaneous factoids of information from these courses—how to use a table of random numbers to select a sample, the definitions of five types of internal validity, and so on—but these are not accompanied by deeper understandings about the importance of sampling, the meanings of relationships between concepts and operationalizations, the meanings of relationships between research questions and techniques for data collection, and so on. Simply stated, students do not understand the principles behind the technical details they have memorized. Courses that successfully convey an extraordinary amount of information are not always so victorious in building a way of thinking. This is unfortunate, because my experiences as a teacher and journal editor have taught me that research projects rarely fail because of one technical error or another. Projects fail because of errors in methodology such as faulty operationalization, posing a question that is too complex, using a research technique not capable of producing appropriate data, and so on.

In describing what I perceive as problems with outcomes of research methods courses, I simultaneously have described my vision of what these classes should accomplish: I want students to understand social research as a set of tools for examining the mysteries of social life. I want them to learn how to think critically, to ask questions about what they see and hear in daily life, and to understand the underlying logic of social research.

My hunch is that many instructors have similar goals of training students how to think, how to question, and how to evaluate. But I also believe that widely available standard textbooks can work against achieving these goals. Books in this standard methods textbook genre are big, with 15 to 18 chapters covering all aspects of research design, research implementation, and data analysis. Often they contain appendixes of random numbers, chi-square distribution tables, tables of areas under the normal curve, and so on. While texts in this tradition do a fine job of introducing students to the vocabularies, general issues, and technical details in social research, they simultaneously lead to the problems I described.

First, standard texts are characterized by a great deal of attention to method and not enough attention to methodology. Sometimes methodology— the underlying logic and principles of research methods—is not covered in any depth; sometimes, methodology is covered but lost in a blizzard of vocabulary definitions and technical details. Second, standard textbook genre books tend to reflect traditional beliefs equating *social* science research methods with *natural* science research methods. At times, standard texts simply define natural science methods as the backbone of social research and contain little discussion of the diversity of research methods in the modern era. At other times, these texts cover *quantitative* methods and *qualitative* methods in neatly separated sections. This encourages students to think in terms of stereotypes; it misrepresents the real world where excellent research often does not fit ideal images; it even can lead students to believe that qualitative and quantitative methods are in a contest and that students must choose between them. This is not good.

I think of the book that follows as a modest attempt to promote methodological thinking, to encourage students to think about research and to learn something about its underlying principles and logic. What I am assuming is that this book will be used as a supplement to a standard textbook in introduction to social research classes, particularly those in sociology, political science, criminology, and communications. It can also be used as a stand-alone book in a variety of classes such as senior seminars or honors seminars at the undergraduate level, as well as content courses at the advanced undergraduate and graduate levels, where students are asked to produce independent research and could benefit from being reminded about the general principles of social research design.

With this in mind, the book that follows has the following characteristics:

1. It brackets the technical details of social research design in order to emphasize logic and general principles. I observed earlier that standard textbooks are heavy on details and light on general principles of research design; the following is heavy on principles and light on details.

2. It develops social research as detective work to explore the mysteries of social life and research methods as a set of tools for that work. Conceptualizing methods as a set of tools leads to my recurring comments that just as it makes sense to use hammers and saws and pliers to accomplish different tasks, it makes sense to develop different forms of research to explore different types of questions. The repeated, explicit lessons throughout these pages state that it is *not* possible to argue that one or another form of research is better than any other and that good researchers understand the differences among—and appreciate the capabilities of—different tools.

3. It draws attention to how all aspects of study design should form a coherent package. While chapters proceed in a logical order—from forming questions to doing reviews of literature to conceptualization and operationalization to choosing data generation techniques to sampling to writing—each chapter concludes by highlighting the relationships among study design components.

4. It develops models of research (positivist, interpretive, and critical) and forms of data (numerical and verbal) in terms of their relationships to research design. In each chapter, I show how different models of research lead to different kinds of questions about social life, different

types of operationalizations, data generation techniques, and so on. I repeatedly discuss the impossibility of evaluating one model of research or form of data as better than any other.

5. It pays attention to teaching students how to develop the skills to evaluate the quality of research done by others as well as to design small-scale research of their own. It is organized to help students become good consumers of research as well as good producers of research.

6. It demonstrates the principles of research by using examples from published research. Throughout this book, I use eight published research articles representing different kinds of research questions and different kinds of data generation techniques. Although I edited the articles to highlight the methods, students can see how real research defines questions, makes use of existing knowledge, conceptualizes and operationalizes, and so on. By using the same articles throughout the book, I hope students can see both how real research is designed and how design is a package of components. A web-based student study site, available at **www.sagepub.com/loseke**, provides access to the full versions of the journal articles that are referenced throughout the text.

In summary, what I hope to accomplish here is encourage students to *think*: to think about social research as set of powerful tools to examine the mysteries of social life, to think about how to ask questions that can be answered using these tools, to think about how to design the best research possible, and to think about how to evaluate the research done by others. Methodological thinking—that is what I was thinking about when I wrote these pages.

ACKNOWLEDGMENTS

SAGE and the author gratefully acknowledge the contributions of the following reviewers:

James David Ballard, *California State University, Northridge*

Ellen Berg, *California State University, Sacramento*

Jacqueline Carrigan, *California State University, Sacramento*

Lance Erickson, *Brigham Young University*

Kenneth E. Fernandez, *University of Nevada, Las Vegas*

Lori Helene Gronich, *The George Washington University*

Kim M. Lloyd, *Washington State University*

Elizabeth Monk-Turner, *Old Dominion University*

Linda Renzulli, *The University of Georgia*

Warren Waren, *University of Central Florida*

Marion C. Willetts, *Illinois State University*

ONE

EXPLORING THE WORLD OF SOCIAL RESEARCH DESIGN

——————•◦•——————

Y ou know from the title that this book is about social research. I will begin by asking some questions to encourage you to start thinking about what social research *is*. This is the first step to thinking about how research can be designed in order to produce information about the social world that is of the highest possible quality.

Most people reading this book will be students, and if you are a student, you probably live in a world where you take endless tests that measure *what* you know. My question is different: *How* do you know what you know? A characteristic of the current world is that we have too much information from too many sources. We know about the world from our practical experiences. We learn about the world as we go through our daily lives, and over time we develop a considerable amount of knowledge from these experiences. We also learn about the world by talking with people we know—family, friends, and coworkers—and we get further information from people we do not know—bloggers, anonymous web page authors, journalists, and talk show hosts. Some people seek information by attending public lectures as well as meetings of religious or social organizations. Students, of course, are in regular contact with textbooks that explicitly teach about the world as well as with teachers whose job it is to teach about the world. I could go on about sources of information, but I probably have made my point: The answer to my question—how do you know what you know?—is that we know through our own experience and through what known and unknown other people tell us. Our environment is saturated with information.

Although we gain much knowledge about the world without explicitly searching it out, my second question is about information that you do actively seek: *Where* do you go when you have a question you need answered? Of course, the answer depends on the type of question being asked. Questions in daily life (Should I apply for this job? Why is my best friend angry at me?) are often answered by relying on prior experiences and common sense or by asking trusted friends or respected elders. There are self-help books, websites, and support groups for questions about personal troubles, and all sorts of questions can be answered in websites such as Wikipedia or Ask.com.

Our technological, mediated world has made it easy to find answers to just about any question at any time. This leads to my next question: How do you know what information can be *trusted*? Our complex era makes assessing the probable truth of information very difficult. Here is a short summary of what I am sure you already know: Anyone can become a blogger, conveying his or her opinions to everyone on everything from how to be a good mother to how to manage foreign policy; any person, group, or organization can set up a website to promote any personal, social, political, religious, or economic agenda. Some online publishers automatically accept *any* manuscript written by *any* person on *any* topic. Indeed, people who wish to be authors do not even need to go through publishing companies, because technology allows self-publishing without any review by anyone. In these and countless other ways, information can come to us unfiltered, without any review, and without even a pretense that it has any relationship to something that can be recognized as truth.

This is not good. In daily life, each of us has countless needs for trustworthy information. Parents need information to help make decisions about sending their children to public or charter schools; patients need information to make decisions about what medical treatments furnish the best hope; consumers need to know how to evaluate the quality of products; citizens need information to decide how to vote on policies that will affect millions, tens of millions, or hundreds of millions of people.

Traditional means of assessing the likely truth value of information—trusting particular categories of people such as elders and church leaders, relying on practical experience, or plain old-fashioned common sense—still can be used as yardsticks to judge the likely credibility of some of what we see and hear. Yet as our world grows larger and more complex, these traditional ways of evaluating knowledge are insufficient. How can we rely on our personal experiences to make decisions about which public policies to support when the policies are targeted to people we do not know, to people we never have met? Does the wisdom of elders extend to knowledge about the benefits and limitations of the most current medical or computer technology? We live in an increasingly complex, global, and technological social order, and many of the questions generated in such places cannot be answered by relying on tradition, the wisdom of elders, personal experience, or common sense.

This takes me to my specific topic of *social research*, which is one way of generating information about the social world as well as one way of evaluating the quality of information about that world. I begin with the obvious: What is social research?

DEFINING SOCIAL RESEARCH

While social research is only one of many ways to search for answers to questions, it is a very important way. Think about how often you have been asked to accept something because it is "based on research." It sometimes seems that merely saying that information "is based on research" is asserting its truth value. From validating statements about what kinds of food and exercise lead to good health to supporting advice about how to have a happy marriage to upholding claims about how and what schools should teach, the term *research* seems to have magical powers in making something true.

What is it about social research that encourages trust? Here is a basic definition of social research, the parts of which combine to give the idea of social research its power:

> Social research is the systematic and empirical exploration of human social life.

Exploration: The central term in this definition is exploration. Social research is about exploring the mysteries of social life. Social life contains countless mysteries: Why do some people become saints while others become sadists? What are the causes and consequences of poverty? What are relationships between gender and crime or between race and voting behavior? How do people fall in love? Social research of any type is detective work in the truest sense; it is detective work to explore the mysteries of social life.

Systematic: As with all detective work, research is not a haphazard search for clues; it is *systematic*. Just as good detectives proceed cautiously in finding and developing clues, good researchers work in ways that can be described as structured, orderly, methodical, coherent, consistent, and logical.

Empirical: The exploration in social research is systematic and it also is *empirical*, meaning that it is evidence-based. Evidence in research is called *data*, and data are defined as what we can sense about the social world— what we can see, hear, smell, touch, and taste. Most data in social research are from sight and sound: what people say (in talk or in writing), what people do, or records of what people have said and/or done in the past. While I will discuss the many types of data and the multiple techniques that can generate data, all research shares the characteristic that it is based on evidence. Stated simply, it is *not* research when people (no matter how smart they are) argue that something is true because they say it is true. In research, something is true because we can sense it—we can see it, hear it, touch it, smell it, or feel it.

Social Life: The final term in the definition of social research describes the types of mysteries that interest social researchers. These are the mysteries of human social life associated with several academic disciplines, including sociology, anthropology, history, criminology, political science, psychology, gender studies, social work, public health, and communications. Although there are major differences in the types of questions associated with each of these academic areas, what they all share is a primary interest in people. So while geologists study the physical causes of volcanic eruptions, social researchers are more interested in how these eruptions influence people. While biologists study physical and chemical workings of human reproductive systems, social researchers are interested in questions about the social nature and social consequences of fertility and reproduction.

Social research is a particular way of obtaining information about the social world. It requires actually looking at and listening to what is in this world rather than merely speculating about what might be in it. Research requires careful, rather than haphazard, detective work. Information from social research can be highly valued precisely because these characteristics offer the potential for generating information that is of the highest possible quality.

Social Research and Other Ways of Knowing

The definition of social research as the systematic, empirical exploration of human social life distinguishes it from other ways of knowing. Knowledge from social research is not generated by the same methods or evaluated by the same criteria as knowledge from philosophy, religion, or art; knowledge from social research only occasionally confirms what we learn from our own practical experience or what seems to be common sense.

> Social research is a particular way of generating knowledge about the social world.

Saying that knowledge from social research is different from knowledge generated by other ways of knowing is *not* saying that other forms of knowledge are inferior. Different means different. However, for two practical reasons, it is important for you to understand how social research works even if you personally evaluate other ways of knowing as more important. First, understanding how social research works will give you a set of skills that can serve you well in your daily life as you do your own research to make decisions, such as where to live or what kinds of household appliances are most economical. The skills you learn by studying social research will be useful in doing detective work on a wide variety of questions. Second, we are often told what we should do and think based on social research. If you understand how research works, you will be able to ask questions about the research producing the results. You will not need to simply accept findings because someone says they are true nor will you be forced to rely only on your personal biases to decide the probable truth value of what you are told. This knowledge gives you the power to make your own evaluations.

This takes me to the next topic: evaluating research. While relatively few people want or need to *design* social research, the skills to *evaluate* research are becoming increasingly important as our information-saturated environment simultaneously produces both more information and fewer oversights on information credibility. For this reason, I think this book is about evaluating research as much as it is about designing research.

EVALUATING SOCIAL RESEARCH

While social research is an excellent method to generate information about the world, not all social research is high quality. One of my primary goals for this book is to help you gain some insight into the characteristics of high-quality research. The general lesson is quite easy:

> Rules and standards define the expectations for high-quality social research.

The results of social research deserve to be seriously considered when— and only when—research design, implementation, and data analysis all have been done according to rules and standards. Although there are many variations in how these rules and standards are defined by different subcommunities of researchers, a large part of the systematic nature of social research comes from rules and standards that are enforced by research communities. To take obvious examples: class projects as well as thesis and dissertation research are evaluated by faculty members who judge the extent to which research meets standards; reports of research submitted to journals for potential publication are evaluated by reviewers and editors and, if published, will be evaluated by the people who read the journal. Although there can be disagreements about the *precise* content of rules and standards, there is no disagreement that social research is rule bound.

THE STUDY OF SOCIAL RESEARCH DESIGN

It is not uncommon for social science students to approach their research methods courses with dread. The term *research* often conjures images of scientists as men in white coats who talk in ways that make them seem much smarter than the rest of us. The term *research* also can be associated with unappealing images of experiments with rats or frogs. For many reasons, some understandable and some simply unfortunate, students can find the actual experience of their research methods courses parallels their negative expectations. Negative experiences are at least partially created by the tendency of introductory methods courses to emphasize learning the vocabularies and technical details of research methods.

To be absolutely clear, facts are important, and communication is not possible unless we all understand and use common vocabularies. So the typical contents of social research methods classes and textbooks are *necessary*. However, a regrettable consequence of stressing the rule-bound nature of research is that it encourages students to memorize vocabularies and technicalities without understanding what anything actually *means*, without understanding research methods as ways of knowing about the social world.

This is where I hope to intervene. My interests are in helping you—the person reading this book—to understand the *reasons* for the rules governing social research, which means learning about the kinds of thinking behind the rules.

I am limiting my focus in two ways. First, I will cover only those topics connected with social research design: the tasks of forming questions, showing why questions are important, conceptualizing and perhaps operationalizing the major study concepts, developing techniques of data generation, choosing a sample, and writing a report of results. I will *not* talk about how social research design is implemented—how interviews or observations are done or how documents are coded—or how data are analyzed.

My second limitation is that I will emphasize what is often ignored in regular methods textbooks or what can get lost in the blizzard of technical details characterizing those texts. While social research textbooks typically are about how to *do* social research, my interest is in how to *think* about it. I will call this *methodological thinking*, which is a way of thinking underlying the rules, procedures, and vocabulary associated with research methods. I have learned from my teaching experience that people who first learn about research as a way of thinking find it relatively easy to then learn the specific rules and technicalities, because these follow logically from the basic principles.

So that is my plan: I will leave it to others to tell you the very important technical information about how to *do* research, and I will focus on encouraging you to *think* about research in particular ways.

BASIC PRINCIPLES OF METHODOLOGICAL THINKING

The remainder of this book will fill in the details and offer many examples of the following basic principles of the kind of thinking I want to promote. Consider these a series of guidelines about how to approach social research design. What I would like you to notice is how these themes are basic and straightforward. As with social research itself, there is nothing mysterious or complicated about these points *as long as you think*.

Think Critically

A book on research methods should begin and end with the importance of critical thinking; everything between the beginning and the end should be about critical thinking. The elements of social research methods are no more and no less important than the consequences of thinking about how to gather information about human social life in ways that will lead to the highest-quality information possible. The best way to think about critical thinking is that it is *thinking about thinking*.

> Critical thinking is thinking about thinking: It is analyzing and evaluating what you think and why you think it.

Critical thinking means analyzing and evaluating; it means not accepting information simply because you agree with it or like the implications and not rejecting information simply because you disagree with it or dislike the implications. Critical thinking requires thinking about biases—your personal biases as well as those from disciplinary and methodological preferences—and how they influence decisions about how to do and evaluate research. Critical thinking as it applies to research also requires understanding that how the general public understands research can be different from how researchers think about it.

Although thinking—questioning, assessing, and appraising—is something humans *can* do, it is not something we do automatically. Scientists studying cognition have found that human brains simply are not capable of consciously processing *all* the information coming from *all* of our senses while simultaneously directing the workings of each and every part of our physical bodies. Brains partially compensate for this physical inability by having "nonthinking" as a default mode for incoming information. Stated in another way, while our brains will automatically do a great many things (such as pull our hands from fire or tell us when we need food), evaluating the possible truth value of abstract information is a higher-order brain function that is *not* automatic. Thinking takes effort and thinking takes time.

The first requirement in developing the skills of methodological thinking is to learn how to think critically, and this means learning how to move from the automatic mode of not thinking to the more difficult and time-consuming mode of thinking.

Treat All Knowledge as Tentative

A hallmark of research is that it is characterized by a *critical/skeptical* attitude.

> A critical/skeptical attitude requires treating all knowledge as tentative and subject to change.

Research is a search for the *negative* (which means disconfirming data) and for alternative explanations (called *rival hypotheses*). What this requires is treating all knowledge as tentatively true or as true only until shown otherwise.

This is one of the ways in which public understandings of research are not similar to how researchers think. In daily life, people often talk about how one or another study *proves* something, but within the logic of research of all types (natural science and social science), it is not possible—or desirable—to prove anything. Research can confirm or disconfirm existing knowledge; new data can add to the existing evidence; new data can challenge existing knowledge, but nothing can be proved. It is necessary to think of research as not being able to prove anything, because there would be very negative consequences if things *could* be proved: If something is proved, there is no need to ever question it, and that—simply stated—is not the way to increase knowledge. Everything in science, even something whose facticity is as assured as gravity, retains a formal status as a *theory*—something that could potentially be disproved. Most certainly, it is not that anyone expects that gravity will be disproved. Treating *all* knowledge as tentative is a general attitude that leads to questioning, to thinking, to not simply accepting what is presented as a "truth."

**Understand the Importance of
Each Element of Research Design**

Public understandings of research are not similar to the ways researchers think in another way: It is common for people in the public to limit their visions of research methods to techniques for generating data. Because of this, many people think of all research as equivalent to surveys, interviews, experiments, and so on. This is doubly unfortunate because the techniques used to obtain data are only one element of research design and because deciding what technique is best often comes at the end of the process of research design. Methodological thinking is being attentive to all elements in the design process, including what lies behind the scenes—theoretical perspectives, types of reasoning, understanding the study in relation to the existing scholarly dialogue, characteristics of the research questions, and conceptualization and operationalization. The likely ability of a research design to generate high-quality data depends upon *all* design elements.

> High-quality research design is a package of components that are logically related to one another.

Think Both as a Scientist and as an Artist

Research methodology is a science because it is systematic, it requires understanding and correctly using a precise vocabulary, and it requires the competent use of rules. But all aspects of research—from design to implementation to data analysis—can reflect creativity. Sociologists talk about the importance of the sociological imagination, I think of this as the *methodological imagination*. How can we study topics such as racism when people are unlikely to honestly answer direct questions? How can we safely do research on dangerous topics, such as terrorism or drug dealing? How can we find people in "hidden" populations, such as immigrants who are undocumented? Answers to such questions are not found in rules governing social research; answers are found by thinking creatively.

Methodological thinking is logical and rule-bound, and people who are skilled at this kind of thinking have a good chance of becoming competent researchers. Yet excellent researchers often are more than technically competent—they are excellent, at least in part, because they are creative; they are driven by curiosity. As with good detectives, curious researchers will think. They will figure out creative ways to circumvent the untold numbers and kinds of roadblocks that social life throws up around its mysteries.

This is yet another way in which public understandings of research—or in this case, understandings of researchers—are partial. Yes, good researchers are very logical and systematic, but like effective detectives, good researchers also are creative.

Know the Appropriate Uses of Social Research Tools

The various components of research, from the different kinds of questions that can be asked to the different ways data and samples can be generated, can be understood as the research detective's set of tools—equivalent to the carpenter's tools of hammers, saws, and pliers. This has many implications. First and most clearly, good carpenters understand how to use more than one or two tools. Carpenters who say, "I like saws, so I won't learn how to use hammers," will be greatly confined in what they can build. The more tools a carpenter understands, the better. So it is in methods: Individual researchers might have personal preferences for some data generation techniques, some kinds of questions, or some forms of data, but it is a very good plan to understand as many as possible. It also is important to understand as many tools as possible to avoid the too-common problem of individuals who have strong skills in some kinds of tools and justify their choices by criticizing others. While it certainly *is* true that particular types of questions can best be answered by particular types of techniques or with particular types of data, it makes *no* sense to talk about how some tools are better than others. Just as it would make no sense for a carpenter to say that pliers are better than screwdrivers or that electricity is better than plumbing, it makes *no* sense for a researcher to say that observation is better than surveys or that inductive reasoning is better than deductive reasoning or any other such evaluation. As with carpenters' tools, methodological tools are specialized: Surveys are the best way to collect some kinds of data but only some kinds of data; numbers tell us some things about the social world but only some things; sometimes we need to measure what people think while at other times we need to measure how people actually act, and so on. Methodological thinking means understanding as many research tools as possible. It is understanding that no one type of question, data, or tool used in research is better or worse than any other.

Understand the Characteristics and Consequences
of Methodological Diversity

These are exciting times in social research. As compared with the not-so-distant past, when there was general agreement that research in the social sciences should mimic the goals and organization of research in the natural sciences, our current world contains many choices in how to think about social research, how to design and conduct studies, how to analyze data, and how to present findings. The one model of social research in the past has been replaced with many models today.

This variety of choices is wonderful, because it allows researchers far more creativity than in the past. Yet possibilities for creativity come at a cost: Because there is no longer one accepted model of research, evaluations of the adequacy of research today often are more difficult than in the past. It is not uncommon for any one particular piece of research to be evaluated as excellent by some people, adequate by others, and perhaps as not adequate at all by still others. Methodological thinking requires learning more than one set of rules; it requires thinking about multiple choices and their consequences.

In this book, I hope to encourage you to develop the skills of methodological thinking. These skills will be the foundation upon which you can design high-quality research. Perhaps most important, I anticipate that most people reading this book will not go on to become social researchers, so the skills to design research might not seem important. Yet all of us are consumers of research in our daily lives. Methodological thinking is a skill that will serve you well in making decisions about the quality of research underlying the information that bombards us in daily life.

PLANNING THE STUDY OF RESEARCH DESIGN

I will again describe my goals just to remind you what I am and am not trying to do. I want to help you understand methodological thinking so that you can develop the skills to evaluate the quality of research done by others and to design your own research projects. My focus on how to *think* about research leads me to ignore or only briefly talk about the details of how to *do* research. I do so not because such details are unimportant. On the contrary, good research design *must* reflect adequate attention to all relevant technical details. Yet because there are many textbooks that do a very good job explaining the *what*s and *how*s of social research, I will attend only to the *why* questions—the underlying logic of research design decisions.

The seven chapters following this introduction parallel the arrangement of chapters in many standard methods texts. Chapter 2, "Foundations," considers foundational issues, including the components of all social research (data, concepts, and theories), relationships between data and concepts/ theories (logic), and underlying models of social life (positivist, interpretive, and critical). These are very much like the foundations of houses—critical yet often all-but-invisible. Chapter 3, "Research Questions," proceeds to the topic of writing and evaluating questions leading to research projects; Chapter 4, "Literature Reviews," shows why and how every new research project should be a part of the ongoing scholarly dialogue. Chapter 5, "Measurement," turns to the issue of measurement: how the events, objects, and people of interest in research are defined (conceptualized) and measured (operationalized), and how the quality of these conceptualizations and opera- tionalizations can be evaluated. Chapter 6, "Data Generation Techniques," is a summary of the most common ways to obtain data in social research proj- ects (experiments, surveys, interviews, observations, and document analysis), and Chapter 7, "Samples," looks at the general issues of samples—be they samples of people interviewed, questions asked, places observed, or docu- ments categorized. Finally, Chapter 8, "Summary: Writing and Evaluating Social Research Design," begins with reminders about the importance of critical thinking and then centers on answering questions about how to write about social research design as well as some general ways in which design is evaluated.

I have arranged my comments into these chapters, which I then put in a particular order. While this is a satisfactory order for learning how to evaluate research done by others, I worry about the unintended consequences of my presentation on those of you wanting to design research yourself. I will com- ment in every chapter how it is incorrect to think of research design as a series of tasks that are done once and that are done in a particular order. People who design actual research often find that their original research questions must be modified based on what they learn by reading the existing literature on the topic and/or that the impossibility of obtaining particular samples leads to modifying research questions or proposed research techniques, and so on. I will return to the following point repeatedly, because it is important: Published reports of research typically are cleaned up; they do not include truthful descriptions of the actual messiness of the research process. If you are new to research design, simply assume that new information or problems arising at one stage of the design process will lead you to make changes in other aspects of your research design. When this happens, it will seem to be a setback. While frustrating, however, often what begins as a problem leads to changes in the research that makes research better. The actual process of designing research looks like the following diagram, with every design com- ponent influencing all others:

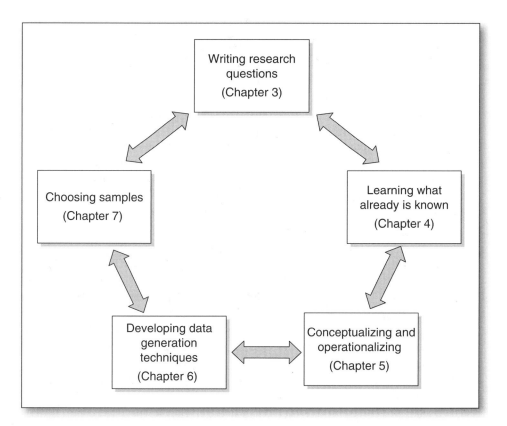

I like this diagram, because the double arrows (⟺) truthfully show that every component of research design influences all others. This is good to remember, because the goal of design is to create research that is a package of ideas with each component—question, existing knowledge, measurement, data generation techniques, and samples—logically related to all others. At the same time, I don't want you to really look closely at this and try to find the way out of the loop: It looks as if this is an endless process! That, of course, is not true; throughout this book I will talk about the very minor modifications that can sometimes be made that will make elements flow together logically.

METHODS IN THEORY AND IN PRACTICE

I think there is similarity between learning about research methods and learning music: You can read a book about how to play a piano, and you can memorize the scale and all the rules about playing the piano, but you will not actually learn how to play until you sit down and do it. Likewise, you can read books defining the characteristics of "good music," but to really understand the differences between good and not-so-good music, you need to listen to a lot of it. So it is with research methods. Abstract talk about methods is not enough to understand what methods look like in real research.

What I want to do is to merge abstract talk about methodology with how design appears in real research. In the appendix, you will find eight (highly edited) published articles that I will use throughout this book to demonstrate my points. A web-based student study site, available at www.sagepub.com/ loseke, also provides access to the full versions of the journal articles that are referenced throughout the text. Because I will return to the same examples over and over, by the end, you should have a fairly detailed understanding of how methodological thinking applies in real-life research.

I used two criteria to choose my eight examples: First, each of my examples has the term *identity* in the title. I chose this topic because it is one of my current interests, because it is a topic explored by researchers in several disciplines, because it can be conceptualized in many ways, and because it leads to many different kinds of research questions. I hope this will encourage you to see an important characteristic of social research: There are multiple and equally good questions about *any* topic. Second, I selected articles in terms of their diversity in order to demonstrate how social research encompasses many varieties of perspectives on social life, types of data, and techniques of data collection.

I did *not* choose articles because I believed they represented especially excellent research. One of my recurring themes throughout this book will be that perfection is not a good standard upon which to evaluate social research. The complicated nature of humans and our lives together leads to many common problems that cannot be wished away. Of course, we always should strive for perfection and find ways to make research better, yet simultaneously we need to understand that less-than-perfect research can offer insights. While the articles I chose are not perfect, each does tell us something about the mysteries of social life.

That is my plan: I hope I can help you develop the ability to think methodologically about designing and evaluating social research.

⊰ TWO ⊱

FOUNDATIONS

⸻•◆•⸻

I titled this chapter "Foundations" because it is about the building blocks of social research design. The foundations of social research design are like the foundations of buildings: They are the base upon which all else is built. I will begin with the most basic point: All social research has three components—data, concepts, and theories—and all social research is about the relationships among these. Then I will continue to two questions that often lie in the background of social research design: To what extent will research be led by theory (deductive reasoning), and to what extent will research be led by data (inductive reasoning)? What will be the model of social life underlying a research project (positivist, interpretive, or critical)? The final major section in this chapter describes two continuing debates about these foundational issues.

THE COMPONENTS OF SOCIAL RESEARCH: DATA, CONCEPTS, AND THEORIES

Social research is about relationships among data, concepts, and theories, so defining these is a good place to start.

Data

Data are concrete reflections of the social world that can be *sensed,* which means that data are what we can see, hear, taste, touch, or smell. You can see the incredible variety of social research data by looking at the articles in the appendix. Data come from asking many people identical questions and having them choose their answers from a limited set of possibilities ("Exploring the Bases of Partisanship," "Smoking Identities and Behavior"); they come from general conversations about topics, such as how former drug addicts experience the process of becoming a non-addict ("Addicts' Narratives of Recovery").

Data from long conversations describe how students think of themselves in relation to computer technology ("The Digital Identity Divide"), and how men in prison understand their membership in gangs ("Gang-Related Gun Violence"). Data also come from magazines ("Unassailable Motherhood, Ambivalent Domesticity") and from watching people walking down busy city streets ("Ethnography of Racial Identities").

> Data are tracings of the physical and social worlds obtained through the senses.

Think of data—all data—as having three dimensions: content, origin, and form.

Variations in Data Content: Thinking/Feeling and Behavior

Much social research data initially come from verbal reports of what people *say* they think or feel. We can hear these data when people talk, and we can see these data when words are written.

Social researchers also are interested in behavior—what people do and how people act. We can see what people do by observing their actions, and we can read reports of behavior, such as records of marriages and divorces, births and deaths, and so on.

Variation in Data Origins:
Researcher Produced and Naturally Occurring

Data also can be distinguished in relation to its origins. Data often are produced by researchers themselves who ask people to talk, answer survey questions, or participate in experiments. These data exist because researchers create them for the particular purpose of answering research questions.

Data also can be naturally occurring, which means their existence does not depend upon researchers. Such data come from speeches and television shows, transcripts of social policy hearings, blogs, Twitter messages, diaries, and organizational documents. Researchers also can watch people walk down busy streets, or they can use official records to examine social patterns and social change. In all these instances, data not originally produced by researchers are used by researchers.

Variations in Data Form: Words and Numbers

Records of data can be kept in the form of words or in the form of numbers. Data in the form of words can be used to describe the content of magazines or other documents, to describe behavior, and to show the content of speech. Data in the form of numbers can offer summaries of how many people answered questions in particular ways, how often people acted in particular ways, and numerical relationships between questions and/or behaviors.

> All data can be categorized in terms of content, origin, and form. These dimensions are independent.

Content, origin, and form are three independent dimensions of data. This means that data measuring thinking/feeling can be researcher produced or naturally occurring, and it can be recorded as words, numbers, or both. Data describing behavior can be the same way— researcher produced or naturally occurring and recorded as words, numbers, or both. Remember these variations when you design research, because they will give you many possibilities for producing data that are the best possible fit for answering your research questions. I will return to data and their variations in Chapter 6, which covers the various techniques to generate data.

Concepts

While direct knowledge of the physical and social worlds comes from our senses, just about everything of interest to social researchers is in the form of *concepts*, which are abstractions that cannot be sensed. Social researchers talk endlessly about such things as social class, discrimination, deviance, and socialization. While such concepts are the building blocks of research and theory throughout the social sciences, none of them have a physical reality.

> Concepts are abstract ideas that cannot be sensed, because they do not have a physical existence.

As you read through the articles contained in the appendix, notice the countless abstractions. Researchers talk about social identity, ideology, and political party identification ("Exploring the Bases of Partisanship"), social hierarchy and deference ("Ethnography of Racial Identities"), and narratives of recovery, non-addict identity, and reconstructing the self ("Addicts' Narratives of Recovery"). In comparison to data, concepts do *not* have a physical existence. You cannot see or touch a concept; concepts exist only when researchers see or hear something and say that what they see or hear is an instance of a particular concept. Stated otherwise, social researchers use data to examine the mysteries of social life, yet data—traces of the physical and social world—are interesting only when they are given meaning (concepts). Researchers are interested in concepts, and concepts are abstractions.

Theories

The third building block of social research is theory. Each theory is composed of a series of concepts that, when taken together, explain something about the social world. Below are three examples of how concepts are brought together to form theories.

> Theories are systems of interconnected concepts that condense and organize knowledge about the social world.

Example 2.1: Researchers Alan Abramowitz and Kyle Saunders ("Exploring the Bases of Partisanship in the American Electorate") are interested in two concepts: political party identification and voting behavior. They theorize that voters have systems of beliefs (the concept of ideology), which they match with the beliefs associated with Republican and Democratic political parties. This is a theory: Political party identification and voting behavior are explained by the alignment between the ideology of voters and the policy preferences associated with political parties.

Example 2.2: Researchers James McIntosh and Neil McKeganey ("Addicts' Narratives of Recovery") offer a theory that creating narratives of a non-addict self (concept) is an important part of the process of coming off drugs (concept).

Example 2.3: Researchers Maya D. Guendelman, Sapna Cheryan, and Benoît Monin ("Identity Threat and Dietary Choices") theorize that when immigrants to the United States feel their identity as Americans is being threatened (concept of identity threat), they eat more American-identified food as a way to demonstrate that they are American.

Data, concepts, and theories are the foundational components of social research. Questions about relationships among them are another foundational issue.

DIRECTION OF REASONING
BETWEEN DATA AND CONCEPTS/THEORIES

Regardless of what research questions and what data generation techniques are used, all research is about relationships between what can be sensed (data) and the meanings of what can be sensed (concepts and theories). This raises a question about the foundational issue called *research logic*, which is the direction of reasoning between data and concepts/theories. Studies informed by *deductive logic* begin with concepts/theories and use them to direct data generation and interpretation; research informed by *inductive logic* begins with data and uses data to form concepts/theories.

Deductive Reasoning

Social research is most commonly informed by *deductive logic*, which begins with concepts/theories (what already is known about the topic) and moves to data (the unknown). The process of deductive research begins with reviewing the existing literature (see Chapter 4). Based on what is already known, researchers develop hunches (a formalized hunch is called a *hypothesis*) of what they will find, then research is designed to test these hunches. Research following deductive reasoning uses existing knowledge as a guide to designing new research.

> Deductive logic: reasoning from a known principle to an unknown;
> reasoning from the general to the specific.

The present state of knowledge (concepts/theories) in deductive reasoning guides social research design. The more research is led by deductive logic, the more researchers know what they are looking for when they begin data collection.

> **Example 2.4:** The research reported in "Smoking Identities and Behavior" is highly deductive. We know this because research respondents were asked only two questions, and for each question, they were offered only a limited number of ways in which they could respond. What is already known about smoking identities and behavior was sufficient to allow the researchers to know what specific questions to ask as well as what answers were possible for these questions.

Deductive reasoning is used by detectives who have a hunch (theory) about how to solve the mystery. They begin with this hunch and then gather clues (data), testing the extent to which the hunch seems true.

Inductive Reasoning

Inductive logic is the reverse of deductive logic. The beginning point for inductive reasoning is data, which are used to develop more abstract generalizations (concepts and theories).

> Inductive logic: reasoning or drawing a conclusion from particular
> facts or individual cases.

Theory in inductive research often is called *grounded theory*, because the theory is grounded in actual data. Inductive reasoning is the method used by detectives who begin with the "crime scene" and form bits and pieces of "evidence" (data) into a theory of what happened. Data in inductive research generate theory.

> **Example 2.5:** "Addicts' Narratives of Recovery" is an example of research that is highly inductive. The researchers began with an interest in how addicts construct stories to make sense of their new, non-addict identity. This general interest in how stories can make sense of new identities led only to general questions to ask research participants, not to a specific series of questions that would characterize deductive theorizing.

While there are two distinct kinds of relationships between concepts/ theories and data, research in practice can be far more fluid. First, it is best to think of inductive and deductive reasoning as a continuum of relationships between concepts/theories and data. While hypothesis testing and surveys with fixed questions and fixed responses are examples of highly deductive reasoning, most actual research tends to be a mixture of deductive and inductive reasoning.

Also, while it might not be clear in final reports, most real-life research is actually done in ways that go back and forth between inductive and deductive reasoning. This makes sense: Research is detective work, and detective work requires both clues (data) and hunches (concepts/theories). Detectives see a clue, construct a theory about the meaning of the clue, check the theory by looking for other clues (which then leads to other theories), and so on.

Logic and Research Design Decisions

If you design research, you will not have much control over the extent to which your research should/must/can rely on deductive and inductive reasoning. Decisions are made by the characteristics of the existing literature. If a great deal is already known about a topic, it would not make sense to use inductive logic—why generate data that are not informed by what already is known? The more that is known about a topic, the more sense it makes to use deductive logic and the types of data generation techniques that go with that form of reasoning (more about that as we continue). Just as certainly, if not much is known about a topic, then deductive logic is simply not possible.

MODELS OF SOCIAL LIFE
AND MODELS OF SOCIAL RESEARCH

Another of the primary foundations of social research design that rarely appears in final reports is the model of social life underlying the research. Different visions of social life lead to different images of how research should be designed and implemented, as well as what the goals of social research should be.

While there are innumerable ways to distinguish the varieties of models of social life underlying research, I have outlined three that I call positivist, interpretive, and critical, which are briefly described in Exhibit 2.1. As you read, think about two things: First, chart your own reactions to these perspectives—do any seem to be more similar to your own views and interests? Methodological thinking requires recognizing your biases and their consequences as you design and evaluate research, so recognizing if you are drawn to a particular perspective is important. Second, think about how different assumptions about the world lead to different ways of thinking about social research design. A recurring problem in social research is that failing to think about these models of social life that underlie research can lead to illogical designs.

Positivist Perspectives

Basic positivist question: How does society influence people?

The origin of all social research methods is in positivist philosophy, originally developed in Europe in the late 1800s. This philosophy is rooted in the methods and epistemology of studies of the natural world (such as biology, chemistry, and physics).

Positivist Perspective Assumptions About Social Life

The basic positivist belief is that the social world is no different from the natural world: Just as there are facts in biology or chemistry, there are facts in social life. Facts—whether about frogs or friendships, thunder or theaters—exist and can be measured. A second positivist belief is that how people think

Exhibit 2.1 Models of Social Life, Models of Social Research

Positivist	Interpretive	Critical
Assumptions About Humans and Social Life:		
The components of society have an objective existence; they are not influenced by human ideas or values.	While there is an objective world of tangible objects, social research is about the social world, which does not have meaning apart from human understanding of it.	The components of society have both an objective existence and a subjective meaning.
Because components of society have an objective existence, they are factual and can be accurately measured.	Facts are fluid and embedded in meaningful systems.	The components of society can be measured, but facts also are embedded in systems of meaning determined by power and politics.
The components of society can influence (weak version) or determine (strong version) human behavior/human understandings.	While human experiences are shaped by the components of society, humans remain creatures who must find meaning in their surroundings.	All society life is oriented around power relations. These relations determine human behavior and experiences.
Assumptions About Social Research:		
Social researchers must use the scientific method as developed in the natural sciences.	Social researchers must look to the humanities, not to the natural sciences, for appropriate research methods.	Science has been a tool of oppression; its methods are not value-free. Yet these methods can be used when they are in the service of freeing oppressed people.
Typical question: How are humans influenced/controlled by the environment?	Typical question: How do humans understand and thereby shape the social world?	Typical questions: How do social structures/social forces/social processes oppress particular groups of people? How does inequality influence consciousness?
The goal of research is to predict and control human behavior.	The goal of research is to understand the complexity of the human experience.	The goal of research is to critique power relations and to change the world by empowering oppressed people.
The researcher is a scientist: objective and impartial. The eyes and ears of the scientist can objectively record the facts of the world.	The researcher is a student of social life and the researcher is a social member; hence, objectivity is not possible.	The researcher is an advocate for oppressed people. Biases helping the oppressed should drive research.

and act is influenced by (weak version) or determined by (strong version) society, which is a very abstract concept composed of other concepts such as roles, norms, socialization, and institutions.

Positivist Perspective Assumptions About Social Research

Because the positivist stance is that the social world is the same as the natural world, it follows that social science research can—and should—be the same as natural science research. Therefore, positivist models stress the importance of precise and reproducible measurements, and they promote experimentation as the preferred data generation technique. Likewise, the goal of positivist-informed social research is the same as the goal of natural science research: to gain knowledge in order to make the world a better place. Indeed, the term *positivism* stems from the belief that research can make society a better place, because research will lead to knowledge that will allow us to know the causes and consequences of behaviors, which in turn can lead to understanding how to eliminate behaviors with negative consequences and encourage behaviors with positive consequences.

Positivist Perspective Assumptions About Social Researchers

The positivist perspective imagines that social researchers can and must be value-free and objective in their search for knowledge.

Although the term of positivism has gone out of style, most current social research remains informed by basic positivist principles. This makes sense, because positivist concern with understanding the causes of human behavior is very much in keeping with practical concerns. Americans—citizens, social service providers, and public policy makers alike—have practical questions that require positivist frameworks: What leads people to vote one way or another? How do threats to identity lead people to make unhealthy food choices? How do failures to identify occasional and social smokers as smokers lead to missed education opportunities? All of these are questions about how society influences people, which is the basic question associated with positivist models of social life.

Interpretive Perspectives

Basic interpretive questions: How do people make sense of the world? How do these understandings shape social life?

Interpretive perspectives can be called "anti-positivist" because their origins, often attributed to the sociologist Max Weber, were *explicitly* opposed to positivist theories. While positivist philosophy is rooted in the natural sciences, interpretive philosophy is rooted in the *humanities* (such as philosophy, history, and literary criticism).

Interpretive Perspective Assumptions
About Social Life

While positivist perspectives assume that the social world is similar to the natural world, interpretive perspectives are strongly rooted in the assumption that the social and natural worlds are distinct and different. This makes sense, because the interpretive focus is on what is distinctly and uniquely human: How do people create meaning? How does the meaning we create then shape us? The focus on meaning leads to questions such as the following: Who creates meaning? What are the characteristics of meaning? How do systems of meaning, once created, influence human understandings of the world?

Interpretive Perspective Assumptions
About Social Research

The goal of interpretive research is to understand the *meaning* of socially circulating systems of ideas, values, symbols, social processes, and so on—not as the objective facts that are of interest in positivist-informed research but rather as meaning as it is created and understood by people themselves. The ultimate goal of interpretive research is to understand the complexity of human experience. So while positivist-informed research would be interested in understanding what causes people to stop using illegal drugs, interpretive researchers would ask how recovering drug addicts themselves experience the recovery process. While positivist researchers might ask what causes teens to become members of gangs, interpretive researchers explore the meanings of gang membership.

Interpretive Perspective Assumptions
About Social Researchers

In comparison to positivist images of researchers as objective, interpretive researchers are assumed to be meaning-making creatures whose own values and biases will influence their research. Hence, there often is considerable discussion in interpretive research about how researchers must be ever aware of how their own values and experiences shape their research.

Critical Perspectives

> Basic critical questions: How does society oppress particular groups of people? How does inequality influence consciousness?

In contrast to positivist models that conceptualize society as governed by order and cohesion, critical theory understands society as groups of people in constant conflict and as the domination of some groups of people by other groups of people.

Critical Perspective Assumptions About Social Life

Critical perspectives share much with both positivist and interpretive perspectives. As with positivism, critical perspectives can be concerned with the real, physical elements of social life, although concern is narrowed to material conditions such as money, housing, education, and employment. As with positivism, critical perspectives view people as shaped by their environments—in this case, by social, political, and cultural factors. As with interpretive research, critical research can be interested in examining how humans make meaning, although critical research's concern is narrowed to how meaning is shaped by real, objective relations and how society works to oppress groups of people. Critical perspectives differ from both interpretive and positivist perspectives in that they begin by dividing the world into only two types of people: the oppressed and the oppressors. The assumption of critical perspectives that is not shared with either positivist or interpretive perspectives is that all social life is oriented around power relations.

Critical Perspective Assumptions About Social Research

In contrast to positivist perspectives that emphasize the importance of objectivity in research, critical perspectives emphasize the need for engagement: The ultimate goal of research from critical perspectives is to change the world by empowering oppressed people.

Critical Perspective Assumptions About Social Researchers

In sharp contrast to positivist perspectives that demand value neutrality from all researchers, researchers working within critical perspectives *must* define themselves as advocates for oppressed people.

In this book I will talk less about critical perspectives than about interpretive and positivist perspectives because in terms of design, critical research often either looks like positivist research or interpretive research. The distinguishing characteristic of critical research, the value-engaged stance of both the research and the researcher, is more noticeable during the implementation and data analysis phases of research.

In summary, Exhibit 2.2 shows the models of social life and type of research logic associated with the eight examples of published research contained in the appendix. Notice how it is possible for a project to have elements of two models of social life (such as critical/interpretive in "Unassailable Motherhood" and positivist/interpretive in "Gang-Related Gun Violence"). Notice also that the apparent strength of research logic can vary from highly deductive ("Exploring the Bases of Partisanship") to highly inductive ("Addicts' Narratives of Recovery").

Research Design Decisions and Models of Social Life

The most important point to keep in mind when thinking about design or evaluating social research is that we live in a world where there are very different models for researching social life. What I call positivist, interpretive, and critical models of social life are competing images of what social research is and what it should be.

While creative research is highly prized, certain types of models are logically associated with particular kinds of research designs. Although it is rare for an underlying model to be incompatible with one design characteristic or another, it certainly is true that different models are associated with particular sorts of design characteristics, as seen in the following:

> **Example 2.6:** Positivist-informed research prizes finding general laws. General laws can be discovered only by data representing a great many people, so positivist research often uses surveys, which are the only method capable of generating data on large numbers of people.

> **Example 2.7:** While nothing prevents positivist-informed research from using in-depth interviews, this is a very time-consuming way of generating data, which means it is not possible to have conversations with the great many people necessary to explore the general laws of interest in positivist perspectives. Conversely, it makes sense that in-depth interviews are closely associated with interpretive perspectives, because understanding how people create meaning (the interpretive question) requires long conversations.

> **Example 2.8:** Although research from critical perspectives is not confined to deductive reasoning, critically informed studies *must* have a dose of deductive logic, because they begin with firm understandings of which groups of people are oppressed and which groups do the oppressing.

The point here concerns thinking methodologically: When designing and evaluating research, it is important to think about how underlying assumptions make some forms of research design more coherent than others. I will do more with this as we go through the explicit design topics in the following chapters.

Exhibit 2.2 Foundational Characteristics in Published Research

Title/Author	Models of Research	Logic
Abramowitz/Saunders: "Exploring the Bases of Partisanship"	Positivist: Social identity *causes* political partisanship.	Highly deductive: Predetermined survey questions have predetermined possible responses.
Bowser: "Ethnography of Racial Identities"	None: This research note is tightly focused on method; there is no underlying theory.	Totally deductive: He begins with hypotheses.
Goode: "The Digital Identity Divide"	Critical: The central argument is there is inequality in education and unequal access to computer technology.	Unclear: Not enough information is given.
Guendelman/Cheryan/Monin: "Identity Threat and Dietary Choices"	Positivist: Identity threat *causes* immigrants to change their dietary choices.	Highly deductive: What is already known was used to design the experiment.
McIntosh/McKeganey: "Addicts' Narratives of Recovery"	Interpretive: Research is interested in addicts making sense of their recovery.	Highly inductive: "The process through which such recovery comes about remains far from clear" (lines 9–10).
Odland: "Unassailable Motherhood, Ambivalent Domesticity"	Critical: Feminist concerns about the oppression of women. Interpretive: How did the *Ladies' Home Journal* construct the meaning of motherhood and domesticity?	Deductive: Criteria from existing knowledge led to data collection (lines 133–135).
Ridner/Walker/Myers: "Smoking Identities and Behavior"	Positivist: Does the number of cigarettes smoked *cause* smoking identity?	Highly deductive: Predetermined questions have predetermined possible responses to them.
Stretesky/Pogrebin: "Gang-Related Gun Violence"	Positivist: How does gang socialization *cause* gun use? Interpretive: How do gang members understand themselves in relation to gang membership?	Somewhat inductive: They were doing research and asked questions, which led them to see the importance of these topics (lines 73–81).

CONTINUING DEBATES IN SOCIAL RESEARCH DESIGN

I will end this chapter about the foundations of research design with a discussion of two debates. My personal belief is that both of them are nonproductive and divert energy from the important job of actually doing research. However, my goal is to encourage you to develop methodological thinking, and because these debates are common, you need to understand them so that they do not hinder your ability to think critically. You need to know the basic issues in order to recognize them when you see them.

Natural Science Versus Humanities

A debate that has gone on for over a century concerns the appropriateness of using the methods of the natural sciences as guides to design research about the social world. On one side of this debate are those who argue that the natural science model, as interpreted through the lens of positivism, is the most appropriate—perhaps the *only* appropriate—model for social research. The evidence for this argument is practical: Researchers in the natural sciences— biology, chemistry, physics, and so on—have been immensely successful in producing knowledge about the physical world, so it only makes sense to use their model as a guide for social research. What this means is that while interpretive researchers might argue that the social world is more complex than the natural world and therefore incapable of being precisely measured, the natural science/positivist response is that the problem is in the measurements, meaning researchers need to develop better ways to measure complexity. While interpretive researchers complain about the impossibilities of being objective and while critical researchers promote value engagement, the natural science/positivist response is that objectivity should be valued and that energy should be spent developing techniques to ensure it.

In sharp contrast to those promoting a natural science model for social research are those identifying with interpretive perspectives, who argue just as strongly that the natural science model as interpreted through positivism is an inappropriate guide for social research. According to this view, rather than attempting to bring social research methods into line with natural science methods, researchers should take the time to develop new research models that are more appropriate for studying the complexity of humans and social life. In this view, we should look to the humanities—to history, literary criticism, and philosophy—for insights about how we might do research that is capable of exploring the complexity and uniqueness of our human experiences.

While each of these extreme views of totally embracing or totally rejecting natural science models of research has its proponents, a middle ground seems far more desirable. Everything about social life is complex, so it makes sense that there would be multiple questions about any topic; it makes sense that different assumptions about social life and research apply in varying degrees at different times. It makes good sense to ask what *causes* crime (a positivist question), *and* to ask how criminals or victims *understand* the experience of crime (an interpretive question), *and* to ask how the organization of the criminal justice system reflects and perpetuates *inequality* (a critical question). I will offer many more examples of this in the next chapter, which discusses how to think about topics when forming research questions. The positivist, interpretive, and critical models are tools in the methodological tool kit. Part of thinking methodologically is realizing that different kinds of questions require different kinds of perspectives. It seems wise to understand that at times it might make sense to design research very much in keeping with natural science models, while at other times such models do not make sense at all.

Qualitative Versus Quantitative Design

It is very common to hear people talk as if all research fits into one of two categories: *quantitative* and *qualitative*. Often, it seems as if the dispute is about whether data should be in the form of numbers (quantitative) or in the form of words (qualitative). I would argue these debates are not always (or even most often) just about data form. Debates are more complex: they are about the direction of reasoning between data and concepts/theories, the underlying models of social life, the purposes of social research, and the kinds of questions that are important to ask. Such issues are *far* more important than whether data are best in the form of words or numbers. The following table provides more detail.

Dimensions of the *Qualitative* Versus *Quantitative* Debate		
	Quantitative	**Qualitative**
Model of social life	Positivist	Interpretive
Model of research	Natural science	Humanities
Preferred data type	Numbers	Words
Preferred logic type	Deductive (theory testing)	Inductive (grounded theory)
Primary research goals	Discovering social patterns Making predictions	Understanding what is distinctly human Understanding social complexity

Rather than getting pulled into this debate, I would encourage you to remember the general principle that I will be demonstrating throughout this book: There are countless mysteries of social life that should be the topics of social research. Some questions are best answered by certain kinds of data, and other questions require other kinds of data. I would argue that choosing sides in this debate is equivalent to a carpenter arguing that saws are better than hammers. While it is quite acceptable—and expected—for individual researchers to be drawn to some kinds of questions and some types of research, becoming too identified with any one model can have negative consequences by hindering critical thinking.

FOUNDATIONS AND RESEARCH DESIGN

So ends the tour through what I am calling the foundations of social research. While published research rarely contains explicit attention to the kinds of logic and the underlying models of social life, the foundations of social research are like foundations of houses. Visible design characteristics—research questions, literature reviews, and data generation techniques—rest upon these structures. Methodological thinking requires attending to the design components that are out of sight.

Calling these topics *foundations* is good to emphasize their importance, yet—in contrast to building a house—when designing research, you might find it necessary to rebuild a foundation. You might assume that little is known about your project, so you begin using inductive reasoning only to find in your review of the literature that a great deal already is known; then your project becomes more deductive in reasoning. Or you might begin with a positivist perspective but find that the most interesting questions about your particular topic are more in line with interpretive or critical perspectives. One of the frustrations of doing research is that because humans and social life are so complicated, designing research is complicated. While I will talk about these kinds of situations, which create the need for change throughout this book, I also will remain forever a cheerleader: What might start as a problem often can become an opportunity to be creative.

Now it's time to move on to a topic that is an obvious central component in all research: research questions.

SUGGESTIONS FOR FURTHER READING ON
FOUNDATIONS OF SOCIAL RESEARCH DESIGN

For additional thoughts on positivist perspectives

Marcuse, H. (1966). Foundations of positivism and the rise of sociology. *Reason and Revolution: Hegel and the Rise of Social Theory* (pp. 323–389). Boston, MA: Beacon Press.

Wallace, W. L. (1971). *The logic of science in sociology.* Chicago, IL: Aldine-Atherton.

For additional thoughts on interpretive perspectives

Blumer, H. (1969). The methodological position of symbolic interaction. *Symbolic interaction: Perspective and method* (pp. 1–21). Upper Saddle River, NJ: Pearson Education.

For additional thoughts on critical perspectives

Harding, S. (1986). *The science question in feminism.* Ithaca, NY: Cornell University Press.

For additional thoughts on the qualitative/quantitative divide

Gusfield, J. R. (1990). Two genres of sociology: A literary analysis of the American occupational structure and Tally's Corner. In A. Hunter (Ed.), *The rhetoric of social research: Understood and believed* (pp. 62–96). New Brunswick, NJ: Rutgers University Press.

Tarrow, S. (2004). Bridging the quantitative-qualitative divide. In H. E. Brady and D. Collier (Eds.), *Rethinking social inquiry: Diverse tools, shared standards* (pp. 171–180). New York, NY: Rowman Littlefield.

Weinberg, D. (2002). Qualitative research methods: An overview. In D. Weinberg (Ed.), *Qualitative research methods* (pp. 1–22). Malden, MA: Blackwell.

THREE

RESEARCH QUESTIONS

—————●○●————

Research is detective work, and every case begins with a mystery, a question about social life. Just as good detective work depends upon a well-defined mystery, high-quality research is led by appropriate and clear questions. Adequate questions are a central component of high-quality research, because characteristics of questions greatly shape other design decisions, such as the types of data (content, origin, form) and data generation techniques that make sense given the question.

> Suitable questions for social research are about the *who, what, where, when, why,* and *how* of social life and can be answered using the methods of social research.

The questions leading social research are simply that—questions about characteristics, causes, consequences, processes, and meanings of social life. Research *can* examine questions about the *who, what, where, when, why,* and *how* of social life; it *can* explore "so what" questions about the consequences of how the world is organized and the consequences of specific human behaviors. What social research *cannot* do is tell us what should be evaluated as moral or immoral. Social research is a toolbox of rules, conventions, and techniques for discovering what *is*; philosophy, ethics, and religion are ways to assess what *should* be. That said, while social research is *not* capable of making moral evaluations, it most certainly is the way to generate data upon which to base such evaluations. Data describing the characteristics, causes, and consequences of events such as prison overcrowding, delinquency, urbanization, and so on can be evidence upon which to make the moral evaluations that in and of themselves lie outside the capabilities of social research.

Methodological thinking requires the ability to identify and evaluate questions written by others as well as the ability to write questions for research you are designing.

IDENTIFYING RESEARCH QUESTIONS IN PUBLISHED RESEARCH

Evaluating the quality of published social research requires evaluating research questions; yet before this can happen, the questions leading the research must be identified. An important skill in reading and evaluating research is the ability to identify research questions.

Because a research question is simply that—a question—it would seem that they should be written as questions. Sometimes that is true. Yet it still can require quite careful reading to find these questions in published research, as seen in the following examples.

> **Example 3.1:** The question leading the research on "Addicts' Narratives of Recovery" is somewhat hidden in a paragraph in the section Sample and Methods. This section is as much about what the researchers are *not* interested in as about what they *are* interested in:
>
>> What we sought to do was not to critically assess individuals' accounts of their recovery experience in order to produce a genuine ex-addict group, but rather to look at the process of coming off drugs from the perspective of the drug users themselves. Our question was not "have they genuinely managed to become ex-addicts," but *"what is the nature of the individuals' accounts of their recovery and in what ways might the recounting of those narratives be part of the recovery process?"* [emphasis added] (lines 94–100)

Rather than writing questions as questions, it is more common for researchers to transform questions into statements.

> **Example 3.2:** In "The Digital Identity Divide," readers are told that "this article considers the complex ways that schools and universities perpetuate the digital divide" (lines 23–24). Quite a bit later, we learn that "this study uses narrative inquiry to investigate how holding a technology identity subtly influences academic and social life at the university setting" (lines 105–107). Although these are statements, notice how easy it is to turn them into questions: What are the complex ways that schools and universities perpetuate the digital divide? How does holding a technology identity subtly influence academic and social life at a university setting?

Example 3.3: In "Identity Threat and Dietary Choices," readers learn that researchers "investigated whether members of non-White immigrant groups choose and consume American food as a way to convey that they belong in America" (lines 17–18). Considerably later in the article, researchers tell us they "investigated whether the motivation to convey an identity can also bring about actual dietary decline" (lines 47–49). Notice, again, how these statements are easily understood as questions: Do members of non-White immigrant groups choose and consume American food as a way to convey that they belong in America? Does the motivation to convey an identity bring about actual dietary decline?

When reading research, it is important that you figure out what questions are being asked. Very often, this requires some detective work, because questions can be in the middle of paragraphs and they might be in the form of statements rather than questions. Often research questions are located in statements beginning with phrases such as "in this study," "here we examine," "we are interested in," "the purpose of this study," and so on. Exhibit 3.1 shows how research questions actually appear in the articles in the appendix. You should notice how common it is for questions to appear as statements—and how easy it can be to translate these statements to questions.

When you cannot locate research questions even with careful reading, consider that perhaps the questions might only seem to be missing, because the article was written for people who have specialized knowledge that you do not have—knowledge allowing them to understand what is not explicitly stated. At the same time, do not assume that the problem is yours, because not all published research is high-quality research characterized by clear and obvious questions. In such cases, slow down in your reading and be very attentive to keeping the critical/skeptical stance, because ambiguous or missing questions can be an indication of less-than-quality research.

The lesson here is when writing research, be sure to include specific questions; when reading research, be sure that you identify the specific questions being examined. Simply stated, you cannot evaluate the extent to which research resolves a mystery if it is not clear what mystery was being investigated.

CONSTRUCTING RESEARCH QUESTIONS

An important skill in designing research is developing the ability to *write* good questions. Unless you will be replicating (simply redoing) research already done by someone else, constructing research questions can be a messy process, often starting only with fuzzy ideas about interesting topics. If you are designing a research project, it is best to expect that writing good

Exhibit 3.1 Research Questions in Published Research

Title/Author	Questions as They Appear in the Article	Question Form
Abramowitz/Saunders: "Exploring the Bases of Partisanship"	[W]e test[ed] the social identity theory by examining the influence on party identification of membership in a wide variety of social groups (lines 63–64).	What is the influence on party identification of membership in a wide variety of social groups?
Bowser: "Ethnography of Racial Identities"	[hypothesis]: There is now a hierarchy of public identities based upon perceived ethnicity and Muslim affiliation . . . This hierarchy is acted out through social interaction . . . in [public] (lines 73–76).	Is there a hierarchy of public identities based on perceived ethnicity and Muslim affiliation? Is this hierarchy acted out through social interaction in public spaces?
Goode: "The Digital Identity Divide"	This article considers the complex ways that schools and universities perpetuate the digital divide (lines 23–24). This study uses narrative inquiry to investigate how holding a technology identity subtly influences academic and social life at the university setting (lines 105–107).	How do schools and universities perpetuate inequality? How does a technology identity influence academic and social life in a university setting?
Guendelman/Cheryan/Monin: "Identity Threat and Dietary Choices"	We investigated whether members of non-White immigrant groups choose and consume American food as a way to convey that they belong in America (lines 17–18). We investigated whether the motivation to convey an identity can also bring about actual dietary decline (lines 47–49).	Do members of non-White immigrant groups choose and consume American food as a way to convey that they belong in America? Does motivation to convey an identity bring about actual dietary decline?

(Continued)

Exhibit 3.1 (Continued)

Title/Author	Questions as They Appear in the Article	Question Form
McIntosh/McKeganey: "Addicts' Narratives of Recovery"	We are . . . interested in the way in which [narratives of recovery] may be used by addicts as an integral part of [their recovery] (lines 24–26).	How do drug addicts use narratives of recovery to help them recover from drug use?
	What is the nature of the individuals' accounts of their recovery and in what ways might the recounting of those narratives be part of the recovery[?] (lines 98–100)	[same]
Odland: "Unassailable Motherhood, Ambivalent Domesticity"	I examine how *Ladies' Home Journal* . . . participated in the discursive construction of maternal identity (lines 38–40).	How did *Ladies' Home Journal* participate in the discursive production of maternal identity?
Ridner/Walker/Hart/Myers: "Smoking Identities and Smoking Behavior"	The purpose of this study was to examine smoking identity and smoking behavior among college students. The specific aim was to explore the relationship between smoking identity and the number of days smoked in the past month (lines 51–54).	What is the relationship between smoking identity and smoking behavior among college students?
		What is the relationship between smoking identity and the number of days smoked in the past month?
Stretesky/Pogrebin: "Gang-Related Gun Violence"	This study considers how gangs promote violence and gun use (lines 1–2).	How do gangs promote violence and gun use?

questions will require considerable time and energy. While there is not one magic formula for how to write good research questions, here is one way you might think about the task: The process of writing questions is that of gradually narrowing down broad topics (say, an interest in why some of your friends love anything to do with computers while others find technology a constant source of frustration) to much smaller topics capable of being empirically examined ("What are the relationships between technology identity and using technology?").

Step 1. Start with a general topic you find interesting. The possible topics for social research are as endless as they are fascinating. Sociologists explore questions about relationships among individuals, groups, social processes, and social structures, including topics such as gender, disability, social class, identity, family, education, politics, social problems, and work. Criminologists examine similar topics with a particular emphasis on understanding the characteristics, causes, consequences, and resolutions of crime and deviance. Social workers also are interested in relationships among individuals, groups, and social systems with the particular goals of understanding the causes, consequences, and solutions to troubles people experience. Because the process of doing research is most appealing if you are interested in the topic, start with something you find intriguing. Perhaps you read something that was exciting for a class? Maybe you always have wondered how something works? Keep your eyes and ears open and be alert to all the mysteries of social life swirling around you.

Step 2. Review the existing literature. The next chapter, "Literature Reviews," talks about the design task of learning what already is known about your topic. What research already has been done? What gaps are there in what is known? What seems to be fairly agreed upon, and what seems to be characterized by disagreements? As you read, pay particular attention to the end of reports, where researchers often offer their opinions about what kinds of questions still require answers. It could be that you will find an excellent question already has been written by someone else. That is good luck.

It might also be helpful to get into the habit of jotting down your thoughts and questions as you read. This will be an informal record of possibilities, and as you read over your notes, you will start to see what kinds of topics draw your attention. In the beginning stages of your exploration, do *not* try to come up with specific questions for your research. Rather, think creatively and broadly about the general topics. Explore possibilities.

Step 3: Write a question. You started only with a general topic. Now that you have some ideas about what others have said and what previous research has shown, can you write a specific research question?

Step 4: Go back to the literature. Once you have a question, you might need to go back to the literature, because now you will be looking for articles about more specific topics.

Step 5: Repeat (and repeat). This is a process—writing questions, reading, and modifying questions. The process ends when questions that are *suitable* for studying by the methods of social research are also *appropriate*, given the characteristics of the researcher, study participants, and practicalities.

ASSESSING THE APPROPRIATENESS
OF RESEARCH QUESTIONS

While there are *technical* characteristics of good research questions, not all technically adequate questions are appropriate. If you are designing research, it would be well to think about your own characteristics, the characteristics of the people who will be participating in your study, and the practicalities of doing the research that would be needed to answer the question.

Thinking About Researchers

While the image of researchers within positivist perspectives is of people who are emotionally detached from the process of research, this is not always the case. If you are designing research, there are some things you might think about as you start to form topics and questions. Thinking about these in the beginning stages of your research can save you much time in the long run.

Research and Personally Meaningful Topics

Researching topics that are interesting is beneficial, because working on mysteries you find interesting is more fun than working on those you do not much care about. Topics that are exciting often include those that are personally meaningful. Recent immigrants can be attracted to questions about immigration; very religious people can be interested in topics surrounding religion and spirituality, and so on. Doing research on personally meaningful topics can be beneficial: Researchers' personal experiences can lead to sensitivities not possible without such experiences; personal relevance can be a powerful motivator and source of energy to do the sustained work required for producing quality research.

At the same time, there can be negative consequences when researchers explore topics that are about their most deeply held values and/or topics that are centrally significant experiences in their lives. The lesson is obvious: If you are designing research on a topic that is *very* important to you, do *not* try to convince others—or yourself for that matter—that you are approaching your work in the dispassionate and objective manner valued within positivist frameworks. You must be honest about how your own values and biases shape your research design as well as the processes of data generation and data interpretation. Such biases are very troublesome within research from positivist perspectives; they are not necessarily problematic in research from interpretive or critical perspectives. Just be honest.

I also suggest that you think very carefully before designing research on a topic that is personally painful. The social research process requires immersion in the subject, and while some people find deep engagement to be therapeutic, others find it very upsetting. Stated truthfully, because the tasks and goals of research are *not* the same as the tasks and goals of therapy, confusing research and therapy can produce both bad research and bad therapy. I have seen students design research projects they are unable to implement: A woman who had been raped found she could not listen to other women talk about their own rape experiences, because listening to their stories led her to recall her own experiences; each interview felt like she was reliving her rape. A man who had grown up with an alcoholic, abusive father found he was not really interested in doing research on this topic—he did not want to listen to the experiences of others, unless they were like his own experience; he found himself arguing with people he was interviewing, trying to change their perspectives to match his own.

The lesson for research design is that it is best to explore topics that are interesting and perhaps personally meaningful yet think carefully about designing research on topics that are *very* meaningful. Ask yourself if you really want to absorb yourself in the topic.

Research and Personal Perspectives on Social Life

A topic in the last chapter was how underlying assumptions about social life associated with positivist, interpretive, and critical perspectives influence research design. While I will return to how these influence other characteristics of research design, I want to make a preliminary comment that whether you are designing research or evaluating the research of others, you will be most comfortable with research that is more or less in line with how you personally view the world. So if you are very concerned about social justice, you will be biased toward having positive evaluations of articles informed by critical perspectives, and you will be most comfortable using this perspective in research you design yourself. What this means is that when designing research, it is best to start with the kinds of questions associated with the perspectives you find most comfortable. You might change your perspective as you develop the project, but start where you feel most comfortable.

Research and Working Styles

At the beginning stages of designing research, you should think about how you prefer to work. Some people do their best and are most comfortable when they have a fairly clear idea of precisely how their research will proceed. If this is you, then you should design research that is securely grounded in the current state of knowledge. This is *deductive* research, where data gathering does not begin until the researcher has a fairly detailed idea of what to look for and for how findings will be understood. In this case, you should write a research question on a topic where a great deal already is known. If you are a person who *really* dislikes the feeling of working without a clear image of what you are doing, then consider doing a *replication* study (where you are repeating a study that has already been done), which is the most deductive research possible.

Other people like the excitement of exploring the unknown; they feel comfortable working on projects without clear expectations of how the project should be done or of what the final product should look like. If this describes you, then you should consider *inductive* research, which is characterized by beginning data generation with only general notions of what might be found. In this case, you should seek a topic where not a great deal already is known.

In my own experiences, I have found that there is *no* relationship between the personal preferences of students to engage in deductive or inductive research and their abilities as researchers. This is another of those instances where *different* simply means *different*, where one preference is not better or worse than another and where one method does not take more—or fewer—skills than another. Doing well with inductive research requires a high tolerance for uncertainty and ambiguity; doing well with deductive research requires careful attention to how the smallest details of current understandings are being supported or refuted. Keep this in mind as you think about your research topic and as you refine your interest to specific questions.

Thinking About Research Participants

Much research uses data produced by researchers who ask people to talk, answer survey questions, participate in experiments, and so on. Whenever research requires participants, it is the responsibility of researchers to ensure that people are not harmed by their participation. I will say more about this in Chapter 6, because questions about protecting research participants are most obviously raised during the process of developing techniques to generate data. What I would suggest is to memorize the following general rule; if you keep it in mind, you will be well along in designing research that protects the people participating in your study:

> The well-being of study participants is the *first, foremost,* and *primary* responsibility of social researchers.

During the early stage of thinking about research, remember that some topics require special sensitivity. Subjects such as religious beliefs and sexual identifications, for example, tend to be associated with strong feelings; topics such as grave illness, death, suicide, abortion, and family troubles of all types can be personally experienced as traumatic and private.

> Focus on how your research project will appear from the perspective of your research participants. Do not assume that they share your experiences, values, and biases.

If you want to propose research on topics that have even the *slightest chance* of being sensitive or upsetting, then you need to seek advice from others who have done such research and/or from people who are familiar with the specific issues pertaining to that particular topic. Expect also that research on sensitive or disturbing topics will be closely examined by institutional review boards, which are local committees charged with reviewing and certifying that proposed research will do no harm to study participants.

I will return to the topic of protecting research participants in Chapter 6. For now, the lesson is that as you start to settle on a topic and begin the process of transforming this topic to specific questions, do not forget that the well-being of your study participants must always remain your first consideration.

Thinking About Practicalities

The process of research often begins rather abstractly—the potential researcher reads, thinks, writes questions, modifies those questions based on readings, and so on. Yet the process ends very practically: Researchers go out into the world and talk with people, watch people, run experiments, analyze magazine articles, and so on. It is not uncommon for "perfect" questions and "perfect" research designs to become somewhat less than perfect, because the practicalities of doing research get in the way of perfection. I will talk about this in several chapters: Some questions that sound appropriate for research turn out to be too complicated (Chapter 5); it might be too expensive to generate data using the most appropriate technique, or ethical questions might be posed by that technique (Chapter 6); the question might require a sample of people who cannot be obtained (Chapter 7). The messiness of real research is that it is about people and social life, both of which are complicated, and so on

The lesson for designing research is that practicalities can make it impossible to examine the exact question researchers wish to pose. If problems are discovered early in the design process, they often are easily resolved. I return to my optimism:

> Problems (of any type) do *not* mean the topic must be abandoned. Consider problems as opportunities to be creative.

RECONSTRUCTING RESEARCH QUESTIONS

Methodological thinking encourages viewing research design as a *creative* process; it involves thinking about the task of overcoming problems (of any type) as occasions for creativity. Think outside the box; think about alternatives.

Modifying Questions to Reflect
Particular Views of Social Life

Earlier I suggested that when designing research, you should think about your own perspectives on social life. If you do this, you might decide that, for one reason or another, the question you have written is drawing from a model of social life that is not the most interesting to you. Perhaps you are drawn to a positivist-linked image of social science as the objective and value-free study of social life, yet the question you have written seems more in keeping with critical perspectives, because it assumes inequalities and promotes particular values. Or maybe you are interested in how people make meaning, but your question seems to assume that people are controlled rather than meaning-makers. You should expect to find a great many such inconsistencies: Social life is complex, so the overwhelming majority of topics can be—indeed, should be—examined through different perspectives. What this means is that it most often is easy to re-write a question in order to slightly refocus it. Consider, for example, Exhibit 3.2:

Exhibit 3.2 Varieties of Research Questions: Drug Addiction

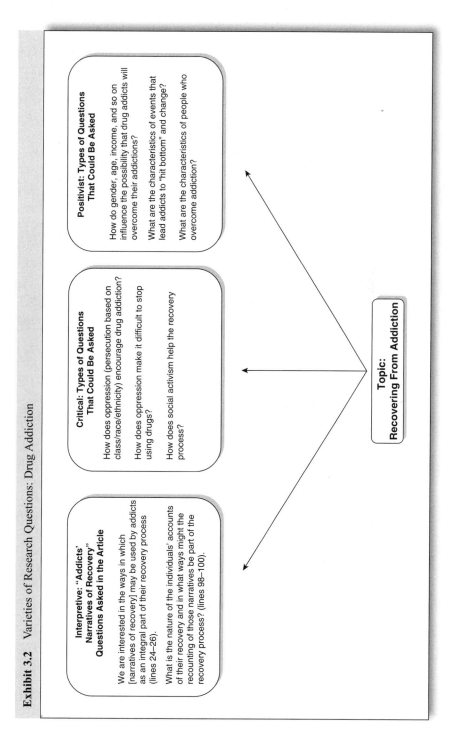

Interpretive: "Addicts' Narratives of Recovery" Questions Asked in the Article

We are interested in the ways in which [narratives of recovery] may be used by addicts as an integral part of their recovery process (lines 24–26).

What is the nature of the individuals' accounts of their recovery and in what ways might the recounting of those narratives be part of the recovery process? (lines 98–100).

Critical: Types of Questions That Could Be Asked

How does oppression (persecution based on class/race/ethnicity) encourage drug addiction?

How does oppression make it difficult to stop using drugs?

How does social activism help the recovery process?

Positivist: Types of Questions That Could Be Asked

How do gender, age, income, and so on influence the possibility that drug addicts will overcome their addictions?

What are the characteristics of events that lead addicts to "hit bottom" and change?

What are the characteristics of people who overcome addiction?

Topic: Recovering From Addiction

We know that "Addicts' Narratives of Recovery" is from an interpretive perspective, because this perspective is interested in how people make meaning, and this article is about how recovering addicts tell stories about themselves, their addictions, and their recovery and how these stories are a part of the recovery process (lines 96–100). Consider how easy it would be to shift the focus from an *interpretive* interest in meaning-making to a *positivist* perspective focus on understanding cause. There are important questions about recovering from addiction from this perspective: How do gender, age, income, and so on influence the possibilities that drug addicts will overcome their addictions? What are the characteristics of events leading addicts to "hit bottom" and change? Likewise, critical perspectives also would contain important questions about recovering from addiction: How does oppression (bias based on class/race/ethnicity) encourage drug addiction? How does oppression make it difficult to stop using drugs? How does social activism help the recovery process?

Are any of these questions better than the others? Certainly not. Questions are simply *different*. As another example, consider Exhibit 3.3, which shows the variety of questions possible for the concept of "identity threat":

"Identity Threat and Dietary Choices" is from a positivist perspective. We know this because the theory is that people (in this case, immigrants) are influenced/controlled by social life (in this case, by reactions to perceived threats to their identities as Americans). The positivist mystery in this study is empirically explored through an experiment involving relationships between threats to identity and eating behavior: Do threats to their American identity cause immigrants to change their dietary preferences from their own (often more healthy) foods to calorie- and fat-laden foods associated with the United States? This is a very good question and one with obvious practical implications, because immigrants tend to become Americanized, which includes changing their food preferences. Over time, this leads immigrants to the same poor diets associated with Americans. An interpretive researcher might think about the topic of identity threat and want to know more about meaning. The researcher might think, "Why are researchers *assuming* that immigrants experience identity threat?" Rather than assuming this, why not talk with immigrants to see how they understand what it means to be an American and how they understand links between their identities and their behaviors. From a critical perspective, this topic is clearly about relationships between experiences and oppression: How are people in immigrant groups treated as outsiders? How does being treated as an outsider negatively influence immigrants' self-evaluations?

Once again, what we have is a general interest in a topic, such as "identity threat," that can be reasonably transformed into many different

Exhibit 3.3 Varieties of Research Questions: Identity Threat

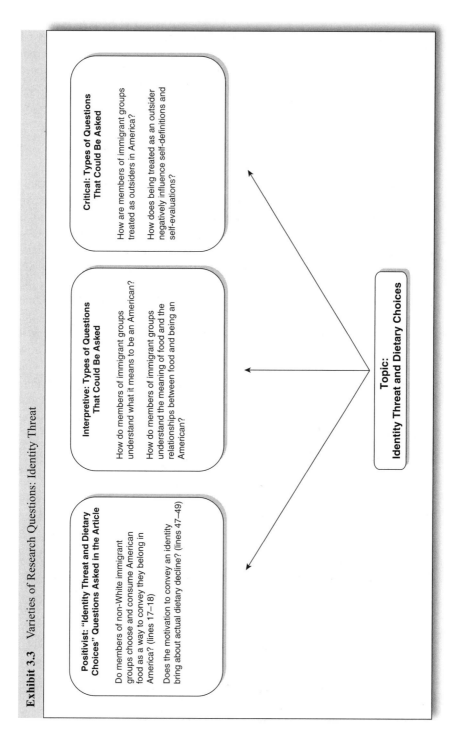

Positivist: "Identity Threat and Dietary Choices" Questions Asked in the Article

Do members of non-White immigrant groups choose and consume American food as a way to convey they belong in America? (lines 17–18)

Does the motivation to convey an identity bring about actual dietary decline? (lines 47–49)

Interpretive: Types of Questions That Could Be Asked

How do members of immigrant groups understand what it means to be an American?

How do members of immigrant groups understand the meaning of food and the relationships between food and being an American?

Critical: Types of Questions That Could Be Asked

How are members of immigrant groups treated as outsiders in America?

How does being treated as an outsider negatively influence self-definitions and self-evaluations?

**Topic:
Identity Threat and Dietary Choices**

kinds of research questions. Questions differ because they reflect different underlying assumptions about social life and because they reflect different visions of the goals of research. What this means is that when you are designing social research, you might find yourself drawn to a particular topic, and once you settle on the topic, an all-but-unlimited number of questions are possible.

Modifying Questions to Reflect Practicalities

In each of the following chapters, I will give examples of how practicalities sometimes require modifying research questions. Here I want to restate the general lesson, because if you are designing research, you need to hear this over and over: Part of the art of research design is modifying questions so that the research topic is as close as possible to what would have been perfect. It might not be possible to locate the exact documents you wanted to examine; it might not be possible to talk with people who have the exact characteristics you are interested in; it might not be possible to find enough such people to serve as an adequate sample. Researchers often find that it simply is not possible to do the exact research they would like. It is at that point that methodological thinking—creative thinking—helps. Allow yourself to feel sad for a moment that you cannot do exactly what you wanted to do, but after that moment, think about how even a small change in your question might give you something pretty close to what you wanted and how it might actually give you more than you originally thought you could get.

It also is necessary to remember the constant problems of practicalities in social research when you are evaluating the social research of others: You might read a report of research and believe that the researchers did not ask the most important question. Before evaluating this as a design flaw, ask yourself, "Would it have been possible to do research on the most important question? Or is this, perhaps, the best we can do?"

EVALUATING RESEARCH QUESTIONS

Here is a summary of the characteristics of good research questions:

1. A good question is about the *who, what, where, when, why,* or *how* of social life.

2. A good question requires data that can be obtained through the senses using the methods of social research.

3. A good question is sensitive to the characteristics of the person doing the research.

4. A good question is sensitive to the well-being of people who will participate in the study.

5. A good question can be explored, given practicalities.

Two remaining qualities of good research questions are topics in the next two chapters:

- A good question is supported by the existing literature (Chapter 4).
- A good question is composed of terms that can be adequately conceptualized and operationalized (Chapter 5).

RESEARCH QUESTIONS AND RESEARCH DESIGN

My continuing comment is that the actual practice of social research design and implementation can be messy, with each design task influencing the others. The process of constructing research questions, as well as the work of evaluating research questions written by others, is related to other components of social research design. Research questions can—and *must*—change in response to other design considerations.

In practice, the actual process of writing research questions cannot be separated from the literature review. So let us proceed to that.

Writing questions ⟷ **Learning what already is known about the topic (literature review)**

⊣ FOUR ⊢

LITERATURE REVIEWS

———◦•◦———

I will start this chapter with what journalists call a *grabber*, a statement meant to gain your attention: The majority of the time needed to design research is spent in finding, reading, and summarizing what already is known about the research topic. If you skip too quickly over this design task, your research will not be as good as it could have been; it might even turn out to be useless, if all you do is rediscover what already is known.

This design task of learning about what already is known is called "reviewing the literature." Recall that in the last chapter, this was every other step in constructing a research question: Think of a topic, review the literature, write a question based on what you read, and then read some more. Writing a research question cannot be separated from reviewing the literature; the tasks are done simultaneously. I will start with defining the meaning of *the literature*.

DEFINING THE LITERATURE

There are many variations in how, specifically, researchers define the meaning of what is called *the literature*. Here I will take a very traditional, conservative approach. In this perspective, *the literature* is shorthand for *the scholarly literature*. In the abstract, the scholarly literature contains the total sum of current social scientific knowledge about the world. In the concrete, the scholarly literature has three general characteristics: First, it contains research and theory that primarily has been written by and for members of *scholarly communities*, which are groups of people who share disciplinary orientations or substantive interests. There are scholarly communities of sociologists, criminologists, gerontologists, and so on; there are also scholarly communities of people interested in particular topics such as identity, American history, gender, and so on. Second, the scholarly literature appears in specific places: it is in books and journal articles whose assumed audiences are members of the scholarly communities concerned with the topics in those books and journals. Third, works in the scholarly literature have often gone through the process of *scholarly review*, whereby manuscripts submitted for possible publication are evaluated by members of relevant scholarly communities. Sociologists respected for their knowledge of race/ethnicity review manuscripts on those topics, social workers known for their knowledge about family dynamics review manuscripts on those topics, and so on. In this way, respected members of particular scholarly communities control what will—and what will not—become a part of the scholarly literature.

This description of what is in the literature simultaneously defines what is *not*: Excluded is work appearing in mass media outlets of all types (magazines, newspapers, broadcasts) and on internet sites sponsored by individuals or corporate, political, or social activist organizations. Most certainly, some of the research reported in these places might be excellent, yet it does not count as *the literature*, because the contents of these places are not controlled by communities of scholars. In addition, information on Wikipedia is *not* a part of the scholarly literature at this time (although it might change in the future).

The definition I just offered leads to an image of the existing literature as elitist, because it is limited to knowledge generated by scholars and evaluated by scholars as important enough to be published. Yes, that is true, and there are good reasons to criticize the process leading to publication in such places: Members of scholarly communities can become isolated from concerns of people outside these communities; community members can be biased and accept work that reflects these biases rather than work reflecting top-rate research. For these and other reasons, it is true that the system of scholarly review ensures neither that what makes it into the literature is excellent nor that what is excluded is inferior. Is high-quality research necessarily produced by people who are members of scholarly communities? No. Is the process of scholarly review or location in a respectable academic journal a guarantee that the work is high quality? No. The lesson is this: You must take the *critical/skeptical stance* on everything you read and not merely assume that academic credentials or particular publication sites guarantee high quality.

If you are thinking critically at this moment, you might wonder why you should continue reading this chapter. If *the literature* does not necessarily contain the truth, if publication in a respectable journal is not a guarantee of truthfulness, then what good is it? To that honest question, I would reply with the honest answer that while certainly imperfect, scholarly review is better than the most common alternatives, which are simply assuming that everything in print is true or evaluating information quality by the extent to which it confirms personal biases or promotes political agendas.

EXISTING KNOWLEDGE
AS A TOOL FOR RESEARCH DESIGN

A major tool of detectives is their personal experiences and knowledge of the past. Some mysteries remind them of other mysteries—already solved mysteries that might offer clues to solving current mysteries. In much the same way, the existing literature offers social research detectives many tools. If you are designing research, think of the literature review more as a task that *saves* time than as a task that *takes* time. The contents of the existing literature offer tools that help in designing research.

Previous Studies Define the Foundation for New Studies

Research is the process of asking and answering questions about social life, so it only makes sense to start the research process by asking what already is known about the topic. If you are designing research, be ready for the possibility that once you start reading, you will find your original question already has been answered. This makes sense, because there is a long history of research on the mysteries of social life, so many of the most obvious questions—What causes crime? What are gendered expectations for women and for men?—have received a great deal of attention. Although the answers to your original questions might already be known, this can be positive: If general answers are already known, you can modify your questions to ask more interesting ones about the details behind the generalities.

> **Example 4.1:** There is much interest in understanding how people recover from drug use. This interest is understandable: It might be possible to use information about how some people recover from drug abuse to help others do the same. If this was your interest and you started reading the existing literature, you would see that a great deal is already known about recovery. Researchers James McIntosh and Neil McKeganey ("Addicts' Narratives of Recovery") report this existing knowledge in the section of their literature review titled "Recovery From Addiction" (lines 31–78). Their research *starts* with what already is known.

The task of reviewing the literature is important, because it shows what is already known about the proposed research topic, which furnishes a baseline upon which to build new research.

Previous Studies Define What New Research Is Needed

The second reason why it is important to know what previous research studies have found is that understanding what *is* known simultaneously defines what is *not* known, and what is *not* known defines what new research is needed. While individual researchers can have personal reasons for doing research (the love of discovery, to pass a course, to obtain a degree, to qualify for a job) and while much research is in the service of answering practical questions, all research is in service of the *social* goal of adding to existing knowledge. An important task in social research design is developing the research mandate, which is the justification for how new research will add to knowledge.

> A design task is justifying the research in terms of how it will fill gaps in the existing literature. This justification is called the research mandate.

Examples of research mandates are seen in Exhibit 4.1, which shows how new research is justified in terms of how it corrects a problem in the existing literature. Also notice how in Exhibit 4.1 there are several ways in which new research can be justified in terms of how it will increase knowledge:

Example 4.2: Research examining how the *Ladies' Home Journal* magazine portrayed images of women right after the end of WWII ("Unassailable Motherhood, Ambivalent Domesticity") is justified by describing how the study *differs from other studies*: "What differentiates my study from previous studies is that I draw a clear distinction between motherhood and domesticity" (lines 89–91).

Example 4.3: Research to develop a method to study social inequality ("Ethnography of Racial Identities") is justified in terms of *what we do not know*: "Are some Parisians 'more equal' than others? . . . For the moment there is no way to answer these questions directly" (lines 30–34).

Example 4.4: Research to examine the influence of social identity and ideology on voting behavior ("Exploring the Bases of Partisanship") is justified by *what other researchers have ignored*: "In fact, [other researchers] never actually test this social identity theory, nor do they compare the influence of social background characteristics with the influence of issues and ideology" (lines 38–41).

Previous Studies Offer Guidelines for Research Design

Reading the existing literature is important to understand the *content* of existing knowledge. It also can be a good way to get help on questions about

Exhibit 4.1 Relevant Literatures and Mandates in Published Research

Title/Author	Topics Covered	Mandate
Abramowitz/Saunders: "Exploring the Bases of Partisanship"	Theoretical: Social identity theory and ideological realignment theories of voters' preferences Empirical: Changes in voting behavior	"In fact, [other researchers] never actually test this social identity theory, nor do they compare the influence of social background characteristics with the influence of issues and ideology." (lines 38–41)
Bowser: "Ethnography of Racial Identities"	Empirical: Recent immigration and changing patterns of inequality in France. This is a research note, which means it only is about method and not theory.	"Are some Parisians 'more equal' than others . . . Are social inequalities in Paris and other cities . . . moving further away from the ideal of equality? . . . For the moment there is no way to answer these questions directly." (lines 30–34)
Goode: "The Digital Identity Divide"	Theoretical: Importance of identity Theoretical/Empirical: Gender, economics, race/ethnic inequalities in education (access divide)	"[we need] a more robust definition of the digital divide which moves away from a technological determinist perspective and toward a framework that examines how the digital divide reflects and reinforces society's social and economic inequities." (lines 66–70)
Guendelman/Cheryan/ Monin: "Identity Threat and Dietary Choices"	Theoretical: Relationship between social identity threat and behavior Empirical: Relationship of weight gain and "American food"	None explicitly offered

Title/Author	Topics Covered	Mandate
McIntosh/McKeganey: "Addicts' Narratives Of Recovery"	Theoretical: Theories of the process of recovery from drug addiction	"Many addicts do eventually recover. However, the process through which such recovery comes about remains far from clear." (lines 8–10)
Odland: "Unassailable Motherhood, Ambivalent Domesticity"	Empirical: history of women during WWII and after WWII Theoretical: Gender identity is shaped by social and historical circumstances.	"What differentiates my study from previous studies is that I draw a clear distinction between motherhood and domesticity." (lines 89–91)
Ridner/Walker/Hart/ Myers: "Smoking Identities and Behavior"	Relationship between theoretical/ empirical: How past studies have measured smoking identity and smoking behavior, problems in measurement	"Despite . . . evidence of discrepancies between smoking behavior and smoking identities, researchers and health care providers . . . use . . . category systems. . . [that] fail to uncover actual smoking behavior, which increases risks for individuals and decreases the effectiveness of smoking prevention . . . efforts . . . It is vital to explore smoking identities." (lines 45–50)
Stretesky/Pogrebin: "Gang-Related Gun Violence"	Theoretical: Relationships between gangs and crime, the process of socialization into gangs, meaning of gangs to people in them	"[the past research] still leaves open the question about why gang members increase their violent behavior after they join a gang." (lines 25–27) "[I]t is interesting to note that little research exists that examines the relationship between guns and gangs in terms of identity formation." (lines 68–69)

research design, because reading what already is known offers tips for designing research. How did other researchers define major concepts? What methods of generating data (surveys, experiments, observation, etc.) have been used? What are the details of these? When you read reports of research understand that they can do more than offer information about the topic—they can be an excellent source of research design help.

> **Example 4.5:** Research reported in "Smoking Identities and Behavior" used survey questions that already had been developed for the National College Health Assessment. This saved the researchers the time it would have taken to develop questions. In this case, the added benefit was that the quality of those questions already had been demonstrated (lines 71–78).

As you read what others have written, jot down details of what they did that might be useful in planning your study. With proper citation, of course, it is acceptable—indeed, it is preferable—to make use of what others have done. Researchers form a community; research is about building knowledge.

In brief, the lessons about the importance of literature reviews for *designing* research are fairly clear. The contents of the current literature are a useful tool; the time spent in finding and reviewing the existing literature is well spent, because you can use what is already known about your topic, and you can build on the works of others.

The lessons about literature reviews for *evaluating* research also are fairly clear. As you read literature reviews, note the extent to which researchers position their research within existing knowledge. Does the author convince you that new research is needed to advance knowledge?

DEFINING THE RELEVANT LITERATURE

Now that I have discussed generalities of literature reviews, I need to be more specific. What I have been calling *the existing literature* is a very abstract concept; it contains tens of thousands of books and probably hundreds of thousands of articles. By containing, in effect, everything that is known about everything, the literature is useless in helping us understand any one particular topic. So rather than talking about the literature as if it is one thing, it is more important to talk about that part of the literature that is *relevant* to the particular study being designed.

What is the relevant literature? The short answer to that question is that the researcher decides. Just as any topic can lead to multiple research questions, most questions can be situated in multiple ways that will each highlight some aspects of social life and ignore others. Deciding what is and is not relevant is about far more than deciding what will be included in the literature review. Think of defining the relevant literature as the process of drawing boundaries around the research in ways that situate it within particular ways of thinking about social life.

Defining Boundaries for the Inclusion of Topics

One of the most difficult aspects of designing research is to decide precisely what should be included in the review of the literature. These always are difficult decisions: Humans and social life are complex, and in very real ways, almost everything is related to everything else. But for two reasons researchers must make decisions about what topics to include/emphasize and what to exclude/ignore:

The first reason is simple and practical: Much social research is reported in journals, where there are very real and nonnegotiable page limits. Although my students tend to believe that writing fewer pages is easier than writing more pages, they find the situation is quite the opposite when writing literature reviews. The less space there is, the more *difficult* it is to summarize all that already is known about the topic; the less space there is, the more information must be excluded.

The second reason why researchers must set boundaries around their research and only include some topics and not others is more important: The literature review sets the stage for research by justifying the research question and placing it within the context of what already is known. So the question is, *which* context?

> **Example 4.6:** The literature review for "The Digital Identity Divide" develops the topics of the importance of technology to college success (lines 1–10), how women, poor students, and students of color can be unprepared to use this technology (lines 11–14), the *access divide*, a term labeling the inequality in access to technology (lines 28–70), and the potential usefulness of examining how students think of themselves in relation to technology (lines 79–97).

First, notice how what is included in the literature review of this report of research nicely sets the stage and justifies the need for the research. The review prepares readers for the data they will see; it places the data within context. This is a characteristic of high-quality research: Design components all fit together into a package. The literature review fits nicely with the research questions, which are, in this case, about how students define themselves in relation to technology, how this influences their school success, and how inequalities are created by schools themselves.

Second, notice how much the researcher might have included but did not: While she says that "the home context trumps school experiences in terms of building technology knowledge" (lines 55–56), she offers no details about these home experiences. And while her primary concept is "technology identity" (lines 17–19), she does not use any insights from the vast literature about "identity." Still further, while she mentions that the digital divide is associated with geographical location, (dis)ability, educational level, and generation (lines 35–37), she ignores these topics and attends only to gender, race, and socioeconomic status. The question for readers to evaluate is, are these exclusions understandable and justifiable? I personally think they are. She situates her research mandate within a critical perspective when she writes "sociology and communication scholars have called for a more robust definition of the digital divide which moves . . . toward a framework that examines how the digital divide reflects and reinforces society's social and economic inequities" (lines 66–70). Such a mandate deflects attention from how home life might be a part of the process of developing a particular orientation to technology. Likewise, the critical perspective tends to focus on oppressions based on race/class/ gender, which diverts attention from the potential importance of other characteristics such as geographical location, (dis)ability, educational level, and generation.

Are the neglected topics important nonetheless? Yes. Yet given space limitations for journal articles, developing anything more would require reducing attention to what she covered; in other words, covering more would mean the information covered would be more general rather than in-depth. There are always decisions to make about what to cover and what to exclude.

If you are designing research, expect that you might need to think long and hard about what to define as the relevant literature, because decisions about what to *include* simultaneously are decisions about what to *exclude*. Methodological thinking requires being aware that you are making these decisions, and aware of the trade-offs and that you are able to logically justify why you included some topics and not others.

When evaluating research, you need to do the same kind of thinking: You cannot expect *any* author to give you, the reader, all the information that already is known about a topic; you cannot expect *any* author to develop each and every related topic. That is not possible. Your evaluation should be informed by practicalities: Given space limitations, did the author tell you enough about what already is known so that the research is placed in an appropriate context, even if that context is one of many? Are the author's decisions about what to include logical? Are exclusions likewise defensible?

A final note: What is excluded in one manuscript becomes the potential topic for another. Even research projects that are quite small often generate enough data and insights for more than one article.

Defining Boundaries of Abstraction

Defining relevant literatures also is about setting boundaries around the extent to which the study is focused on the abstract/general versus the concrete/particular. At times, researchers interested in very broad topics find they need to think "smaller" in order to find a manageable number of articles about the topic and—most important—to locate their research in something that is not too abstract.

> **Example 4.7:** A few years ago, one of my students was interested in the experiences of African American student scholar-athletes. He started his review of the existing literature by assuming that he would locate his research in the topic of race, but that proved to be far too large. The topic of race is so multidimensional and so complex and is the subject of so much theory and research that he got lost in the immense literature. He then thought he might place his research within the topic of sports, but that, too, proved to be too large and complicated. He found that he needed to think less abstractly and more concretely. His literature review started with a fairly short paragraph about race and then moved directly to reviewing what we know about the topics of race *and* college sports.

If you find yourself getting lost in a literature that seems enormous and never-ending, think about being less general and more concrete.

> **Example 4.8:** Research on "Identity Threat and Dietary Choices" is grounded in the literature on obesity as a problem (lines 4–8), on the tendency of immigrants to adopt unhealthy American eating habits (lines 8–14), and on what is known about the consequences of "identity threat" (lines 19–49). Notice how there is nothing about far larger topics such as the general experiences of immigrants, differences among immigrants due to place of origin, the general processes of claiming and maintaining identity, the negative consequences of obesity on health, and so on.

When designing research, you will want to draw boundaries around the extent of conceptual abstraction in order to make the task of reviewing the literature manageable and—more important—to make your study conceptually clear. It is *not possible* to do research on topics such as race or immigration or health—those topics are too large.

If you design social research, realize that just as you might need to reduce your vision in order to make the literature review manageable, you may need to think more *generally* in order to locate your research in the ongoing scholarly dialogue. Every research topic and its accompanying concepts are lodged in increasingly larger concerns. Searching for these larger topics/concepts is necessary to do the literature review, and this is critically important to locate research in the ongoing scholarly dialogue. A good sign that you need a higher order of abstraction is if you find that no one has written anything on your topic.

> **Example 4.9:** Another student story: One of my students was interested in the experiences of women who work at Hooters Restaurants. Strongly grounded in a critical, feminist perspective, she wanted to understand the problems facing women who are expected to do the difficult physical work of waitressing while simultaneously acting and appearing as sexual objects. Her initial look into the literature was frustrating because she could not find any past research about Hooters. She had to think more abstractly and expand her vision to thinking about Hooters as a *kind* of place rather than as a *specific* place. For example, Hooters is a restaurant, and there has been considerable attention paid to the experiences of women waitresses. Hooters is also a place where a work requirement is displaying feminine characteristics, which is very similar to expectations for women who work in bars, and considerable research has looked at those kinds of jobs.

In summary, defining the relevant literature requires deciding how to draw boundaries in your research. Boundaries are about what topics are and are not relevant and about the extent to which the concepts you are examining are abstract or concrete. These all are decisions researchers make. I will get back to these in Chapter 7, where the topic turns to samples. Deciding what to include/exclude and deciding levels of abstractions for literature reviews also influences the characteristics of populations and samples that will be relevant for the research.

THINKING ABOUT THE REVIEW TASK

The sheer magnitude of the existing literature, even when reduced to the *relevant* literature, can make the thought of doing a review overwhelming. Here is the tightrope: When designing research, you *should* want to do a very good job of finding and reading the literature—because it is in your best interests to do so—but you do *not* want to dedicate your life to it. I offer some general suggestions on how to think about this task.

My most important suggestion is that Step 1 of your literature review should be talking to a librarian. They are trained in how to do these reviews, they can direct you to the most useful resources, and they generally make your life much easier than if you attempt to go it alone. You should always begin with librarians and not wait until you have problems.

> The most important tool for doing literature reviews is librarians.

Where to Look

In the not-so-distant past, the books and journals comprising the scholarly literature were physical objects located in libraries. Today, increasingly digital libraries are competing with physical libraries. If you are designing research, your initial conversation with a librarian should include asking about the availability of digital resources.

Search engines, such as Google, are a primary way to locate information to answer questions in daily life. However, when I talk about the virtual library or the digital library, I am talking about something that is more specific: There are search engines that track and retrieve objects in the world of scholarly research. This is *not* the same world as the commercial world of Google. Other than my advice to enlist the help of librarians, the most important time-saving advice I can offer is the following:

> While Google Scholar is becoming a decent research tool, a general Google search is *not* useful, because you will be slammed with commercial and popular treatments of your topic, which is *not* helpful if you are looking for *scholarly* literature.

There are many search engines for scholarly literature, and I have included a listing of some of the most common ones at the end of this chapter. What you will notice is that many of these track hundreds of journals. Because the technology tends to be user-friendly, obtaining *basic* competence in using these will not require much of your time (and once again, librarians can be very helpful in getting you started). Realize that each search engine has advantages and disadvantages, strengths and weaknesses, limitations, and quirks. Also, although these search engines are fantastic tools for finding literature that appears in countless places, they are not perfect: Because each database tracks a different combination of journals, the *same* search done through two search engines can yield *different* results. Not all potentially relevant journals are included in every search engine: the more mainline the journal is (such as those sponsored by professional associations), the more likely it will be tracked by many search engines.

How to Read

I have two general kinds of advice for how to read the articles you find. First, if you are a student used to reading textbooks, you might find that journal articles are more difficult to read. In comparison to textbooks that assume audiences know little or nothing about the topic at hand, the assumed audience for journal articles is professionals who have preexisting understandings of the topic as well as some level of general theoretical and methodological sophistication.

Readers who do *not* have this knowledge will have problems evaluating the meaning and quality of research reports, because it will seem as if too much is missing. What you will note in all the examples I am using is that authors tend to summarize a great deal of research very quickly. Such quick summaries will be enough if you already know something about the topic but might not be enough if you know little or nothing about the topic. Likewise, when researchers assume that their readers are statistically sophisticated, they can merely cite statistical procedures used and not discuss details of their use, but this will leave the statistically unsophisticated in the dark. This is one reason why articles include citations to other work: You can find other articles and read them if you want to know more.

While there is no magic resolution to the problem of how to understand research in professional journals without having the knowledge held by members of professional communities, *critical thinking* can help. Even with little knowledge of the specific content, you might be able to evaluate the logical nature of the research questions, the fit between the questions and methods, the quality of the sample, and the extent to which the research and the author's interpretation make sense in a common sense type of a way. Granted, it is not perfect, but it is better than simply ignoring everything that seems difficult to read.

Second, when reading for literature reviews, you should *skim* a great many articles. Start with the abstracts, which are the summaries at the beginning of reports of research. Abstracts are short, so you can read them carefully. Look for the research question, the data generation technique, the sample, and the major findings. Some articles that have interesting titles will turn out to be of little or no use to you. If that is the case, then go on to the next article. Only if there seems to be something interesting should you continue to actually read the article. Some articles will be important because they have excellent summaries of existing knowledge; others will be important because they are using a data generation method you are considering; still others will be important because they make you think in new ways. Just as you will skim some articles, assume that there will be others that you will read very carefully.

What to Read for

You will be looking for published articles and books on your topics of interest. Read research on your topic that is from different models of research (positivist, interpretive, and critical) and that uses different techniques to generate data. The more views you have of your topic, the easier it will be to see where your particular research will fit.

> Your goal in reviewing the existing literature is to understand the range of theories and the range of empirical findings on your topic

A serious problem is reading only those articles that seemingly confirm what you already know or believe about the world. Maintain the *critical/skeptical stance* and keep the detective image in mind as you read and be open to clues that could send your research in an unanticipated direction. Literature reviews that merely build a line of reasoning without attending to complexity are not convincing to readers. Reviews that do not attend to complexity also are a very poor foundation for the research itself: They will not prepare you for the complexity you will find in the social world, or (even worse) they will encourage you to ignore complexity, which will distort your findings. Indeed, I would even suggest that you explicitly seek out articles that have theories and/or data generation techniques that you are not attracted to. Force yourself to read things you do not agree with; such articles will make you think.

THE CONTENTS AND FORM OF LITERATURE REVIEWS

The best way to understand how to write a review of the literature is to read how others have done it. I suggest that you look at the articles I have been using as examples and study them for their form. While you should notice that there are many possible models for writing reviews, all of them share both particular contents and forms.

Literature reviews have a particular *content*. They clearly describe the questions that are being asked (see Chapter 3). They also locate the research within the ongoing scholarly dialogue. This is done by summarizing current understandings and by discussing why what we already know leads to the need for the present research (which we have discussed in this chapter). In relation to what is already known, literature reviews also define the primary concepts (see Chapter 5). These are the elements in *all* literature reviews.

Again, while there are many specific models for writing reviews, what all of them share is that they are in essay form and characterized by the following:

1. The content should proceed from topic to topic. While a primary task of the literature review is summarizing what already is known, this should *not* be presented as a series of paragraphs that each summarizes a particular piece of prior research. The object is to offer summary statements of existing research as a *whole*, not summaries of particular articles or books.

2. The content should include what is necessary for readers to understand the context of the research, and it should include only what is necessary. For example, particular methods used in a reviewed study should not be discussed *unless* they are important to establish why the current proposed method is better; specifics about samples in previous studies should not be discussed *unless* they are important to the particular project, and so on.

3. The content is characterized by good writing. In the real world of journal publishing, reviewers will refuse to review a manuscript that is poorly written. Do not allow problems in writing to stop your audience from understanding your good ideas.

4. The content is properly cited. Properly citing the work is critical for two reasons: First and foremost, ideas and knowledge are the products of academic labor, so citations give credit to the original author. Second, citations are important for scholarly work in general, because they are the way for readers to trace back the ideas contained in a report.

LITERATURE REVIEWS AND RESEARCH DESIGN

Reviewing the literature is rarely something done only in the beginning of the process of research design. Expect that you will frequently return to the literature throughout the research process and that particular literatures that seem important at one stage in the process might seem not as important later. Data analysis can lead to unanticipated findings requiring attention to new topics.

Rather than thinking of reviewing the work of others as an endless task, try thinking of the existing literature as your friend, somewhere you can go to help you think.

Just as the process of writing questions cannot be separated from the literature review, the literature review cannot be separated from the design task called *measurement*, which is about defining key concepts and deciding how they will be measured in the research. Measurement is our next topic.

| **Conceptualization/ operationalization in existing studies** | ⟹ | **Conceptualization/ operationalization decisions for current study** |

EXAMPLES OF SOCIAL RESEARCH ARTICLE DATABASES

Academic Search Primer

This is the world's largest scholarly, multidisciplinary, full-text database and contains more than 3,600 peer-reviewed publications as well as indexing and abstracts for more than 8,200 journals.

Criminal Justice Periodicals

This is a professionally compiled periodicals database for criminal justice scholars. It provides total access to 45 criminal justice journals, plus complete abstracts for over 100 additional titles.

NCJRS: National Criminal Justice Reference Service Abstracts

These abstracts are published by the Office of Justice Programs, U.S. Department of Justice's National Criminal Justice Reference Service, an information clearinghouse for research, police, and practice related to criminal and juvenile justice and drug control.

PsycINFO

This database covers the professional academic literature in psychology, medicine, psychiatry, nursing, sociology, education, pharmacology, physiology, linguistics, and other such topics. It also contains over 1,300 journals and dissertations in over 30 languages and book chapters that are written in English.

Social Sciences Full Text

This is a database that covers 756 core periodicals in the following subjects: anthropology, economics, geography, law and criminology, political science, social work, sociology, and international relations.

Social Services Abstracts

This database provides indexes and abstracts of current research (1980 to present) in social work, human services, social welfare, social policy, and community development.

Sociological Abstracts

This database abstracts and indexes the international literature in sociology and related disciplines in the social and behavioral sciences and contains citations from 1963 to present, journal articles, book reviews, books, book chapters, dissertations, and conference papers.

Web of Science/Web of Knowledge

This database accesses Science Citation Expanded, Social Sciences Citation Index, and Arts & Humanities Citation Index; it also contains links to approximately 8,500 of the most prestigious, high-impact research journals in the world.

Wilson Omnifile Full Text Mega Edition

This multidisciplinary database provides the complete content—indexing, abstracting and full text—from six of Wilson's full-text databases: education, general science, humanities, readers' guide, social sciences, and business.

Worldwide Political Science Abstracts

This is a database that contains citations, abstracts, and indexing of the international literature in political science and its complementary fields, including international relations and public administration/policy. Its major areas include comparative politics, developing nations, disarmament, economic policy, electoral systems, environmental policy, international relations/ trade, labor relations, and military policy.

ᴥ FIVE ᴥ

MEASUREMENT

⸻ ⋅◆⋅ ⸻

While social research requires *data*, which are traces of the *physical* world, everything of interest to researchers—social class, ethnicity, inequality, narrative, identity, deviance, crime, migration, and so on—are *concepts,* which are abstractions that do *not* have a physical existence.

> All social research from all perspectives is about the relationships between the physical world that can be captured through the senses (*data*) and the abstract world of meaning (*concepts*).

A central question in designing and evaluating social research of any type is, how do we move from the physical world, which is the source of data, to concepts, which are located in the nonphysical world of meaning? Put another way, how do we know that what we sense in the physical world has a particular meaning?

> Measurement is the process of linking the physical world and the social world of meaning.

Social research of all kinds is about linking the physical and social worlds. For example, my eyes can see a piece of cloth in particular colors (red, white, and blue) and with a particular design (stars and stripes in a specific order). Such a physical object is not of much interest to researchers until it is given meaning; in this case, what my eyes see is an example of the concept of "the American flag." Pieces of cloth do not have any inherent meaning; flags have meaning, and in this case, meaning leads to many questions: *What* does the flag symbolize? *What* and *how* and *why* does it inspire and motivate? *Who* and *when* does it inspire and motivate?

Social researchers are interested in meaning; yet research must use data from our senses, and what we can sense does not have any inherent meaning. All social research is about translations between data and concepts, between what we can sense and the meanings of what we can sense. Recall from Chapter 2 that there are two ways to link data and concepts. *Deductive* research begins with concepts and uses them to interpret the meaning of data; *inductive* research begins with data and uses these to form the meaning of concepts. While I will return to how these different directions of reasoning influence the process of social research design, for now the important point is that all research requires moving from what we can sense to meanings; the only choice is whether to move from concepts to data (deductive reasoning) or from data to concepts (inductive reasoning).

This social research design task of linking the world of physical objects with the world of social meaning is called *measurement,* which is an appropriate term because the question is how research can measure elements in the physical world in ways that allow us to know something about the abstract, intangible world of concepts. Measurement has two components called *conceptualization* and *operationalization*. I will begin where research using deductive reasoning begins: conceptualization.

CONCEPTUALIZATION AND CONCEPTUAL DEFINITIONS

One of the major ways in which methodological thinking is different from how we think in daily life is that research requires a far more careful use of language. Research requires precision, and it is the design task of conceptualization that transforms our usually fuzzy use of language to the careful, precise language required for research.

> Conceptualization: the process of translating imprecise and ambiguous ideas into precise and clearly defined concepts.

Conceptualization is a process, a task, the outcome of which is *conceptual definitions*, the precise definitions of terms.

> Conceptual definition: a careful, exact, logical definition of a concept.

The obvious example: What I have just done is offered conceptual definitions of the concepts of *conceptualization* and *conceptual definition*. While knowing what I mean does *not* require that you agree with my definitions, you now know precisely what I mean when I use the terms *conceptualization* and *conceptual definition*.

Identifying and Writing Conceptual Definitions

An important skill in evaluating reports of research is recognizing conceptual definitions. At times, this does not take much detective work.

Example 5.1: Researcher Sarah Odland ("Unassailable Motherhood, Ambivalent Domesticity") complains that the concepts of motherhood and domesticity are often confused. Her goal is to distinguish between these, which she does explicitly when she writes the following:

I define motherhood as it relates to activities involving the care of children—both physical and emotional—and I define domesticity as it relates to the physical location of women within the home, tending to the daily chores of managing a household, excluding the care of children. (lines 111–115)

Example 5.2: Notice the clarity of the conceptual definition of *technology identity* in "The Digital Identity Divide":

A technology identity represents a blend of four areas of an individual's belief system: beliefs about one's technology skills, about opportunities and constraints to use technology, about the importance of technology, and about one's own motivation to learn more about technology. (lines 19–22)

I highly recommend that you follow these models of writing explicit conceptual definitions in your own research. Explicit definitions help keep researchers focused, and they are the easiest for readers to follow. That said, it is common for researchers to be less than explicit in presenting conceptual definitions, so readers sometimes need to do detective work to find them. Conceptual definitions, for example, can be explicitly defined but not obvious if you are reading too quickly.

Example 5.3: A key concept in "Exploring the Bases of Partisanship" is that of *social identity*, a term used from line 3 onward but not explicitly defined until lines 49–52, which are at the end of a fairly long paragraph: "[social identity is] that part of an individual's self-concept which derives from his knowledge of his membership in a social group together with the value and emotional significance attached to the membership."

Example 5.4: Notice how the definition of the key concept of gang socialization in the study of "Gang-Related Gun Violence" appears in the middle of a sentence summarizing the review of the literature (lines 32–33). I have highlighted the conceptual definition in italics:

> Research on gang socialization—*the process of learning the appropriate values and norms of the gang culture to which one belongs*— suggests that group processes are highly important.

You will not be able to understand the research you are reading if you do not know how the authors are defining their key concepts. Yet there will be times when you will not find conceptual definitions, even when you are reading very carefully. This is quite common when concepts might seem simply commonsense—gender, deviance, social class, family—and therefore not need formal definition. While it is acceptable practice to not offer explicit definitions of concepts whose meaning often is simply assumed to be widely shared, this is risky because commonsense understandings are those from daily life, where our use of language is sloppy and lacking in the specificity needed in research. Indeed, much research from interpretive perspectives has demonstrated widespread disagreement on seemingly simple ideas such as deviance, family, and violence. What is and what is not *deviant*, what does and what does not count as *family* or *violence* are deeply political debates.

The lesson here is that when reading research, you should train yourself to look for conceptual definitions. If you do not find them, slow down because the author is assuming that you share common meanings, which may or may not be true.

In the same way, when designing your own research, I would suggest that you list all your concepts from the most simple to the most complex and think carefully before deciding that you do not need to define any particular concept because its meaning is widely shared. It is better to err on the side of assuming lack of agreement and, therefore, the necessity of explicitly defining the concept than assuming agreement. When in doubt, be explicit.

A final point about conceptual definitions concerns language: The words used to label concepts carry with them entire systems of meaning. The same people, for example, can be called *freedom fighters* or *terrorists*; the behavior of spanking children can be called *punishment* or *abuse*, and so on. Choose your language carefully, and be aware of the meanings behind language when you read reports written by others.

OPERATIONALIZATION
AND OPERATIONAL DEFINITIONS

While all social research asks questions about *meaning*, what we can actually measure is limited to records of the *physical* world. Operationalization is a task—a process of deciding what, precisely, in the physical world will be taken as a sign of the concept.

> Operationalization: the process of deciding what particular data will indicate the presence of a particular concept.

The outcome of the process of operationalization is called the *operational definition*. These outcomes are sometimes are called *indicators*, because they tell us what in the physical world will indicate the presence of a concept. Operational definitions are a recipe of sorts; they bridge the gap between the abstract concept and the physical world of the senses.

> Operational definition: the definition of a concept in terms of what will measure it in the physical world. A fully operationalized concept is called a *variable*.

Types of Operationalizations in Social Research

Operationalization is about how the meaning of data will be classified. Recall from Chapter 2 that data in social research have two general kinds of content: what people think/feel and what people do. While there are countless variations, three basic kinds of operationalizations follow: criteria for classifying things people say (either verbally or in writing), criteria for classifying behavior, and criteria for classifying documents and other physical objects that can be records of what people say and/or what people do.

Operationalizations as Criteria for
Classifying Things People Say

Much social research data come from listening to people talk and/or from reading what people have written. The most obvious operationalizations of this content are in terms of answers to specific questions contained in surveys.

Example 5.5: Researchers in "Exploring the Bases of Partisanship" include a section in their review of the literature titled "Ideology in the American Electorate: Meaning and Measurement." This leads readers to expect that this section will contain conceptualizations and operationalizations of the concept of ideology—and it does. The conceptual definition of *ideology* is "a set of beliefs about the role of government that shapes responses to a wide range of specific policy issues" (lines 95–97). Ideology is then *operationalized* by survey questions measuring "[citizens'] positions on a wide range of domestic and foreign policy issues" (lines 136–154). The section also lists the specific policy issues that are included in the survey (lines 148–154).

Example 5.6: "Smoking Identities and Behaviors," contains a section called "Measures" (lines 69–96). Notice how readers are *not* offered explicit conceptual definitions of the two key concepts of *smoking status* and *self-described smoking identity*, but the concepts are quite concrete, and their operationalizations—defined as particular responses to written survey questions—are clear and straightforward:

Concept: *s*moking status (lines 80–89)
   Measurement: The question on the survey was, "Within the last 30 days, on how many days did you use cigarettes?"
Response Choices

   a. Responses of "have never used" and "have used but not in the last 30 days" are operationalizations of the smoking status category called "not a current smoker."
   b. Response choices of "1-2 days," "3-5 days," "6-9 days," "10-19 days," "20-29 days," and "all 30 days" are operationalizations of the smoking status category called "current smoker."

Concept: Self-described smoking identity (lines 91–96)
   Measurement: The question on the survey was, "Which of the following best describes you?"

   Response choices: "nonsmoker," "smoker," "occasional smoker," and "social smoker." Each of these is the operationalization of *self-described smoking identity*.

Operationalizations as Criteria for Classifying Behavior

Because social research data can be measures of what people do, operationalizations can come in the form of criteria for categorizing *behavior*.

Example 5.7: According to researcher Benjamin Bowser ("Public Indicators of Social Hierarchy"), we need ways to measure a concept he variously calls *social hierarchy*, *social inequality*, and *ethnic inequality*. How can researchers *see* social hierarchy? First, he narrows the concept of social hierarchy to the more specific concept of *deference*. Then he offers a precise operational definition of precisely what researchers need to see in order to say they have seen deference:

> Deference is defined here by altering ones' walking speed and course by turning left or right for an oncoming walker; that is by stepping out of their path or slowing down to let them by or speeding up to get out of their way. (lines 91–94)

Example 5.8: A key concept in "Identity Threat and Dietary Choices" is dietary choices, which is operationalized as *behavior*: the amounts of "American" and "Asian" food participants ordered during an experiment (lines 213–216).

Operationalizations as Criteria for Classifying the Content of Documents or Other Physical Objects

Social research data can include the contents of documents (transcripts of government hearings, magazines, blogs, and so on) and other physical objects (inscriptions on gravestones, messages on T-shirts, music videos, and so on). Operational definitions for such data are in the form of rules for categorizing document content.

Example 5.9: "Unassailable Motherhood" contains a listing of operationalizations used to examine how issues of *Ladies' Home Journal* portrayed women after WWII. The researcher explicitly defines these as the "set of criteria to identify text and visual images that made explicit reference to motherhood." (lines 123–131)

- references to the word *mother* or *mom*
- images depicting a woman and child together
- the hailing of *you* in advertisements for children's products in which the implied *you* is the mother of the child
- advertisements for children's products in which no person is hailed, but . . . it can be assumed that the advertisement's target is mothers.

Notice again the precision that allows readers to know exactly what the researcher was looking at in these magazines.

In summary, measurement is the process of linking the physical and social worlds. Conceptualization (precise definitions of concepts) and operationalization (what measures the concepts in the physical world) are the two components of measurement. Exhibit 5.1 shows the conceptualizations and operationalizations in the published research examples contained in the appendix.

Exhibit 5.1 Conceptualization and Operationalization in Published Research

Title/Author	Conceptualizations	Operationalizations
Abramowitz/ Saunders: "Exploring the Bases of Partisanship"	**party identification:** "an emotional attachment grounded in enduring group loyalties" (lines 6–7)	**party identification:** voting
	social identity: "that part of an individual's self-concept which derives from his knowledge of his membership in a social group together with the value and emotional significance attached to the membership" (lines 49–52)	**social identity:** objective membership in specific groups: "theorists . . . view objective membership as a necessary condition for identification with a group" (lines 47–48)
	ideology: "Set of beliefs about the role of government that shapes responses to a wide range of specific policy issues" (lines 95–97)	**ideology:** 7-point liberal-conservative scale (lines 136–140) or 3-question exit poll (lines 140–143)
Bowser: "Ethnography of Racial Identities "	**social hierarchy:** used synonymously with the terms *social inequality* and *ethnic inequality*; reconceptualized as *deference*	**deference:** "altering one's walking speed and course" to allow others to walk without interference (lines 91–94)
Goode: "The Digital Identity Divide"	**digital divide:** "females, low-income students and students of color are the ones most underprepared for the digital college environment" (lines 12–14)	**digital divide:** citations to research (lines 28–70)
	technology identity: "beliefs about one's technology skills, about opportunities and constraints to use technology, about the importance of technology, and about one's own motivation to learn more about technology" (lines 20–22)	**technology identity:** through examples from the data (the study uses inductive logic, where data define the concepts)

Title/Author	Conceptualizations	Operationalizations
Guendelman/Cheryan/Monin: "Identity Threat and Dietary Choices"	**identity threat:** "having one's membership in a social group doubted" (line 23)	**identity threat:** Experiment 1: A white experimenter approached participants and asked them if they spoke English (lines 106–111). Experiment 2: "the experimenter told those in the identity-threat condition, 'Actually, you have to be an American to be in this study'" (lines 205–207)
	American food: (not defined)	**American food:** Rated in a separate study (lines 113–116)
McIntosh/McKeganey: "Addicts' Narratives Of Recovery"	**addiction, dependence, recovery:** undefined because interest is in the addicts' understanding of these terms (lines 85–90)	**addiction, dependence, recovery:** through examples from the stories addicts told of their own recovery (inductive logic)
	ex-addict: the individual's own sense of recovery (lines 88–90)	**ex-addict:** "addicts' own definitions of whether they had given up using" (lines 85–88)
	narratives of recovery: addicts' own accounts of their recovery (lines 23–24)	examples from data

(Continued)

Exhibit 5.1 (Continued)

Title/Author	Conceptualizations	Operationalizations
Odland: "Unassailable Motherhood, Ambivalent Domesticity"	**motherhood:** "the activities involving the care of children" (line 112)	**motherhood:** references to words *mother* or *mom*, images depicting woman/child together, using "you" in advertisements, advertisements for children's products (lines 123–131)
	domesticity: "physical location of women within the home, tending to the daily chores . . . excluding the care of children" (lines 113–115)	
Ridner/Walker/ Hart/Myers: "Smoking Identities and Behavior"	**current smoker:** smoked at least once in past 30 days (lines 86–89)	**smoking status:** survey question: "Within the last 30 days, on how many days did you use cigarettes?" (lines 83–85)
	occasional smoker: smoked at least once in past 30 days but not daily (lines 7–9)	**Self-defined identity:** survey question: "Which of the following best describes you?" (nonsmoker, smoker, occasional smoker, social smoker) (lines 91–94)
Stretesky/ Pogrebin: "Gang- Related Gun Violence"	**gang socialization:** "the process of learning the appropriate values and norms of the gang culture to which one belongs" (lines 32–33)	**socialization and identity:** through examples in the data. Data operationalize the concepts (inductive logic).
	identity: "The perceived social location of the person" (line 49–50)	

Operational Definitions and Research Logic

Regardless of whether the research is positivist, interpretive, or critical in perspective, regardless of data content, origin, or form, *operational definitions* are rules for moving between data and concepts. There are, however, major differences in how operationalization is carried out depending upon the extent to which research is informed by inductive and deductive logic.

Operationalizations in Deductive Research

When research is *deductive*, what already is known (existing theories/concepts) leads decisions about what questions to ask, what data to collect, and how the meaning of data will be interpreted. Stated another way, the more research is characterized by deductive reasoning, the more decisions about how to operationalize concepts are made on the basis of the *existing literature*.

> When research is deductive, operationalization is a task for research design. The existing literature offers the guidelines for decisions about operationalization.

Operationalization is all-powerful in deductive research: If researchers decide to operationalize "smoking behavior" as the number of *days* smoked in the past month, they will not have data on the number of *cigarettes* smoked. As with decisions about what to include and exclude in literature reviews, decisions about how to operationalize concepts simultaneously are decisions about how to *not* operationalize them. These decisions simultaneously determine what data *will* be generated and what data will *not* be generated.

Operationalizations in Inductive Research

While all research is (or at least should be) informed by the existing literature, there are instances when this literature does not contain sufficient information to allow clear operationalizations or researchers may want to look at something in a way that differs from what has been done in the past. In these instances, prior research is not a good model upon which to base proposed research. These are the kinds of cases calling for inductive logic, where decisions on how to operationalize concepts are made on the basis of the *data*.

> When research is inductive, operationalization is a task for *data analysis*. The data operationalize the concept.

Example 5.10: While researchers in "Addicts' Narratives of Recovery" include a review of the literature describing how researchers conceptualize the process of recovery from drug addiction, they say their interest is *not* in how experts understand this process. Rather, their interest is in what I am calling *interpretive* questions: "What is the nature of the individuals' accounts of their recovery and in what ways might the recounting of those narratives be part of the recovery process?" (lines 97–100). Rather than beginning with specific questions, they ask their study respondents to "describe, in their own terms, how they had come off drugs" (lines 109–110). What they found—the respondents' own words about how they began thinking of themselves as *ex-addicts*—becomes the operationalization for the concept *narratives of recovery*. In other words, the operationalization of *narratives of recovery* is what respondents said.

I want to include a word of warning here about inductive research. Because operationalization is not a design task for these studies, it is true that inductive research is easier to design than deductive studies. However, there is a heavy cost to generating data without the guidance provided by operationalizations: Researchers are left with the task of figuring out the meaning of data without much support. While deductive studies do take more time to design, inductive studies tend to take far more time to analyze data.

In summary, quality research often is more or less inductive and more or less deductive. To the extent that it is deductive, operationalizations are made on the basis of the existing literature, and they guide the tasks of generating data; to the extent research is inductive, operationalizations come from the data, so they are a task for data analysis. What is important when you design and read research is that you look for the logical relationships between what we sense in the world (data) and the meanings of what we sense (concepts).

MEASUREMENT PROBLEMS IN SOCIAL RESEARCH

If research were perfect, what we *actually* measure in the physical world (the implementation of operationalizations) would correspond perfectly to what we *say* we are measuring (concepts). In this perfect world, we would measure exactly what we say we are measuring, and we would measure only what we say we are measuring. Given the complexity of people and social life, however, it is not surprising that such a perfect state is rarely achieved. While specific forms of data generation techniques are characterized by specific measurement troubles, I will focus on the generalities—the measurement problems for all social research that arise from the diversity and complexity of people and social life.

The Problem of Meaning

While social researchers are interested in concepts (which are about meaning), meaning is not inherent in the physical world. A few examples: a cat is understood as a pet by some people and as a food by others; some people are certain that gender is fixed and biological, while others are just as certain that gender is a choice. The concepts of interest to social researchers do not have a fixed meaning; their meaning depends on a wide variety of conditions, so meaning is constantly changing and subject to disagreement. This is a problem for measurement, of course: How do we measure something whose meaning is not fixed and is subject to disagreement?

The Problem of Multidimensionality

In contrast to the clarity and specificity of many concepts in the natural sciences (there are few disagreements about the meaning of *gravity* or *oxidation*), social research involves topics with multiple dimensions. How, precisely, should we define *racism*? Is it a subjective feeling? An objective behavior? What is *family*? Should we define it in terms of legalities? Biology? Feelings of belonging? The mysteries of social life involve biology, psychology, relationships, social structures, history, and so on. While no one research project can look at any concept in its full range of dimensions, ignoring some dimensions might interfere with our abilities to understand other dimensions. What do we measure when we cannot measure everything that could be important?

The Problem of Interconnectivity

The elements of social life are interconnected. The meaning of any particular object, event, behavior, or person most often cannot be isolated from surrounding objects, events, behaviors, or people. This leads to the common measurement problem of *confounding* (also called *mis-specification*), which happens when two concepts that are highly interrelated in real life become confused within research. The influences of race/ethnicity, for example, are commonly confused with the influences of economic class; gendered characteristics of particular jobs often are confused with gendered characteristics of people in jobs, and so on. While there are a variety of techniques to measure *statistical* confounding in quantitative data, the problems for social research are not confined to statistical measurements. How do we know we are measuring what we say we are measuring and not something else?

The Problem of Measurement Imprecision

Human social life is complex; so unsurprisingly, social research often involves concepts that are difficult to conceptualize and operationalize. There is not one right way to conceptualize or operationalize deviance or social class or many other concepts of primary concern to social researchers. While careful attention to measurement is a characteristic of quality research, conceptual and operational imprecision will remain simply because the complexity of social life cannot be eliminated. How can we have precise concepts and precise measurements when humans and social life are so imprecise?

The lesson here is complex: We cannot expect perfect measurement in social research, yet we clearly cannot simply ignore measurement problems.

EVALUATING MEASUREMENT

Conceptualization and operationalization are central in all social research, because they create the link between the physical world we can measure and the abstract world of meaning that we study. Yet the complexity of social life, coupled with disagreements and imprecision in how to define and measure this complexity, means that social research of all varieties is characterized by measurement problems. Indeed, measurement problems often are a specific topic of concern for researchers who complain about how even a seemingly concrete concept such as smoking behavior can be defined and measured in multiple ways ("Smoking Identities and Behavior," lines 14–35); how there are conflicting interpretations of the central concepts of addiction, dependence, recovery, and behavior change in research about the process of recovering from drug addiction ("Addicts' Narratives of Recovery," lines 18–21); and how we do not have ways to directly measure the new forms of social inequality surrounding ethnicity ("Ethnography of Racial Identities," lines 23–25).

How can conceptualizations and operationalizations be evaluated? Positivist and interpretive perspectives approach this question in different ways.

Evaluating Measurement Validity in Positivist Research

Recall that positivist frameworks begin by assuming that the physical world exists apart from how humans understand it and that it can be measured. Given this, it is not surprising that there is considerable concern in this perspective for *correctly* measuring the world. This is called *measurement validity.*

In positivist perspectives, measurement is evaluated in terms of its validity. A valid measure is one that actually measures what the researcher says it is measuring.

Because operationalizations are the measure of concepts, it follows that a basic type of validity (called *content validity*) refers to the relationships between the concept and its operationalization: Does the operationalization adequately measure the concept? While various technical tests exist, underlying each test is *thought* about what is being measured and what it is being called: Measuring shoe size and calling it "intelligence" is not valid.

> **Example 5.11:** The concept of smoking behavior ("Smoking Identities and Behavior") was measured by asking people the number of days in which they smoked during the past month. Is knowing the number of days smoked an adequate measure of something called *smoking behavior*? If it is, then "number of days smoked" is a valid measure of smoking behavior.

> **Example 5.12:** The concept of social identity in research on voting behavior ("Exploring the Bases of Partisanship") was defined as "that part of an individual's self-concept which derives from his knowledge of his membership in a social group together with the value and emotional significance attached to the membership" (lines 49–52). Notice how this concept has two components: an *objective* membership in a group (such as religion, gender, or geographical residence) *and* a *subjective* feeling that membership in this group has "value and emotional significance." Researchers measured only "objective membership in a large variety of social groups" (lines 63–65). Is that a valid operationalization of the concept of social identity?

Evaluating Measurement Trustworthiness in Interpretive Research

The purpose of interpretive research is to understand the complexity of human experience, so measurement is evaluated on the extent to which it explores complexity while recognizing the social nature of research itself.

Within interpretive perspectives, measurement is evaluated in terms of its apparent *trustworthiness*.

While there is no rule book for how to establish trustworthiness in interpretive research, there is an underlying logic that is sensible. First, the image of researchers within interpretive perspectives is of people whose own values and biases will influence the research. You will notice how reports of interpretive research often contain information about the personal characteristics of researchers, which serves to establish the trustworthiness of the *researcher*. Next, in comparison to research from positivist perspectives (where readers often are offered very little information about the process of research), interpretive research often contains detailed descriptions that serve to establish the trustworthiness of the *research process* (lines 86–109 in "Gang-Related Gun Violence" are a good example). Finally, because a goal of interpretive research is to understand the complexity of social life, the trustworthiness of *data analysis* is established by emphasizing the complexity of findings.

Problems in Evaluating Measurement

While readers should be concerned with evaluating the quality of measurement in research they read, the actual task of evaluating measurement can be difficult.

Conventions for reporting studies using numerical data often make it hard for readers to evaluate measurement quality. Readers typically are not told much about what researchers did to prepare the data for analysis (a process called *data cleaning*) nor are readers told how many statistical models researchers tried but discarded. Also, published articles reporting the results of large-scale surveys rarely list all of the survey questions and their possible responses. It therefore is not possible for readers to judge the extent to which the questions adequately—or accurately—measured the concepts.

Studies from interpretive perspectives pose other kinds of problems for evaluators, the most tangible of which is that journal articles allow each author a very limited number of pages. Researchers do not have enough space to adequately establish the trustworthiness of themselves or of the data collection process. Indeed, even in the journal articles I am using as examples, I could not offer examples of evaluating measurement. The general principles— demonstrating the trustworthiness of researchers, of the research process, and of data analysis—are quite obvious in books, but journal articles are not long enough. I will return to this problem in Chapter 8, which considers the task of evaluation.

CONCEPTUALIZATION AND OPERATIONALIZATION AND RESEARCH DESIGN

In this chapter, I covered the design task typically called *measurement*, which includes the two elements of *conceptualization* and *operationalization*. It makes sense to think of conceptualization and operationalization as a joint task because good measurement—whether called *valid* or *trustworthy*—depends upon logical relationships between the operationalization (what is being measured) and the conceptualization (what the measurement is taken to mean). And, because most research is more deductive than inductive, it makes sense to think of conceptualization and operationalization as coming after the literature review, because conceptualization and operationalization are based on what is discovered in the existing literature.

At the same time, operationalization in deductive research is about the task of developing techniques for data generation. After all, if research is to use written surveys, then *operationalization* means writing survey questions; if the research is to examine document content, then *operationalization* means developing criteria for classifying content. Just as writing research questions cannot be separated from reviewing the literature and just as reviewing existing knowledge cannot be separated from conceptualization, operationalization cannot be separated from the design decisions of how to generate data. Designing research is not a series of isolated tasks; it is a process of interconnected parts. This takes us to our next topic: techniques for generating data.

Existing knowledge ⟹ **Operationalizations** ⟸ **Data generation techniques**

SIX

DATA GENERATION TECHNIQUES

———•◆•———

Regardless of research questions, perspectives, and direction of reasoning linking concepts and data, all research requires data; this chapter considers how to think about obtaining it. In the methods tool kit, different ways of obtaining data are similar to carpenters' tools: Just as hammers, saws, and screwdrivers each are designed for some purposes and not others, each data generation technique produces specific kinds of data that can answer some research questions and not others.

I begin with a note about terminology. While it is most common to talk about ways of *collecting* data, that term is unfortunate, because it encourages images of researchers carrying baskets into the world to pick up data that are simply lying around. This certainly is not an accurate image of the actual research process, which always is about making decisions. I have decided to use the term *data generation*, because it will encourage you to remember that a complex process lies behind data used to address social research questions.

RESEARCH QUESTIONS AND DATA

In Chapter 2, I talked about how data had three dimensions: content (what people say/what people do), form (words/numbers), and origin (produced by researchers/naturally occurring). Research questions determine what data content are necessary.

Research Questions and Data Content

Although it might seem too obvious to require mentioning, the two different contents of data (reports of what people say and reports of behavior) correspond to two types of questions—how people think/feel and how people act. This is the lesson you should take with you:

> Empirical evidence for how people think/feel comes from asking them; empirical evidence for how people act comes from watching them.

Clearly distinguishing between measuring thinking/feeling and measuring behavior is important for two reasons. First, researchers repeatedly have found that self-reports of behavior can be less than truthful: People commonly *over-*report socially valued behaviors (such as attending church) and *under*report socially devalued behaviors (such as alcohol consumption). The second reason for distinguishing thinking/feeling from behavior is more subtle: People are not always aware of the meanings or consequences of their behaviors.

> **Example 6.1:** "Ethnography of Racial Identities" is about relationships between ethnicity/social class and social hierarchy, operationalized in terms of "walking patterns" (lines 91–94), "line jumping" (lines 215–224) "counter-crashing" (lines 246–249), and "service jumping" (lines 278–284). It is possible that people who were allowed to walk in a straight line were not aware that others were modifying their walking patterns; those who subtly changed their course of walking to allow others to walk in straight lines might not even have been aware they were doing this.

People cannot answer questions about their behaviors when they do not realize these behaviors exist. Behaviors we often are unaware of are also strongly associated with gender, race, and class. These behaviors are important to study precisely because they work outside the realm of consciousness. They are powerful, but people cannot talk about them because they are not aware of them.

Just as we cannot know how people act by asking them, we cannot know what people think or feel by watching them. Consider again the article "Ethnography of Racial Identities." The empirical findings are that some types of people are more likely than others to change their walking paths or experience others moving in front of them in lines or diverting the attention of sales clerks. Do we know that these behaviors are experienced as problems? No. Do we know why people so rudely act this way? No. Behavior does *not* tell us motivation; behavior does *not* tell us meaning.

What should be measured—the content of data—depends upon the research question. In real life, of course, it is not always possible to observe people when researchers would like to observe them nor is it always possible to talk with people when researchers would like to talk with them. At times, the best we can do is to ask people to report behavior or to watch people without knowing the meanings or motivations for the behaviors. The lesson, though, for both designing and reading research is to understand that reports of behavior are reports and not direct indications of behavior and that observation cannot tell us meanings or motivations.

Research Questions and Data Form

Another dimension of data is its form: We can generate descriptions of what people say or do either as words or as numbers. The form of data should be determined by the research question.

Data in the form of words are necessary when questions are about complex meaning and when concepts are not understood well enough to allow them to be operationalized as survey questions, especially those with a limited number of response choices. On the other hand, data in the form of numbers are obviously necessary to address questions about quantity. Such data also are necessary for answering questions requiring large amounts of data, because only data as numbers allow statistical analysis, and only statistical analysis can handle large amounts of data.

The third dimension of data takes us to the topic of techniques for data generation. Data have two origins: Some are *produced* by researchers and some are *naturally occurring* and used by researchers.

Exhibit 6.1 describes relationships among data content, origin, form, and specific techniques of data generation. It shows, for example, how records of

Exhibit 6.1   Data Content, Origin, Form, and Techniques of Data Generation

Data Content	Researcher Produced	Data Form	Naturally Occurring	Data Form
Verbal reports	Laboratory experiments (when the dependent variable is verbal reports)	Words/ numbers	Naturally occurring field experiments	Words/ numbers
	Fixed question surveys	Words/ numbers but typically numbers	Overheard talk	Words/ numbers but typically words
	In-depth interviews	Words	Document analysis	Words/ numbers

Data Content	Researcher Produced	Data Form	Naturally Occurring	Data Form
Behavior	Experiments (when the dependent variable is behavior)	Words/ numbers	Observation in natural settings	Words/ numbers
			Official records (marriage, divorce, births, immigration, voting)	Numbers
			Documents describing behavior (court documents, policy hearings transcripts)	Words

what people say (verbal reports) can be researcher produced (from data generation techniques of laboratory experiments, surveys, or in-depth interviews) or naturally occurring (from naturally occurring field experiments, overheard talk, or document analysis) and how some of these data will be in the form of words while others are in the form of numbers.

I had two reasons for talking about forms of data before moving to the main topic of techniques for producing data. One is about the *science* of research design: High-quality design is characterized by logical consistency among various design components. Different kinds of questions require different kinds of data. My second reason for talking about dimensions of data before talking about techniques is the *art* of research design. It is important to think creatively when designing research. There are so many possibilities to explore and consider.

DATA GENERATION TECHNIQUES

Just as different types of questions require different kinds of data, different kinds of data are obtained in different ways. Also, as with hammers, saws, and so on that are best used for specific purposes, each data generation technique produces data that best answers particular kinds of questions. While there are countless variations, here are five primary ways to generate social research data: experiments, fixed-question surveys, in-depth interviews, observation, and document analysis. Each has particular uses, strengths, and weaknesses.

Experiments

Experiment is a method originally developed in the natural sciences and most closely associated with positivist perspectives in social research. The defining characteristics of experiments are the *physical control* and *physical manipulation* of the environment, which allow the empirical verification that one concept (called the *independent variable*) causes another (called the *dependent variable*) to react in a certain way.

> **Example 6.2:** The question in Experiment 1 of "Identity Threat and Dietary Choices" is, will Asian Americans whose identity as American is threatened change a seemingly stable part of themselves—their favorite food—to appear more American? (lines 83–85). The study found that Asian American partici-pants whose identity as an American was threatened listed favorite foods that were more associated with America than Asian American participants whose identity was not threatened. How do we know the difference in food selection was because of the concept called *identity threat*? The power of experiments is the logical power of experimental control and manipulation: Research partici-pants were *randomly assigned* to either the threat group, where a white experimenter approached them before the study to ask, "Do you speak English?" or the nonthreatened group (who were not asked anything before the experiment). Random assignment means we would expect there to be no dif-ferences in these groups before the experimental manipulation (threat/no threat). With all other factors the same (control), except the manipulation, it logically follows that any difference in food selection must be due to the threat.

The logic of experimentation makes it the only method capable of directly assessing cause-and-effect relationships. This strength, however, leads to limitations: The questions for experiments must be very narrow, and the envi-ronment must be completely controlled. This leads to the problem of *external validity:* Does what we learn from experiments say anything about the causes and consequences of events outside the controlled laboratory?

> **Example 6.3:** In "Identity Threat and Dietary Choices," Asian American students whose identity as Americans was threatened then went immediately into the experiment, where they showed more preference for American-identified food than did Asian American students whose identity was not threatened. How many times in real life is a person's identity threatened immediately before being asked to choose between two types of food? Is being asked, "Do you speak English?" by an experimenter equivalent to anything that anyone experiences in real life?

Fixed-Question Surveys

When surveys (a method developed by sociologists) contain written ques-tions and fixed answers, many people can be asked the same questions, so results can be analyzed using statistics. The strength of these surveys is that they are the only technique capable of generating large amounts of data that allow generalizing the results of studies (more about this in the next chapter).

> **Example 6.4:** In "Smoking Identities and Behavior," researchers asked 4,000 students the same two questions: "'Within the last 30 days, on how many days did you use cigarettes?' and 'Which of the following best describes [your identity as a smoker]?'"

Achieving the strength of the fixed-question survey method requires asking questions that will likely be understood in the same way by a large number of people as well as forcing people to choose their answers from among a predetermined set of responses. Yet the more questions and their answers are predetermined, the less the survey can measure the complex meanings, feelings, behaviors, and attitudes that are the defining characteristic of people and social life: How much do we learn about the meaning of identity when we only ask people to check a box indicating they identify themselves in a particular way? Does it matter? Do we even know how the people checking the boxes corresponding to identities understood the meanings of these terms?

In-Depth Interviews

This method was originally developed by psychologists and now is highly identified with research from interpretive perspectives. Viewed as extended conversations between researchers and research participants, in-depth interviews are the only method to allow researchers to explore how people understand topics that are too complex to be reduced to the relatively simple and straightforward questions asked on surveys.

> **Example 6.5:** How addicts make sense of their recoveries from addiction and how men in prison understand the influences of gangs in their lives are complicated questions. It would be difficult to translate such questions about meaning-making into survey questions. "Addicts' Narratives of Recovery" and "Gang-Related Gun Violence" feature examples of data generated from in-depth interviews, which are long conversations between participants and researchers, with the person being interviewed doing the majority of talking.

In-depth interviews pose problems that are the reverse of those associated with surveys: In comparison to surveys that can generate a large amount of data from a great many people, in-depth interviews require so much time (both to do the interviews and to analyze the data) that this technique generates too little data to allow much generalization.

> **Example 6.6:** In "The Digital Identity Divide," knowledge about how college students understand their relationships to technology comes from interviews with three students. Because there is no way of knowing the extent to which

the experiences and understandings of these three students are typical in any way, we cannot assume that this research tells us anything more than how three individuals understood the meaning and uses of technology in their lives.

Observation

A method developed by anthropologists, observation is simply that: observing people in order to gather data about how they behave. Only observation allows the researcher to empirically explore how people *actually* act rather than how they *say* they act.

Example 6.7: How can we see social inequality? "Ethnography of Racial Identities" is about developing a measure to examine inequality as a way of acting rather than a way of thinking.

The strength of observation is that it allows us to examine what people actually do, but like in-depth interviews, the method is time-consuming, so it tends to produce an insufficient quantity of data to allow much generalization.

Example 6.8: "Ethnography of Racial Identities" tells us about patterns of interaction on "busy commercial streets" in Paris. We do not know if there is anything specific to Paris (or France, or Europe, etc.) that creates these patterns.

Document Analysis

Document analysis, a method developed by historians, is a way to examine the content of documents put together for purposes other than for research.

Example 6.9: After the end of WWII, there were major shifts in expectations surrounding the proper roles of women. How do we know what these expectations were? "Unassailable Motherhood, Ambivalent Domesticity" uses the contents of the 1946 issues of *Ladies' Home Journal* magazine as data to examine this question.

The strength of document analysis is that it allows us to examine the content of an incredible variety of documents put together for purposes other than research, but the questions for this analysis are quite limited. Document analysis *cannot* show the motivations of the people producing them; it cannot show how contents are/were interpreted by members of the intended audience.

Example 6.10: Did the editors of *Ladies' Home Journal* in 1946 know they were presenting particular images of domesticity and motherhood? Were they trying to present these particular images? How did women in 1946 understand the meanings of the content of these magazines? The documents cannot tell us the answers to questions such as these.

The general lesson about techniques producing data is that each has particular uses, particular strengths, and particular weaknesses. Not surprisingly, much excellent research involves *triangulation*, which means two or more techniques are used to generate data. So for example, written survey questions answered by many people can be accompanied by in-depth interviews with a few people. The survey data can be used to examine generalities and the interview data can show the details. Social life is complex, so it follows that measuring it in more than one way is beneficial.

> No method of generating data is perfect. Use critical thinking to choose the technique that makes the most sense given the questions that you want to answer.

Exhibit 6.2 summarizes what types of research questions can be addressed with each of the most common data generation techniques as well as the methodological strengths and weaknesses of these techniques.

VARIATIONS IN DATA GENERATION TECHNIQUES

Learning the *science* of research design requires understanding the technical details and proper use of techniques to produce data. Learning the *art* of research design requires thinking about the variations in these techniques, which brings possibilities for creativity, as seen in Exhibit 6.3.

Variations to Match Research Questions

Methods for obtaining data can vary according to the specific research questions. The technique of in-depth interviews, for example, most often involves a researcher talking with one person at a time. Yet if the research question is about how people together construct meaning, then a focus group composed of several people who are encouraged to talk about a particular topic would produce data actually showing the process of the meaning-making. Data showing how people actually do this would be better than data showing how people simply talk about it. Or there are different ways to examine documents: Depending upon the research question, researchers can look at the specific content of documents (called *manifest coding*) and/or they can look at the underlying meaning (called *latent coding*).

Exhibit 6.2 Data Generation Techniques: Requirements of Research Questions and Technique Methodological Strengths and Weaknesses

Technique	Question Requirements	Technique Strengths	Technique Weaknesses
Experiment	Questions about causal relationships between variables; questions must be narrow in scope and involve few variables.	Only technique that can empirically establish cause/effect relationships.	Many social research questions are too broad for experiments; controlled laboratory settings raise questions about external validity: Do findings from experiments accurately depict findings outside laboratory setting?
Fixed-question survey	Questions about how people think/feel about relatively straightforward topics; used to obtain self-reported attitudes, beliefs, and personal characteristics.	The more the questions and responses are fixed, the more the survey can be given to many people, which allows generalization.	The more the questions and responses are predetermined by the researcher, the less the survey can measure complexity.
In-depth interview	Questions about how people think/feel about complex topics; questions about topics that cannot be fully operationalized into a series of predetermined questions.	Extended discussion with interview respondents can measure the complexity of how people think/feel about complicated topics.	This is a very time-consuming method of generating and analyzing data from a small number of cases, which means results cannot be generalized beyond the sample.
Observation	Questions about how people act.	Only technique to empirically examine how people actually act, not how they report they act.	Same as interviews; cannot measure motivation or meanings
Document analysis	Questions about the content/meanings of documents; questions from history; questions about social change.	Documents are the only records of history; court/policy transcripts can show processes leading to social products; document analysis can be a fallback if interviewing is not possible.	Documents do not show motivation or meanings of those producing them; documents do not show how they are/were interpreted by people in their intended audiences.

Exhibit 6.3 Variations in Data Generation Techniques

Technique	Variations

Experiment	Variations in experiment location:
	    laboratory (totally controlled environment)
	    field (ongoing settings such as schools)
	
	Variations in the *content* of dependent variable measurement:
	    thinking/feeling
	    behavior
	
	Variation in the *form* of dependent variable measurement:
	    words
	    numbers

Fixed-question survey	Variations in the method of asking questions:
	    written (survey can be self-administered)
	    verbal (respondent can be asked questions)
	        in person
	        on phone
	
	Variations in types of answers:
	    fixed response (respondents given limited choices)
	    open-ended (respondents supply their own answers)

In-depth interview	Variations in number of people simultaneously interviewed:
	    one (traditional)
	    several (focus group)
	
	Variations in relationship between researcher/person interviewed:
	    positivist: researcher is distant, keeps control of the conversation
	    interpretive: researcher is engaged, participant controls the conversation

Observation	Variations in relationship between researcher and observational site:
	    pure observer: researcher is not part of the setting
	    participant observer: researcher is a member of the setting
	
	Variations in data content:
	    thinking/feeling
	    behavior
	
	Variations in data form:
	    words
	    numbers

(Continued)

Exhibit 6.3 (Continued)

Technique	Variations

Document analysis	Variations in what is of interest in the document:
	    what is physically present in the document (manifest)
	    underlying meaning of physical content (latent)
	Variations in data form:
	    words
	    numbers

Variations to Match the Current State of Knowledge

Techniques can vary depending on how much is known about the topic. For example, surveys asking people to choose their responses from a predetermined list of possibilities (as in "Smoking Identities and Behavior": "Are you a smoker, a non-smoker, a social smoker, or an occasional smoker?") require researchers to know what questions are important as well as what answers are possible. There are many times, though, when existing knowledge is sufficient to know what questions are important but not adequate to predict the range of possible answers. In such cases, researchers can ask questions and allow respondents to write in their own answers. While this will make data analysis more time-consuming than if answers were predetermined and limited, it will produce more data than if researchers used in-depth interviews, where respondents do not all answer the same questions. As another benefit, allowing respondents to write in their answers allows researchers to think inductively by using the answers supplied by people to understand the range of possible answers.

Variations to Match Models of Research

Techniques can be sensitive to differences in the perspectives underlying research. For example, researchers in positivist-informed studies are expected to be objective and impartial and maintain distance from those they research. In such cases, researchers would begin interviews with many questions and lead respondents through them while maintaining emotional distance. In contrast, because the image of researchers in interpretive-informed research is of people who are engaged in the research process, interviews informed by this perspective look more like informal conversations with the research participant controlling the conversational topics and the researcher being emotionally involved.

Variations to Match Practicalities

There are many characteristics of individual research projects or their participants that might create particular issues for data generation. For example, if it is anticipated that respondents might have problems understanding survey questions, researchers can read the surveys to respondents and answer questions respondents might have. While this means participants will hear different information and will not all be treated the same, valid responses result when they understand what questions they are being asked. As another example of how data generation techniques can be modified to handle practicalities, data from observation can come from researchers who are pure observers to those who are a part of the setting being observed; experiments can take place in ongoing settings such as schools or other organizations rather than in laboratories.

As you learn about research techniques, stay alert to variations. While no variation will overcome all limitations and while each variation will be associated with trade-offs, you can use variations to generate data that are the best fit for your particular study. When evaluating research, learn to appreciate the artful use of variations. Think critically/skeptically, but think creatively.

ASSESSING THE APPROPRIATENESS OF DATA GENERATION TECHNIQUES

My recurring comments have been that design tasks—writing questions, doing literature reviews, and so on—do not happen only once and that these tasks can happen in many different orders. As with all else in the research process, developing the technique to generate data might lead researchers to rethink decisions about what techniques to use; it might even lead back to slightly modifying the research questions. There are three general types of problems in developing techniques for generating data: danger to research participants, danger to researchers, and problems with practicalities.

Danger to Research Participants

Concern about research participants must be central in *all* research design. In Chapter 3, I talked about the importance of thinking carefully about the well-being of research participants when choosing research topics. Many subjects are sensitive and require special care. The well-being of research participants was not a topic in the chapters on literature reviews or measurement, because these design tasks are about how researchers think. Now I return to this concern for research participants, because (with the exception of the analysis of documents not produced by researchers and observations made by researchers in distinctly public places) every data generation technique relies on people—people who will talk with researchers, participate in experiments, or complete surveys. The well-being of study participants must remain the first and foremost consideration when developing techniques for producing data.

If you are designing research, think of the possible harm that your proposed techniques for generating data could cause. While social science research is typically not as physically dangerous as medical research, physical harm *can* come from putting people with health problems (including problems that are unknown to researchers) in conditions that could lead to emotional stress.

While it is possible for social research to produce physical harm, harm tends to be *psychological.* Psychological harm can come from placing people in embarrassing, anxiety-producing, or unpleasant situations, which include asking people to recall painful events, falsely telling them that something bad has happened in order to measure their reactions, placing people in situations where they feel social pressure to deny deeply held convictions, or asking them to talk about something they feel is too personal and private to discuss with a researcher.

Although social research can and sometimes does create harm, researchers typically are very surprised when this happens. What I have seen all too often are researchers—both new and established—who get so caught up in the excitement of their projects that they simply *forget* to think about their research participants, or they *assume* that their research participants share their experiences and values. Both can lead to research that creates harm. When designing research, you must keep the well-being of your research participants in mind, and you must always be aware of the possible differences between your own experiences and values and those of your participants. I wrote this in Chapter 3, but it is worth repeating:

> You must focus on how your research appears from the perspective of your research participants.

Not surprisingly, from time to time researchers will come to the conclusion that the research they would like to do cannot be done, because it would pose a risk of harm to research participants. To take the most obvious example: Unless a researcher is a trained mental health counselor, it would be irresponsible to ask people suffering from depression to participate in a study about depression. In the same way, unless a researcher is a trained grief counselor, it would be irresponsible to ask people who have recently lost a loved one to participate in a study about grief. If you are designing research, err on the side of worrying *too much* about possible harm, and when in doubt, assume that harm will be done.

Concern about the well-being of study participants should lead to creative thinking: How can the desired research question be answered using another technique, or how can the question be transformed in a way that would examine a similar mystery—even if it is not the same? Perhaps it is not possible to talk with a particular type of person, but there might be organizations or self-help groups that speak on their behalf; often blogs or other documents are publicly available. Will such places/documents offer the same data? No. But they might be the best that is possible to obtain while keeping the well-being of people in mind

Danger to Researchers

Although I like to think of researchers as detectives solving the mysteries of social life, there is a limit to my metaphor. While detectives can find themselves in situations of extreme danger, they are trained in how to be aware of danger and how to protect themselves. In comparison, social researchers most often do not know how to avoid or handle danger. For multiple reasons, most of us should not plan to do research requiring observation or interaction with many types of people—members of violent gangs, drug dealers, and neo-Nazis come immediately to mind. It is foolish to expect such people to take kindly to researchers; my point here is that the dangers of obtaining such data—as well as the unethical behaviors that almost necessarily surround obtaining it—mean that in these situations, *it is not possible to have researcher-generated data*. In such instances, researchers must redesign their questions in ways that allow data to come from documents of some kind. For example, various white supremacist and neo-Nazi groups have organizational newsletters available to the general public; there are also statistics collected by government agencies, testimonies (such as those in court cases and public policy hearings), and so on available for the public to view. While such data are different from those generated by direct interviewing and observation, they might be the best possible options.

Problems From Practicalities

The task of developing data generation techniques should include thinking about the practicalities of implementing them. A particular technique that sounds perfect in the abstract might be impractical—or maybe impossible—to actually use.

One typical problem is cost. Unless you are lucky enough to have funding to pay for research, some techniques are too costly to use. For example, a student of mine was interested in the experiences of people who went through programs that help minority students succeed in college. She had access to a very nice—and very large—sample of over 2,000 alumni of these programs. Because these folks lived all over the United States, she planned to do a mail survey. It seemed a very good idea until she started to work out the details: Each survey would cost 44¢ to mail and each would need to include return postage of 44¢. The response rate for mail surveys is very low, so she had to expect to send second—and perhaps even third—requests to a majority of people to get a decent rate of return. She came to a conservative estimate that the postage cost for her plan would be close to $3,000—in addition to the cost of copying the survey and buying envelopes. This was simply not possible. But because she managed to obtain the e-mail addresses of these people, she did not need to change her research questions; she only needed to change the method of delivering the survey from mail to e-mail. Because she had to hand-enter the e-mail addresses, she could not survey all 2,000 of the alumni; instead, she developed a sample and found that with e-mail, she could do repeated follow-ups, so her return rate was no doubt better than she could have expected if the survey had been mailed.

Another student arranged a series of interviews with environmental activists across Florida, South Carolina, and Georgia. This was shaping up to be a very nice project until she realized that she would need money for gas as well as to stay in motels and buy food as she traveled to these interviews. She ended up doing in-person interviews only with activists in the local area and doing phone interviews with others. While phone interviews did not allow her to get the depth of information she could have gotten during in-person interviews, the data were good enough.

Also anticipate problems in obtaining access to places that are not public, with *public* meaning that *any* person can be there; shopping malls, public parks, and football stadiums are examples of public places. Classrooms, dormitory dining rooms, parties requiring invitations, and child day care centers are examples of places that are *not* public. Ethics require researchers to obtain permission to do research in any place that is not public, and not all people are particularly enthusiastic about becoming topics of research. Proposed research in schools can be especially troublesome, because it requires obtaining layers of permission—from students, their parents, teachers, principals, and district supervisors. Researchers do manage to obtain this permission but anticipate that it might take considerable time and energy to get it. Understandably, it also is very difficult to gain access to observe self-help groups of all types. These groups are created with the purpose of helping their members; people in these groups most often do not want to transform their personal troubles into data for research.

While it is not uncommon to experience problems generating data that would be perfect, these can be opportunities for creativity. If you encounter problems, think about all the possible variations—both in research techniques and in question rephrasings—and consider it a challenge to circumvent your problems. It might not be possible to generate measures of behavior, so questions about behavior might need to be changed to questions about meanings obtained from surveys or interviews, or conversely, questions about meanings might need to be changed to questions about behavior. Naturally occurring data might need to be exchanged for researcher produced data. True, there must be a fit between the research questions and the contents and forms of data necessary to examine them, yet this does not stop the possibility of creativity. Think critically/skeptically, but think creatively.

There also is a lesson here for evaluating research: It often is not possible to do perfect research. We must work with what we have, with what is possible. Do *not* hold real research to the standard of perfection. As long as researchers are modest in what they claim and as long as they are logical in what they do, then you should appreciate what they are able to do and forgive them for not being able to do what is not possible to do.

DATA GENERATION TECHNIQUES
AND RESEARCH DESIGN

At the end of each chapter, I have talked about how all elements of research design are connected. The relationship between data generation techniques and research questions is the most clear—what data are needed depends upon what questions are asked; questions might need to change if data appropriate to answering them cannot be obtained. There also are clear links between data generation and operationalization: Depending upon the data generation technique, operationalizations can take many forms. In surveys or interviews, operationalizations are answers to questions; in observation, operationalizations are particular behaviors; in document analysis, operationalizations are particular document contents. The point is that operationalizations depend upon data generation techniques.

We now move on to the final design task: choosing samples. Research questions, as well as the data generation techniques, influence what samples are needed as well as what characteristics of samples are desirable.

Research Question

⇕   ⇕

Technique ⟺ **Sample**

⊰ SEVEN ⊱

SAMPLES

———•◦•———

S ocial research is about commonalities and their variations in large groups of people, places, and things: Why do some students understand and feel comfortable with technology and others do not? Why do some people consistently vote for Republicans and others for Democrats? How do magazines, blogs, and newspapers construct the meaning of the world for their readers? What do interactional patterns on busy city streets tell us about inequality? This interest in commonalities and variations leads to a problem: It is not possible for researchers to talk with each and every college student; they cannot carefully examine the contents of each and every magazine, blog, or newspaper; researchers cannot see all the interactions on all busy streets all over the world.

This is an *unchangeable fact*: Social researchers are interested in questions about patterns and their variations in people, places, and things. However, for a variety of reasons, we are not capable of directly examining all instances of any particular type of person, place, or thing. Critical thinking about the relationships between the parts of social life we can examine and the whole represented by those parts is important in understanding the logic of social research. I start with defining the central concepts of population and sample.

POPULATIONS AND SAMPLES IN SOCIAL RESEARCH

Recurring questions in social research are about relationships between the whole, called a *population*, and the part studied, called a *sample*.

The Concept of Population in Social Research

In daily life, the term *population* most often is used to talk about people who live in particular places such as cities (the population of Tampa), states (the population of Florida), or nations (the population of the United States). As used in research methods, the term *population* includes this and far more. Population means the entire collection or every case—of people, places, behaviors, things, or time.

Population can refer to types of *people*: The population of "college students" includes every college student; the population of "vegetarians" includes every vegetarian. There are populations of first-generation immigrants in the United States as well as populations of Republicans, Catholics, college athletes, abused children, and so on. In each instance, *population* is a term used to refer to every person with specific characteristics.

As used in research methods, population can refer to types of *places*. The population of "public universities" includes all such universities; the population of "women-owned businesses" includes all such businesses. There are populations of juvenile courts, college classrooms, city streets, law firms, and so on. The population of a particular type includes each and every instance of that type of place.

Population can refer to types of *behaviors*: There are populations such as marriages in 2012, divorces in the past decade, crime in New York City in the 1990s, and so on. Populations of specific behaviors are all the instances of that behavior.

Population can refer to types of *things*, such as television programs, *New York Times* stories about Hurricane Katrina, romance novels, Wikipedia pages, and so on. The population of *things* includes all instances of that thing.

Finally, population can refer to *time*: The population of time is 24 hours a day, 7 days a week; it includes all time from the beginning of the earth to today.

> Whether referring to types of *people, places, behaviors, things,* or *time*, population is a term for the whole, for every case and instance.

Conceptualizing Populations in Research Design

Population is a concept, an abstract idea with no fixed meaning. As such, the relevant population for any particular research project depends upon how the concepts *in that study* are defined. For example, researchers often define the concept of "college student" to pertain only to *American* college students. Often, researchers further narrow the concept to those in particular types of colleges (such as public universities, community colleges, or private colleges), and/or to those with specific personal characteristics, such as a specific race/ethnicity and/or gender. My point is that each of these are different ways of *conceptualizing* the concept of "college student," and each defining point simultaneously serves to limit the relevant population for that study. Each narrowing of the concept narrows the population.

> Definitions of concepts determine definitions of populations.

Narrowing conceptual definitions with the accompanying narrowing of relevant populations can bring conceptual clarity.

> **Example 7.1:** The general concept/population of "television programs" would include *all* programs on *all* television stations from the beginning of television to the present. It would be very difficult to say much of relevance, because the concept is too large. More meaningful would be smaller definitions of concepts/populations such as those of particular *kinds* of programs (situation comedy, reality, drama, etc.), programs on specific *types of channels* (network, cable, public broadcasting, etc.), and/or programs in particular *years*. A concept such as "situation comedies on network television in the past five years" is much more conceptually clear than the concept of "television programs."

> **Example 7.2:** Many researchers note that the way "courts" (a concept) are formally supposed to work is not the way they truly work. This has led to considerable research. However, the concept/population of *courts* is too large and too varied to allow the kind of specificity that is the hallmark of research: There are family courts, criminal courts, civil courts, and juvenile courts; there are local courts, state courts, federal courts, and international courts. Each type of court has its own distinct characteristics, so combining them into a general concept called *courts* requires a very high level of abstraction. And, because so much is known about each of these different kinds of courts, it would be very difficult to do an adequate review of the literature. Narrowing the concept to a particular type of court brings conceptual clarity, which is a hallmark of quality research. It narrows the research, which will be relevant for the literature review, and it narrows the relevant population to one that is more concrete and therefore will be easier to sample.

The general lesson is that population is a concept and as such, researchers can/should define it to suit their purposes. One of the creative aspects of designing research is to define concepts and their accompanying populations in ways that are not so abstract that they are meaningless ("all college students") yet not so concrete that they are trivial ("married immigrant women students in Hillsborough County, Florida community colleges who are majoring in sociology").

> Define concepts and their accompanying populations so that they are important (large enough) and meaningful (small enough).

Each item in a population—an individual person, a specific place, a specific thing—is called an *element*, and rarely can researchers obtain data on each element in a population. It is *not possible* to interview each and every student or each and every voter; it is *not possible* to observe interactions on every street in every city at every hour; it is *not possible* to examine the content of every magazine. This leads to the concept of sample.

The Concept of Sample in Social Research

Because researchers are often unable to examine each and every element in a population, they focus instead on examining samples of populations.

> A sample is a subset of a population; it can refer to study participants, places, times, survey questions, and documents.

Samples in social research most obviously apply to the *people* who participate in studies. Researchers must choose who will be interviewed ("The Digital Identity Divide"), who will participate in experiments ("Identity Threat and Dietary Choices"), and who will complete surveys ("Smoking Identities and Behavior").

Samples in social research also can be about *places* and *times*: For example, researchers must choose the streets they will observe and the days and times they will make these observations ("Ethnography of Racial Identities").

Samples in social research also can apply to *survey questions*. Researchers often work with data from large surveys that contain respondents' answers to literally hundreds of questions. Researchers choose the sample of questions they will use from this population ("Exploring the Bases of Partisanship").

Finally, samples in social research can apply to *documents*: Researchers examining documents must decide what *kinds* of documents to examine as well as which *individual instances* of those documents they will examine ("Unassailable Motherhood, Ambivalent Domesticity").

The design task of sampling is the work of making decisions about which specific people, places, times, questions, and documents will be a part of the study.

> Sampling: the design task of deciding *which* elements in a population will be chosen and how those elements will be chosen.

THE IMPORTANCE OF SAMPLES
IN SOCIAL RESEARCH

Statistical generalization from sample to population is centrally important in positivist-informed research, whose goal is to discover the *general laws* of human behavior. While such generalization is not important at all in research from an interpretive perspective, *all* research from *all* perspectives must be sensitive to consequences of sample characteristics. I start with the general lesson: Decisions about sampling are very similar to decisions about how to operationalize study concepts in that both decisions highly influence what *can* be found as well as what *likely* will be found. Data generated from a website representing the National Association for the Advancement of White People *will* show distinctive and clearly racist images of the world; stories presented in the *New York Times* will be different from those in *Oprah* magazine; there *will* be very different ideas about what government should do to help the American economy depending upon whether data are coming from CEOs or public school teachers.

While my examples might seem too obvious to require mentioning, social research very often relies on samples that greatly affect study findings. One example includes studies of children of divorce, which often are authored by psychologists and clinical social workers who use the children in their care as their research participants. It should not be surprising that these studies invariably find that children experience many problems associated with divorce. *Of course they do*: Children would not be in psychiatric care unless they had problems. The sample determines the findings. Likewise, studies about women victims of violence often generate data by talking with women living in shelters for abused women. Such studies invariably find'these women are poor. *Of course they do*: Women would not be living in shelters if they had money. The sample determines the findings.

In the same way, whether thinking about data from research you have designed or reading research written by others, keep focused on sample characteristics, so you can understand what data do—and do not—mean. If study respondents were teachers talking about students, then beware of sentences that seem to convey that this is what students themselves would say. Also remember there are multiple perspectives on social life. Questions about the work of any social service agency, for example, can be answered from the perspectives of agency supervisors, direct-service workers, and clients; schools are very different places depending on whether data come from principals, teachers, students, or parents.

The lesson for designing and evaluating research concerns the need for critical thinking in relation to sample characteristics: What biases are predictable given sample characteristics? Remember when reading the research of others that it is not uncommon for researchers to briefly mention sample biases, then proceed as if these biases did not exist.

In the last chapter, I argued that researchers causing harm to research participants was rarely a consequence of researchers knowingly putting their participants at risk for harm. Rather, harm typically comes from failing to think about the project from the participants' perspective. There is a parallel here: Researchers do not knowingly mislead their readers; they do not knowingly misrepresent the meaning of their data. The errors come from not thinking through all the implications from samples. As with all else, whether designing research or evaluating the research of others, think critically about the samples upon which data are based.

TYPES OF SAMPLES

Social researchers typically talk about two kinds of samples: probability and nonprobability.

Probability Samples

Probability samples—also called *representative samples* and *random samples*—are the kinds of samples required if researchers want to use inferential statistics to talk about the characteristics of a population based on findings from a sample.

> Probability sample: The sample is selected in such a way that every element in the population has an equal chance of being included in the sample. The sample is a miniature of its population.

The logic of probability samples is statistical, and the logic of statistics is probability: If every element in the population had an equal chance of being included in the sample, then—*probably*—the sample is a miniature of the population from which it was drawn. This means that *probably* what we find in the sample is *more or less* (given a margin of error) what we would find if we did research on each and every element in the population.

There are several ways to actually obtain a probability sample with the idea uniting all ways being that of *random selection*. Why do some elements in the population end up in the sample and others do not? There is no reason, because the selection of individual elements is done in very precise ways that ensure inclusion is not the result of obvious or nonobvious bias. The meaning of random sampling is, again, statistical and probabilistic: *If* each population element has an equal chance of being included in the sample *and* *if* individual elements are randomly chosen to be in the sample, there is no reason to believe any bias worked to make the sample nonrepresentative of the population.

When designing or evaluating research, remember to think about the links between samples and populations and generalizing from samples to populations.

> Only inferential statistics offer empirical evidence of the extent to which something is found in a population based upon data from a sample; the logic of inferential statistics assumes probability samples.

Nonprobability Samples

The second type of sample in social research, the *nonprobability* sample, is defined in terms of what it is not.

> Nonprobability sample: The relationship between the sample and its population is unknown; a nonprobability sample is not necessarily a miniature of the population.

While there are a fairly limited number of very specific ways to select probability samples, there are countless ways in which nonprobability samples can be constructed.

Because much research is done by people who work in colleges and universities, many studies rely on students who are registered in subject pools ("Identity Threat and Dietary Choices") or who respond to e-mail surveys ("The Digital Identity Divide"). Other researchers locate study participants by recruiting in places likely containing the types of people they have an interest in ("Gang-Related Gun Violence"). At times, it can be difficult to locate particular types of people, so researchers might begin with asking social service providers to recommend clients and then use a snowball technique, where people who consent to be interviewed are asked to recommend others ("Addicts' Narratives of Recovery").

Nonprobability samples also can refer to the selection of places to observe ("Ethnography of Racial Identities) as well as to documents selected for examination ("Unassailable Motherhood, Ambivalent Domesticity").

SAMPLING AND SAMPLE PROBLEMS
IN SOCIAL RESEARCH

Samples are critical in research design, yet the process of sampling (choosing what will be included) is often difficult, and the final characteristics of samples can be less than perfect. Different kinds of problems are associated with probability and nonprobability samples, and as with other design tasks, problems can require rethinking other elements of research design.

Problems in Probability Sampling

While probability samples are the most valued in social research and the kind of sample necessary for statistical generalization, actually obtaining such samples can be difficult and sometimes even impossible.

> Probability *samples* are difficult to obtain because of the requirements of probability *sampling*.

The process of developing a probability sample (of people, places, or things) must begin with a list of every element in the population (called a *sampling frame*). This is because a defining characteristic of probability samples is that any particular element in the population has the same chance as any other element of being chosen for inclusion in a probability sample. It is not possible to randomly choose elements without knowing *how many* elements there are and *what* and *where* these elements are. There can be no random sample of men in prison without a list of all men in prison; it is not possible to have a random sample of Methodist churches without a list of all such churches.

Rarely is it easy to obtain a probability sample of any meaningful group of people or collection of places or things. At times, it might be easy to *imagine* a particular population but very difficult to actually construct a sample. For example, while it is theoretically possible to make a list of every high school student in the United States who plays on his or her school's basketball team, it is difficult to imagine the amount of work it would take to construct such a list. Likewise, it is theoretically possible to construct a list of every presidential speech broadcast on radio or television, but it would take a great deal of work to actually construct such a list.

The problem for social researchers is that it often is too difficult, too time-consuming, and too expensive to construct probability samples. Further, there are many instances where no amount of time and money could lead to a probability sample, because the population is unknown.

> Probability samples are possible *only* when the dimensions of the
> population are known.

Knowing all the elements in the population is necessary in order to construct a probability sample. Yet it is not possible to identify all "teens who are members of gangs," or "drug addicts who now think of themselves as *recovered*," or "students who have had bad experiences with technology." When the dimensions of the relevant population are unknown, it is not possible to construct a probability sample.

When researchers are unable to develop probability samples they have two choices: First, they can change their *research questions* from those requiring statistical generalization from probability samples to other questions that are appropriate for data from nonprobability samples. Second, they can change their *topics* so that they can use data generated by governments, public agencies, and large research groups that have the money and means to do the work necessary to gather probability data from large populations. Data from the Population Reference Bureau, the World Bank, National Opinion Research Corporation (NORC), the General Social Survey (GSS), and the Detroit Area Studies are examples of the many existing data sets containing large amounts of data generated from probability samples. If I could offer one word of advice to new researchers interested in inferential statistics, it would be to take the time to learn about existing data sets. Why generate a small amount of new data if large amounts of data reflecting top-rate research already are available? Massive amounts of data from extremely well-done surveys and other data sets are available to all social researchers. Librarians often know about these things and can help you with your search.

Positivist-informed research most highly values probability samples, because the mathematical logic underlying such samples makes it possible to statistically generalize from sample to population. Yet it can be difficult—or even impossible—for social researchers to obtain such samples. Of the eight articles I have been using as examples throughout this book, only two use data from probability samples. One, "Exploring the Bases of Partisanship in the American Electorate," uses data from the 1952–2004 National Election Studies as well as from the 2004 U.S. National Exit Poll. The second article in my examples using a probability sample is "Smoking Identities and Behaviors." Researchers sent a questionnaire to a random sample of 4,000 students at a "large southeastern university" (lines 58–62). However, only 741 of those 4,000 students completed and returned the questionnaire (line 67), which raises a question common to survey research: The survey was *sent* to a representative sample of students, but can we assume that the students returning the survey were a random sample of those sent the survey? If students with particular characteristics tended to return—or not return—the survey, then the sample of *responses* does not represent a random sample of *students.* The authors themselves mention that the low response rate limits generalization (lines 188–190).

The problems of obtaining probability samples for social research leads to the expected consequence: Most social research uses nonprobability samples. Compared to probability samples, it can be far easier to obtain nonprobability samples, yet nonprobability samples can be associated with questions about their quality.

Problems in Nonprobability Samples

Because nonprobability sampling is not governed by detailed rules defining how sample elements are selected, it is up to researchers to tell readers how samples were selected and to convince readers that these samples are adequate. As always, readers should critically evaluate sample adequacy.

> Nonprobability sampling *procedures* should be justified as logical given research questions; characteristics of obtained *samples* should be justified as adequate to explore research questions.

While nonprobability samples cannot be used to statistically generalize results from samples to larger populations, nonprobability samples can be good enough—and sometimes excellent—for exploring many other questions about social life. Two good skills to develop for both designing and evaluating research are that of thinking critically about the kinds of samples that make sense given research questions as well as of thinking about what limitations are posed by particular types of samples.

Example 7.3: "Unassailable Motherhood, Ambivalent Domesticity" contains justifications for why the *Ladies' Home Journal,* rather than other magazines, was chosen for analysis: This was the top-selling women's magazine in 1946, and it focuses on issues related to home and family (lines 103–106). The article also contains justification for choosing the issues from just one year: 1946 was a "turning point in U.S. history," the postwar year marked by a return to family and to traditional gender expectations (lines 98–99). While not a probability sample, the sample is logical and sensible given research questions. Furthermore, the author makes modest claims about what she found: While academics talk about *motherhood* as if it were the same as *domesticity*, the content of a popular women's magazine during an era characterized by vast social change constructed motherhood and domesticity as two separate concepts.

Example 7.4: In "Addicts' Narratives of Recovery," researchers James McIntosh and Neil McKeganey offer careful justifications for their sample. Research participants were "recruited from across Scotland by . . . snowball sampling and follow up of ex-clients of drug services and newspaper advertisements" (lines 101–104). These participants were chosen because they defined themselves as having given up drugs (lines 85–88). This self-definition of being a "recovering drug addict" is important, because the research is about examining "the nature of individuals' accounts of their recovery" and the ways narratives might be a "part of the recovery process" (lines 98–100). Notice also how the authors point out a sample limitation: Because some of these research participants had been recruited through agencies helping people overcome addiction, their stories "may have been constructed in interaction with representatives of drug treatment agencies" (lines 275–278). Again, this is *not* a probability sample—there can be no probability samples when the population (in this case, self-identified recovering drug addicts) is unknown. Yet the sample is not haphazard: the sample is logical; it is justifiable.

Example 7.5: In "The Digital Identity Divide," readers are told the sample started with students "solicited online through the official residential hall mailing list and through residential hall floor meetings" (lines 113–115). Readers also are told that 513 students completed the survey and that although this was only 24% of all surveys sent, those returning the survey were "representative of the student population at the university" (lines 118–120). All this information, though, is not important, because the authors do not use these survey data in this particular manuscript. Rather, the researcher presents this as a case study, an in-depth look at only *three* students who were selected because "they represented different points on the spectrum of technological fluency, cultural identity and experience" (lines 123–125). What we read are three stories, each one representing a different relationship among childhood experiences with technology, how students define themselves in relation to technology, and how schools/universities create and perpetuate the "digital identity divide." Do we know how many students there are with these kinds of identities/experiences? No. Does the study empirically demonstrate links between experiences and identities? Not really. Three examples are hardly sufficient to support the complex arguments here about the creations and consequences of the concept of "technology identity." Yet three examples are sufficient to alert us to the potential usefulness of a new concept called *technology identity*.

My point here is that social research often—most often—relies on nonprobability samples and that these samples can be adequate—even excellent—when examining a range of questions. If you are designing research using a nonprobability sample, I would suggest that you tell readers why you decided to use the sampling you did. While readers make their own evaluations about sample adequacy, it is helpful to know the reasoning behind researchers' design decisions.

Exhibit 7.1 describes the characteristics of samples used in the published research examples. It also shows the justifications for as well as the limitations of these samples noted by researchers.

Exhibit 7.1 Samples in Published Research

Title/Author	Sample	Justification/Limitations Noted by Author
Abramowitz/Saunders: "Exploring the Bases of Partisanship"	National Election Studies (NES)	No justification offered. No limitation offered.
Bowser: "Ethnography of Racial Identities"	Five months of participant observation on "crowded streets" in Paris (lines 43, 90–91)	Justification: Saint-Germain (the name of the street), is like hundreds of similar streets throughout the world (lines 104–108)
Goode: "The Digital Identity Divide"	Three students selected to do in-depth interviews from 513 students responding to survey portion of larger study (larger study not discussed)	Justification: selected because they had different technology identities (lines 123–125). College was "ideal site as it attracts academically elite students. . . . [and] the site [also] enrolls a high rate of low-income students" (lines 109–113). No limitations noted
Guendelman/Cheryan/Monin: "Identity Threat and Dietary Choices"	Experiment 1: Sixty-four students at Stanford University (lines 97–98) Experiment 2: Fifty-five U.S.-born Asian Americans recruited through subject pool at University of Washington. To be in experiment, they had to be U.S.-born and self-identified as Asian (lines 158–161).	No justifications noted. No limitations noted. [Note: It is accepted practice within the discipline of psychology to use students as research participants]

(Continued)

Exhibit 7.1 (Continued)

Title/Author	Sample	Justification/Limitations Noted by Author
McIntosh/McKeganey: "Addicts' Narratives Of Recovery"	Interviews with 70 recovering addicts, recruited from across Scotland via snowball sampling, ex-clients of drug services, and newspaper advertisements (lines 101–104)	Justification: "We deliberately selected our sample on the basis of addicts' own definitions of whether they had given up [drugs]" (lines 85–88). Limitations: "The addicts' account of their recovery may have been constructed in interaction with representatives of drug treatment agencies" (lines 275–278).
Odland: "Unassailable Motherhood, Ambivalent Domesticity"	12 issues of *Ladies' Home Journal* from 1946 (line 98)	*Ladies' Home Journal* was the top-selling magazine for a white, middle-class, female audience; 1946 was a turning point year, shifting from war to peace (lines 98–106). No limitations noted.
Ridner/Walker/Hart/Myers: "Smoking Identities and Behavior"	Random sample of 4,000 full-time students at "large southeastern university" (lines 58–61). Response rate of 18.5% ($N = 741$) (line 67)	No justifications noted. Limitations: predominantly featured educated Caucasian women from a tobacco-producing state; low response rate limits generalization (lines 186–188)
Stretesky/Pogrebin: "Gang-Related Gun Violence"	Interviews with 22 gang members taken from larger study of 75 Colorado prison inmates who used a firearm in the commission of their most recent offense. The list containing the 75 inmates was a "random sample . . . of all inmates incarcerated for a violent crime in which a firearm was involved" (lines 73–85).	No justification noted. Limitation: A paragraph on problems of the ability to generalize; however, this study was not trying to generalize, so this was not a problem (lines 118–130).

Practical Problems in All Sampling

Regardless of what type of sample is being constructed, there can be practical problems in putting together a sample, and at times, these problems force researchers to rethink other aspects of research design.

In the last chapter, I talked about how the practical problem of cost could make it impossible to generate data in particular ways. The examples I gave there—the costs of sending mail surveys and of conducting face-to-face interviews with people who live far from the researcher—also can be understood as sample problems.

If you plan to design research, be alert to four general kinds of problems you might encounter in obtaining people to participate in your study.

The first is *locating people whose characteristics or experiences are interesting because they are not typical.* Several years ago, I was working with a student who was designing her final project for a graduate degree in medical anthropology. She wanted to talk with women who were Anglo-American, had a college education, and were HIV/AIDS positive. This is an important group to study, because most HIV/AIDS-positive people do not have those characteristics. Her plan was to do in-depth interviews to learn how these women understood themselves and how they sought help, given that they were different from common images of HIV/AIDS-positive people. It was a fascinating project, but it had a fatal flaw: She could not find women in the local community to talk with. The very reasons leading these women to be of interest to social researchers—there are few of them—were why the research was not possible. My student remained interested in this group of women, and she did not want to change her basic research questions. She set up a website and used networking techniques to find women with these characteristics. Granted, she could not obtain the depth of information she would have in face-to-face interviews, yet her new data gathering technique yielded the unexpected benefit of allowing her to establish contact with women who lived throughout the United States as well as in other countries. She discovered something the existing literature had not led her to expect: Women's experiences varied dramatically depending upon where they lived. This was an insight she would not have gained if she had managed to find her original sample of women in the immediate area.

A second type of problem comes from *asking research respondents to do too much.* This can be a problem with any type of data generation technique. For example, I received a mail survey a few weeks ago. Although it was on an interesting topic (how college teachers manage their time to allow them to do both research and teaching), I took one look and saw that it was 25 pages long. Without hesitation, I tossed it in the recycle container, thinking it was odd that a questionnaire about balancing time wanted to take so much of mine. As another example, one of my students could not get even his friends to volunteer for his proposed study, which required people to keep a diary of everything they ate for a month. Another student could not find people to participate in her proposed life-story interviews. She asked participants to commit to talking with her three or four times, for 2–3 hours each time. The lessons here are obvious: The more researchers ask of people, the less likely people will agree to participate in the study.

Third, there are *hidden populations* of people who, although numerous, are hard to find. How do researchers find "women who operate child daycares without a license"? Because these women are working illegally, they do not have sponsoring organizations. How do researchers find "undocumented immigrant women experiencing spouse abuse"? Fearing deportation, such women do not go to shelters, and they hide from authorities—and from researchers.

Fourth, there are people who *do not want to participate in social research.* Not everyone believes in the goals of social research; people who are socially and economically marginalized can worry that social research is about finding ways to control and further oppress them.

The general lesson here for designing research is that you should start thinking about your research participants quite early in the design process: Who will they be? How will you find them? What will you require of them? How will you convince them to help you? If you are designing research and find that it not possible to obtain the sample you need, then you will be back to thinking about how you can subtly change your question or your data generation technique in ways that will make it work.

There also is a lesson here about evaluating research samples. Although I complained earlier in this chapter about tendencies to use samples of people who were easy to find (such as clients in social service agencies), the fact remains that at times, this is as good as it gets. Although researchers certainly must point out the limitations and biases in their samples and while researchers certainly must be modest in what they claim, evaluators should recognize that perfection is not a good standard upon which to evaluate research.

SAMPLES AND RESEARCH DESIGN

I included this chapter on samples at the end of my description of the process of research design, because in many respects, sampling decisions come at the end of the design process. You will not know if you need to recruit people to participate in your study or what you need to recruit people for until you decide what data generation techniques you will use. You will not know if you want to examine court records or newspaper articles or magazines or blogs until you work through questions about data generation techniques. At the same time, I will close this chapter with the way I have concluded all chapters: If you are designing research, do not expect that you will make design decisions once and only once or that decisions are made in a particular order. Keep what you have learned about sampling and samples in mind as you think about your research questions, as you conceptualize and operationalize your major concepts, and as you decide what data generation techniques make the most sense. Research is a package, and the highest-quality research is characterized by logical consistency. Particular research questions are best answered by particular data generation techniques; particular research questions are also best answered with data from particular types of samples.

I have one more short topic before I conclude this tour through the world of social research design: writing and evaluating research. This is a summary of what this book has been about, and I hope it offers ways to think about the general issues of how to evaluate research quality.

EIGHT

SUMMARY

Writing and Evaluating Social Research Design

————◆◆◆————

Design is only one component of research. Design is the plan, and the plan must be *implemented*, which means that data must be generated and then analyzed. While quality research depends upon design *and* implementation *and* data analysis, the importance of design should not be minimized for the simple reason that nothing else matters if the research design is flawed. Although there are differences in how various subcommunities of social researchers define the exact characteristics of quality research design, there are no disagreements that design must be adequate or findings will be not *valid*, as evaluated through criteria associated with positivist perspectives, or *trustworthy*, as evaluated through criteria associated with interpretive perspectives.

In this final chapter, I will summarize my major points by focusing on two tasks that apply to each of the design tasks I have discussed: the work of *writing* about design and the work of *evaluating* its quality.

I thought it was important to cover writing in this last chapter, because the kinds of writing associated with research can be quite different from writing done in daily life. Most certainly, the forms and contents of social media updates, text messages, and e-mails have little in common with the types of writing needed to explain social research design. While learning how to write about research design might be difficult, I would argue that it is worth the effort: Skills to clearly and precisely describe and justify design decisions transfer to such practical tasks as writing cover letters to apply for jobs or complaining to governments or companies about injustice or inferior products.

I also will talk about evaluation in this chapter, because it is a good way to review what I have covered in this entire book. There are many reasons you might find yourself evaluating research design. Most obviously, evaluation is a part of the design process itself. The literature review, after all, is about reading and evaluating what others already have done. It is obvious that you want to base any research you are designing on published research that is high quality; you do not want to carry into your own project the problems in others' research. So *reviewing* the literature must include *evaluating* it. Also, when designing research, it is a good idea to stand back after every design decision and take a long look at it to evaluate the design adequacy. Really look at your research questions and your conceptualizations, think carefully about how you plan to generate your data, and so on. If you do this at each stage in the design process, you likely will discover any problems early enough to be able to remedy them without much trouble.

My final point, but most important because it is so commonly needed, is that understanding how to evaluate the quality of research is a skill we each need in daily life as we are bombarded with facts said to come from scientific research. How should research be evaluated? What questions should be asked? When should findings be accepted, and when should they be rejected? My goal has been to encourage you to think about how to ask and answer such questions.

Because *writing* and *evaluation* both rest on these ways of *thinking*, I will start there.

FOUNDATIONS OF RESEARCH DESIGN AND EVALUATION: METHODOLOGICAL THINKING

Designing and evaluating research of any type depends upon what I call *methodological thinking*. Rather than thinking about research methods as a series of technical procedures and words to memorize, *methodological thinking* emphasizes understanding the logic underlying research.

Methodological thinking is the foundation of social research design, and *critical thinking* is the foundation of methodological thinking. As used in research methods, the term *critical* means to analyze, to question, to assess, or to appraise. Critical thinking is *thinking*—analyzing and evaluating what you think and why you think it.

Our information-saturated world contains countless needs for evaluation: How can we evaluate the advice of countless so-called experts who appear on television, write blogs, and author books to tell us how we should live our lives? How can we evaluate the possible truth of statements made by politicians and commentators who tell us who we should help, who we should punish, and how public money should be spent? How can we judge the value of countless research reports we hear about, especially when they often have contradictory findings? Complex questions require complex evaluations; complex evaluations require critical thinking.

Barriers to Critical Thinking

I talked about the first barrier to critical thinking in Chapter 1: While the human brain automatically does a great many things, evaluating the truth of abstract information is not one of them. We must tell our brains to evaluate truthfulness, and such evaluation takes energy and time. A barrier to critical thinking is that it *is* thinking; it is harder to think than to not think.

The first barrier to critical thinking is easy to overcome. Our brains *can* think critically if we need to do so; therefore, if you want to think critically, then slow down and do it. The second barrier to critical thinking is far harder—maybe even impossible—to eliminate: These are barriers from biases. We each view the world through our own places in it. Our personal characteristics (such as gender, race/ethnicity, age, religion, nationality, and so on) are associated with particular experiences and ways of viewing the world. These can be obstacles to critical thinking. Research consistently shows a strong tendency for people to overlook flaws and to somewhat automatically agree with statements that seem to confirm what we already believe about the world and—unsurprisingly—to search for flaws and to somewhat automatically reject findings we do not personally agree with. Biases create filters; filters hinder critical thinking.

While biases from personal characteristics and experiences can hinder critical thinking on a range of topics, some biases are specific to thinking critically about the methods and findings of social research. Consider, for example, different visions of what research is and what it should look like that are associated with positivist, interpretive, and critical frameworks (as discussed in Chapter 2). Some researchers feel strongly that one or another of these frameworks is better than the others; at times, the strength of their beliefs result in biases that might lead them to evaluate some kinds of research as higher quality than others, simply due to research frameworks. Further biases result from differences among academic disciplines. Psychologists, for example, often prefer to generate data through the technique of experimentation, while social workers often prefer in-depth interviews. Sociologists and criminologists talk about the importance of sampling, a concept that is not central to historians, who are far more concerned about assessing the reliability of sources that produced the documents they examine, and so on. Methodological variations and preferences are understandable, because they reflect differences in the types of questions asked about people and social life. Yet strong identifications with particular disciplines can lead to biases praising research associated with that discipline and condemning research associated with others.

In brief, regardless of their source, biases can interfere with critical thinking, which is the foundation upon which to think about the meanings of social research.

The three primary perspectives on social research (what I call positivist, interpretive, and critical) each have their own way of understanding and responding to biases. True to their name, positivists are positive: They believe researchers can be impartial and objective, and they have developed various techniques (such as double-blind experiments) to ensure objectivity. In comparison, people working from interpretive perspectives challenge this hopefulness about the possibility of non-bias and argue that researchers are human and as such should be expected to see the world in ways corresponding to their experiences. From an interpretive perspective, all that can be asked is for researchers to recognize biases and be honest about them. Finally, while positivists define bias as bad but feel it can be overcome, researchers working in critical perspectives believe that biases are what researchers *should* have. The purpose of research from critical perspectives is to right social injustices, so researchers *should be* biased in ways that help the powerless.

My suggestion is that it is best to assume that there are biases and to take them seriously. This is methodological thinking:

> Train yourself to think about thinking.

Just as critical thinking requires training yourself to switch from an *automatic* to a *thinking* mode, as you design research and evaluate the research designs of others, think about how your own experiences, social positions, and professional commitments influence your evaluation. A trick I use is when I am evaluating research that confirms what I already think, I force myself to look for *problems*; when I am evaluating something that challenges what I already think, I force myself to look for what is *positive*. Clearly and most certainly, these tricks do *not* erase the biases from personal positions and personal beliefs, but they may help you see where your biases are. Truthfulness is to be valued, and acknowledging biases stops them from working without our knowledge. The major lesson is the point I state below:

> You must be honest and admit your biases to yourself and to others throughout the process of research design and evaluation.

In summary, methodological thinking is the foundation of social research, and critical thinking is its core characteristic. While it might *not* be possible for any of us to be truly objective in our evaluations, it certainly *is* possible to be aware of the criteria we are using to make our decisions and to be honest about it.

VARIATIONS IN CRITERIA FOR EVALUATING
REPORTS OF RESEARCH DESIGN

How should reports of research design be written? *What* needs to be written? Questions about writing can be addressed only within context: It is not possible to know what to write or how to write it without knowing the expectations, or the *standards*, for evaluation. Variations in standards stem from differences in *types* of research, in the *purposes* of reports, and in the *audiences* for these reports.

> *How* a report of research should be written and *what* it should include will depend upon the type of research, the purpose of the report, and the audience doing the evaluation.

Variations From Types of Research

A recurring topic throughout this book has been the considerable variation in how research can be designed. Design differences lead to different expectations about *what* should be written.

Variations From Foundational Characteristics

Chapter 2 considered how social research is informed by different models of social life (positivist, interpretive, and critical) and how social research uses different ways to link data and concepts/theories (*deductive* and *inductive* logic). While reports of research design rarely explicitly discuss these design characteristics, each characteristic influences what must be included in reports.

Example 8.1: When research uses *deductive* reasoning, the design precedes data generation. This means researchers need to operationalize concepts (typically called *variables* in this variety of research) in terms of survey questions, experimental manipulations, what will be examined in documents, and so on. These operationalizations should be presented in reports of design. In contrast, reports of research using inductive reasoning do not include operationalization as a component of study design, because specifying relationships between data and concepts (operationalization) is a task in the data generation/data analysis research phase.

Example 8.2: Interpretive researchers are very sensitive to how researchers themselves influence studies. Design reports for interpretive research often include descriptions of the researcher and reflection about biases in that particular study. In comparison, because research from positivist perspectives assumes that researchers are objective, it is rare to find concern about researcher bias; any concern is typically limited to descriptions of how bias is controlled (blind coding, double-blind experiments, and so on).

Example 8.3: There are variations in writing styles associated with research perspectives. Research from positivist perspectives (and often from critical perspectives) is written in a *scientific* style, which is a formal writing style. ("Exploring the Bases of Partisanship" and "Identity Threat and Dietary Choices" are good examples.) Research from interpretive perspectives (and sometimes from critical perspectives) often is written in more *informal* style. ("Addicts' Narratives of Recovery" is an example.) While I did not include any examples, some research from interpretive perspectives and from critical/feminist perspectives forgoes all formalities and is written in the form of personal essays.

Variations From Data Generation Techniques

Chapter 6 considered data generation techniques, and it only makes sense that different techniques would be accompanied by different expectations of what should be included in reports of research design.

Example 8.4: If the research is an in-depth interview study or an ethnography, then readers should expect researchers to include sufficient information to answer questions about relationships between the researcher and the data collected.

Example 8.5: If the research is a written survey, there typically are few—if any—questions about relationships between researchers and data collection, but there are central questions about relationships between conceptualizations of major study variables and their operationalizations (the survey questions).

Example 8.6: Questions about the representativeness of samples are important when—and only when—researchers will analyze data via inferential statistics, which require probability sampling.

This is the lesson you should take with you:

What should be described about study design depends upon the characteristics of the specific research.

Variations From Report Purposes and Audiences

What should be included in reports of research design as well as *how* reports should be written depend upon the reasons reports are written and the characteristics of the audiences for those reports.

There are many reasons why reports of research design are written. Some reports, such as thesis proposals, dissertation proposals, and grant applications, are written to convince particular people (thesis or dissertation committee members or grant evaluators) that the research is needed, that it is methodologically sound, and that it is practical to do. Reports of design also are the front section of reports of research that have actually been implemented; these can be written to report research done as part of a class or as a thesis or dissertation; they can appear as journal articles, as technical reports, or as books.

Here is one word of advice that can save you much time and frustration:

> Before writing a report of research design, be sure you clearly understand the expectations of your audience.

The audience will be the evaluators, so you need to know what they expect; the more you learn about their expectations, the better. If you are doing the research as a part of a class, pay attention to the instructions; if you are doing a thesis or a dissertation proposal, then talk with your committee members and with students who already have gone through the process. You should also read examples of successful projects.

If you are planning on submitting a report of research to a journal for possible publication, then you need to read journals to see what articles look like. The world of academic publishing mimics the world of research insofar as there is considerable variation among journals. Some journals require sophisticated theoretical mandates for research and others do not; some require data in the form of numbers analyzed by state-of-the-art statistical procedures; others want numerical data conveyed only in simple descriptive form; still others do not publish research containing numbers of any type. Some journals require the formal writing associated with the natural sciences, while others expect the more lyrical prose associated with work in the humanities. If you want to publish research, you need to decide which journal is best suited for your particular research, because what you write and how you write it will depend upon where you are submitting it. A place to start is with the reference list for your study: Are there any journals that seem to publish many articles that are similar to yours?

QUALITY WITHIN VARIATIONS

While it is important to understand variations in how research design should be written, it also is important to understand that there are generalities that hold across variations. What are the generalities in how research is evaluated?

I am prone to using the term *adequate* when I talk about research evaluation, because I want to avoid implying that social research should be judged by the standard of *perfection*. I personally believe that while much social research is pretty good and some of it is excellent, research rarely reaches a standard of perfection. As I discussed throughout this book, social life is so complex and multidimensional that it is difficult—and sometimes impossible—to isolate particular concepts of interest; it can be difficult and sometimes impossible to obtain desired samples; it always is possible for interview questions to have been a bit tighter, for samples to have been larger, for multiple methods of data generation to have been included to add depth to findings, and so on.

What this means is that while it is good to strive for perfection and to keep perfection as an ultimate goal, perfection is an *inappropriate standard* upon which to evaluate social research. If you expect perfection—from your own studies or from those of others—you will be disappointed. At the same time, although we cannot expect research to be *perfect*, we certainly can hope for it to be *very good* or even *excellent*. Social research ranges from the excellent to the very good to the acceptable to the inadequate. Upon what grounds are those evaluations possible?

I will begin with the minimum standards of acceptability (what I am calling *the standard of adequacy*) that I tried to develop in every chapter of this book. An adequate *research question* is not ambiguous and is capable of being empirically examined; an adequate *conceptualization* is clear and precise; an adequate *operationalization* is logically compatible with the conceptualization; an adequate *data generation technique* is capable of generating the kind of data that will answer research questions; an adequate *sample* is appropriate for the question being addressed and for the data generation technique being used.

When components of design do not reach the minimum standard, we say that the research is *fatally flawed*, which means resulting data are useless. In positivist terms, such data are *not valid*; in interpretive terms, data from such studies are *not trustworthy*.

Of course, no one would want to strive for mere adequacy—we need to strive to design and implement high-quality research. All the multiple variations in evaluating quality mean that it does not make sense to evaluate all research by the same criteria. Instead, critical thinking is required. When writing and evaluating research, begin by asking, what are the important issues in this *particular* research? Those are what should be discussed; those are what should be evaluated.

Adequate descriptions and evaluations of research design require critical thinking, and they require sensitivity to characteristics of the particular research being evaluated. Clearly and most certainly, being sensitive to variations does *not* mean you can ignore problems in your own research or in research you read. Being sensitive to variations does *not* mean ignoring evaluative criteria; sensitivity means holding research to standards that are appropriate.

If you plan on becoming a researcher, it is important for you to understand how your specific discipline defines and evaluates high-quality research. This is a part of *professional socialization*; I will leave it at that and suggest that you can begin to develop ideas about the characteristics of high-quality research in your particular discipline by reading a great deal of published research. It is like learning what is and what is not good music: If you listen to a great deal of music—or if you read a great deal of research—over time, you will know what separates the deficient from the adequate and what separates the adequate from the excellent.

WRITING RESEARCH DESIGN: CHARACTERISTICS OF HIGH-QUALITY REPORTS

While *what* and *how* design should be written are subject to considerable variation depending upon the type of research, report purpose, and audience, there are some characteristics of high-quality research reports that apply across variations.

Displaying Care in Communication

To answer my students' often-asked question about the importance of writing: Yes, writing counts. This is especially true in the world of research, which values precise communication. Simply stated, if research is not written in ways that are clear and understandable, then nothing else matters. I review a lot of articles sent to journals for possible publication. I have seen reports with many misspellings, with sentences 15 lines in length, and reports that go page after page after page with no headings to help readers to know where they are in the argument. If you are writing research, you want your readers—whether they are instructors, thesis committee members, or journal reviewers—to evaluate you as competent. Sloppiness is a sign that you did not take care in crafting the report. This, in turn, can be taken as a red flag indicating you also were not careful in doing the research. Regardless of the writing style, quality research reports should show that the author has taken language seriously.

This is something to pay attention to when writing research. You will not have many reasons to think about this when reading published research because low-quality writing will prevent those reports from being published.

Containing Appropriate Contents

While I have discussed variations in what information should be included, the contents of high-quality reports tend to contain everything readers need to know—and only what readers need to know—in order to understand and evaluate research. In particular, high-quality reports have the following characteristics:

- **High-quality reports are self-contained documents.** High-quality reports include everything a knowledgeable reader of the particular topic matter needs to know to evaluate the report. These reports also include sufficient references so that readers who are *not* familiar with the particular topic can become knowledgeable by finding and reading these references.
- **High-quality reports are narrowly focused.** They do *not* contain information that is irrelevant (or only superficially connected) to the research topic. In other words, readers are told what they need to know; they are not told anything they do not need to know. Deciding what to include—and what to exclude—is important.

Containing Adequate Information on Design Characteristics

Even though there are multiple variations of what must be included and what should be emphasized, most high-quality reports nonetheless are characterized by particular content centering on research design. Here is what you need to tell your readers when you are writing your own research and what you need to look for and evaluate when reading published reports of research:

1. **Explicit research question(s):** Clearly describe the questions. It is preferable if you write them as questions, so they are obvious to readers. (See Chapter 3 for more detail.)

   Evaluation: Are the questions clear? Are they capable of being examined by social research? If there are several questions, are they logically related to one another?

2. **Grounding of the topic in the theoretical and empirical literatures:** Give enough information about current scholarly knowledge to locate the study in the literature. Be sure you include *mandates*—specific reasons why the study is necessary given existing knowledge about the topic. (Note: Chapter 4 covered in detail what to include in literature reviews and how these reviews should be written.)

   Evaluation: Are you convinced that the author has located the relevant literature and given an adequate description of it? Has the author convinced you this study is needed given what we currently know about the topic?

3. **Conceptualization:** Include conceptual definitions of each of the major concepts (see Chapter 5).

   Evaluation: Are all major concepts defined? Are the definitions carefully written and precise?

4. **Operationalization (only if research is deductive):** Give enough information for readers to know precisely how concepts are being measured (see Chapter 5).

   Evaluation: Are operationalizations defensible? Do they make sense given both existing understandings and the conceptualizations in this particular study?

5. **Description of data generation techniques:** Describe the techniques of data generation. Include enough detail for another researcher to replicate these techniques (see Chapter 6).

   Evaluation: Are you convinced that the data generation techniques used are capable of producing the kinds of data necessary to answer the questions posed in the study?

6. **Sample:** Describe both the sampling techniques and the characteristics of the final samples, of study respondents, and/or of documents, questions, observations, and so on. Justify the techniques and the adequacy of the samples. Also note any limitations in the study (Chapter 7).

   Evaluation: Are the samples (of study respondents, and/or of study materials such as documents to be examined, places to be observed, and/or of survey questions used) adequate to address research questions?

Demonstrating the Logical Coherence of Design Components

I have argued throughout this book that all design elements should fit together. The research question, the literature reviewed, the conceptualizations, technique used to produce data, and characteristics of samples should form a *package of design elements*. So if the research question is about how people act, then data should measure how people act rather than how people think or feel; if the question is about the complexity of how people make meaning, then in-depth interviews, not fixed-question surveys, are needed; if questions are about *how many*, then data must be in the form of numbers, which can be counted, and so on.

This is why designing high-quality research requires *thinking*: The goal of research design is for research questions, data, concepts, existing understandings, data generation techniques, and samples to all fit together in rational, reasonable, and consistent ways. The many rules for research are simply ways to encourage this kind of design.

ENDINGS AND BEGINNINGS

I think of this concluding chapter as both an ending and a beginning. It is the ending of this particular book, but I hope it also will be a beginning, because you will feel you have learned something here that you can use when you design your own research and when you evaluate the research written by others. I hope you will remember that research methods is not simply a list of technical details and words to memorize; it is a tool kit containing ways to think about and explore the mysteries of social life. While very few people work as social researchers, modern life is such that we all need to think of ourselves as detectives—as people who can think critically about what we see and hear and as people who do not need to simply accept what others say. This is the promise of learning the meaning of methodological thinking.

SUGGESTIONS FOR FURTHER READING ON WRITING AND EVALUATING SOCIAL RESEARCH DESIGN

General thoughts about writing research

Becker, H. S. (1986). *Writing for social scientists: How to start and finish your thesis, book, or article.* Chicago, IL: University of Chicago Press.
Przeworski, A., & Solomon, F. (1995). *On the art of writing proposals: Some candid suggestions for applicants to Social Science Research Council competitions.* New York, NY: Social Science Research Council.

Thinking about evaluation criteria

American Educational Research Association. (2006). Standards for reporting on empirical research in AERA publications. *Educational Researcher, 35,* 3–40.
Baker, C., & Pistrang, N. (2005). Quality criteria under methodological pluralism: Implications for conducting and evaluating research. *American Journal of Community Psychology, 35,* 201–212.
Rothman, S. B. (2008, April). Comparatively evaluating potential dissertation and thesis projects. *PSOnline,* 367–369.

APPENDIX

Articles Used as Examples

Abramowitz, A. I., & Saunders, K. L. (2006). Exploring the bases of partisanship in the American electorate: Social identity vs. ideology. *Political Research Quarterly, 59*, 175–187.

Bowser, B. P. (2007). Ethnography of racial identities in Paris: Public indicators of social hierarchy. A research note. *Social Science Information, 46*, 591–605.

Goode, J. (2000). The digital identity divide: How technology knowledge impacts college students. *New Media & Society, 12*, 492–513.

Guendelman, M. D., Cheryan, S., & Monin, B. (2011). Fitting in but getting fat: Identity threat and dietary choices among U.S. immigrant groups. *Psychological Science, 22*(7), 959–967.

McIntosh, J., & McKeganey, N. (2000). Addicts' narratives of recovery from drug use: Constructing a non-addict identity. *Social Science & Medicine, 50*, 1501–1510.

Odland, S. B. (2010). Unassailable motherhood, ambivalent domesticity: The construction of maternal identity in *Ladies' Home Journal* in 1946. *Journal of Communication Inquiry, 34*, 61–84.

Ridner, S. L., Walker, K. L., Hart, J. L., & Myers, J. A. (2010). Smoking identities and behavior: Evidence of discrepancies, issues for measurement and intervention. *Western Journal of Nursing Research, 32*, 434–446.

Stretesky, P. B., & Pogrebin, M. R. (2007). Gang-related gun violence: Socialization, identity, and self. *Journal of Contemporary Ethnography, 36*, 85–113.

EXPLORING THE BASES OF PARTISANSHIP
IN THE AMERICAN ELECTORATE:
SOCIAL IDENTITY VS. IDEOLOGY

Alan I. Abramowitz and Kyle L. Saunders

Political Research Quarterly, 59, 175–187

1   In *Partisan Hearts and Minds: Political Parties and the Social Identities of Voters,*
2   Donald Green, Bradley Palmquist, and Eric Schickler (2002) argue that party
3   identification in the United States is based on voters' social identities rather than
4   on a rational assessment of the parties' policies or performance in office. . . .
5   In proposing this social identity theory, Green, Palmquist and Schickler view
6   party identification as an emotional attachment grounded in enduring group
7   loyalties rather than a deliberate choice based on a preference for one set of
8   policy positions over another—a choice that can be modified if parties' policy
9   positions change or new issues arise. . . . [They] downplay the role of issues and
10   ideology in the formation of party identification. While recognizing that party
11   loyalties can be influenced by dramatic changes in the parties' policy stands or
12   ideological positions, Green, Palmquist and Schickler argue that such shifts are
13   relatively rare and generally confined to periods of major realignment such as the
14   New Deal era in the United States. In this regard, the social identity theory stands
15   in sharp contrast to the ideological realignment theory which claims that as a
16   result of the growing ideological polarization of the two major parties since the
17   1980s, Americans have increasingly been choosing a party identification on the
18   basis of their ideological preferences (Abramowitz and Saunders 1998).
19   According to Green, Palmquist and Schickler, even the one exception to the
20   rule of partisan stability in recent American political history, the dramatic realign-
21   ment of southern white voters' party loyalties since the end of World War II, was
22   based more on changing perceptions of the parties' ties to social groups than on
23   issues or ideology. They argue that as southerners began to assume leadership
24   positions in the Republican party during the 1980s and 1990s, Republicanism
25   came to be seen as a respectable affiliation among white southerners. . . . [They]
26   argue that "the growing correlation between liberalism-conservatism and party
27   [among southern whites] reflects cohort replacement as older conservative
28   Democrats pass away" (2002: 161). . . .
29   We find much that is persuasive about the evidence presented in *Partisan
30   Hearts and Minds*. However, we take issue with the claim that partisan change in
31   the American electorate in recent years has been limited exclusively to southern

32   whites. We present evidence in this work that there has been a substantial
33   increase in Republican identification among white voters outside of the South
34   over the past three decades and that this shift has been quite dramatic among
35   several major subgroups including men, Catholics, and the religiously
36   devout. . . . Most fundamentally, we take issue with the claim that party identifi-
37   cation in the U.S. is based mainly on the social identities of citizens rather than
38   their ideological orientations or policy preferences. In fact, Green, Palmquist, and
39   Schickler (2002) never actually test this social identity theory, nor do they com-
40   pare the influence of social background characteristics with the influence of
41   issues and ideology. They argue that, "we lack the luxury of examining a broad
42   range of social identities [because] social class, ethnicity, religion, and party
43   exhaust the list of social categories about which we have adequate longitudinal
44   data" (83). We find this argument unpersuasive. While measures of identification
45   with social groups may not be widely available, measures of objective member-
46   ship in a large variety of social groups are widely available and social identity
47   theorists generally view objective membership as a necessary condition for iden-
48   tification with a group and the development of group political consciousness. . . .
49   Tajfel (1981), for example, defines social identity as, "that part of an individual's
50   self-concept which derives from his knowledge of his membership in a social
51   group together with the value and emotional significance attached to the mem-
52   bership" (255).
53   In addition to social class, ethnicity, and religion, data on age, race, gender,
54   region, urban-rural residence, and union affiliation are available in the American
55   National Election Studies (NES) and many other surveys conducted over the past
56   50 years. Along with social class, ethnicity, and religion, these are precisely the
57   social characteristics most commonly associated with support for the major par-
58   ties in the United States. Social identity theory clearly implies that voters who
59   belong to groups generally associated with one major party or the other—groups
60   such as the poor, union members, single women, and Jews in the case of the
61   Democratic party, or the wealthy, married men, and evangelicals in the case of
62   the Republican party—should be more likely to identify with that party. Based on
63   this reasoning, we test the social identity theory by examining the influence on
64   party identification of membership in a wide variety of social groups that are
65   closely aligned with the two major parties. . . .
66
67   **Trends in Party Identification**
68
69   One of the key claims made by Green, Palmquist and Schickler (2002) is that
70   outside of the South there has been little change in partisanship since the 1960s.
71   However, this claim appears to be contradicted by a considerable body of
72   research that has documented changes in partisanship based on such factors as
73   gender (Wirls 1986; Kaufmann and Petrocik 1999), marital status (Weisberg
74   1987), religiosity (Guth and Green 1990; Layman and Carmines 1997), and
75   social class (Stonecash, Brewer, and Mariani 2003). . . . Between 1976 and 2004,

76   the percentage of non-southern whites identifying with the Republican party in
77   national exit polls increased from 28 percent to 43 percent [consult original for
78   supporting statistics]. . . .
79
80   **Ideology in the American Electorate: Meaning and Measurement**
81
82   The evidence . . . indicates that since the 1970s there has been a substantial
83   increase in Republican identification among whites outside the South as well as
84   among those in the South and that this increase has been quite dramatic among
85   certain subgroups such as Catholics. But why has this shift occurred? Contrary to
86   Green, Palmquist and Schickler (2002), we believe that ideology has played a
87   major role in producing a secular realignment of party loyalties in the U.S. since
88   the 1970s. According to this ideological realignment hypothesis, the increasing
89   clarity of ideological differences between the parties during the Reagan and post-
90   Reagan eras has made it easier for citizens to choose a party identification based
91   on their ideological orientations. Before examining the impact of ideological
92   orientations on party identification, however, we need to demonstrate that mem-
93   bers of the public, or at least a substantial proportion of them, have meaningful
94   ideological orientations. While the concept of ideology has been defined in many
95   different ways (Gerring 1997), political scientists generally view an ideology as a
96   set of beliefs about the role of government that shapes responses to a wide range
97   of specific policy issues (Converse 1964; Peffley and Hurwitz 1985). . . . However,
98   the extent of ideological thinking in the public has been a subject of debate since
99   the publication of Converse's (1964) seminal study of belief systems in mass pub-
100   lics which suggested that awareness of ideological concepts and use of such
101   concepts by ordinary citizens were quite limited. Although some subsequent
102   studies have supported Converse's conclusions about the lack of ideological
103   sophistication among the general public in the U.S. (Axelrod 1967; Bishop,
104   Oldenick, Tuchfarber, and Bennett 1978; Sullivan et al. 1978; Conover and
105   Feldman 1981; Knight 1985; Jennings 1992), other studies have suggested that
106   the ability of ordinary citizens to comprehend and employ ideological concepts
107   depends on the extent and clarity of ideological cues provided by political elites.
108   According to this view, the greater the prevalence and clarity of ideological cues
109   in the political environment, the higher the level of ideological comprehension
110   and reasoning should be among the electorate (Field and Anderson 1969; Nie
111   and Anderson 1974; Nie, Verba, and Petrocik 1979; Nie and Rabjohn 1979;
112   Craig and Hurley 1984; Jacoby 1995). From this standpoint, the increased ideo-
113   logical polarization of the parties in recent years and the increased salience of
114   ideological conflict in the media should have produced an increase in ideologi-
115   cal comprehension and reasoning among the American public.
116   [O]ur evidence does point to a substantial increase in the ability of citizens
117   to apply ideological labels to the political parties, an increase in the coherence
118   of citizens' views across different issues, and a growing connection between the
119   ideological labels that citizens choose and their positions on a wide range of

120   domestic and foreign policy issues. In 1972, when the NES began asking respon-
121   dents to place themselves and the two major parties on a 7-point liberal-conser-
122   vative scale, only 48 percent of respondents were able to place themselves on the
123   scale and to place the Democratic party to the left of the Republican party. By
124   1996 and 2004, however, 67 percent of respondents were able to place them-
125   selves on the scale and to place the Democrats to the left of the Republicans. . . . The
126   NES data also indicate that there has also been an increase in the ideological
127   coherence of citizens' policy preferences and in the correlation between ideo-
128   logical identification and policy preferences [consult original for statistical
129   supports]. . . . In addition, contrary to the claim that ideological labels have little
130   policy content for most Americans (Conover and Feldman 1981), the evidence
131   shows that liberal-conservative self-identification was strongly related to prefer-
132   ences on every policy issue in every survey and that this relationship has grown
133   stronger over time. These results indicate that there is an ideological structure to
134   Americans' opinions on policy issues and that ideological self-identification is a
135   valid indicator of the liberalism or conservatism of citizens' policy orientations.
136   In testing the ideological realignment hypothesis, we use the seven-point
137   ideological identification scale to classify respondents in NES surveys as liberal
138   (1–3), moderate (4), or conservative (5–7) since this question is correlated with
139   preferences on a wide range of policy issues and it has been included in every
140   survey since 1972. We use a similar ideological identification question with three
141   response categories—liberal, moderate, and conservative—in our analysis of
142   2004 national exit poll data because the split-sample procedures used in the exit
143   poll make it impossible to create a multiple-item scale for the entire sample.
144   However, in our analyses of the 1992–1996 NES panel survey and the 2004 NES
145   survey we measure ideological orientations with multiple-item scales that
146   include the 7-point ideological identification question along with a number of
147   questions about specific policy issues. The 1992–1996 ideology scale is based on
148   eleven items included in both the 1992 and 1996 waves of the panel: liberal-
149   conservative identification, abortion, government aid to blacks, defense spend-
150   ing, the death penalty, laws barring discrimination against gays and lesbians,
151   allowing gays and lesbians to serve in the military, government vs. personal
152   responsibility for jobs and living standards, government vs. private responsibility
153   for health insurance, government spending and services, and the role of women
154   in society [consult original for tests of reliability].
155
156   **Group Membership, Ideology, and Partisan Change**
157
158   In order to test the ideological realignment hypothesis, we will first examine
159   trends in party identification among some of the white subgroups that have expe-
160   rienced the largest Republican gains since the 1970s, while controlling for ideo-
161   logical identification. If the ideological realignment hypothesis is correct, we
162   should find that Republican gains have been greatest among conservative identi-
163   fiers and smallest among liberal identifiers. The evidence [offers] strong support

164 for the ideological realignment hypothesis. For every subgroup examined, the
165 increase in Republican identification was much larger among conservative iden-
166 tifiers than among moderate or liberal identifiers. In fact, Republican identifica-
167 tion declined among liberal identifiers in every subgroup except Catholics
168 [consult original for statistical supports].
169
170 **Ideological Realignment vs. Partisan Persuasion Among**
171 **White Southerners and Catholics**
172
173   The evidence indicates that the relationship between ideology and party iden-
174 tification became considerably stronger among both northern and southern whites
175 who remained in the electorate between the 1970s and the 1990s. However,
176 cohort analysis does not allow us to determine whether ideology was influencing
177 party identification, as the ideological realignment hypothesis suggests, or whether
178 party identification was influencing ideology, as Green, Palmquist and Schickler
179 suggest. . . . Moreover, evidence from National Election Study surveys indicates
180 that for white southerners and Catholics, two subgroups within the white electorate
181 that experienced substantial increases in Republican identification between 1972
182 and 2004, ideological realignment rather than partisan persuasion was the primary
183 mechanism of change. If partisan persuasion was at work, increases in Republican
184 identification among white southerners and Catholics between 1972 and 2004
185 should have led to substantial increases in conservatism in these groups as the
186 growing ranks of Republican identifiers adopted the conservative ideology of their
187 new party. But the data . . . show that there was no increase in conservatism
188 among either white southerners or white Catholics [consult original for supporting
189 statistics]. . . . Contrary to the partisan persuasion hypothesis, white southerners
190 and Catholics did not become much more conservative between 1972 and
191 2004; however, conservative white southerners and Catholics did become much
192 more Republican. Between 1972 and 2004, the proportion of conservative southern
193 whites identifying with the Republican party increased from 39 percent to
194 80 percent. . . . During the same period, the proportion of conservative Catholics
195 identifying with the Republican party increased from 48 percent to 82 percent. . . . This
196 evidence clearly indicates that ideological realignment rather than partisan persua-
197 sion was responsible for the increasing correlation between ideology and party
198 identification among white southerners and Catholics. . . .
199
200 **Social Identity, Ideology and Party Identification**
201
202   According to the social identity theory, party identification is based largely
203 on membership in social groups—citizens choose a party identification based on
204 their perception of the fit between their own social characteristics and the social
205 characteristics of supporters of the two major parties. Since the New Deal, the
206 Democrats have generally been viewed as the party of the poor, the working
207 class, union members, urban dwellers, racial and ethnic minorities, Catholics,

208   and Jews while the Republicans have generally been viewed the party of the
209   wealthy, business executives, small town and rural residents, and white
210   Protestants outside of the South. However, the social images of the Democratic
211   and Republican parties have undergone considerable change in recent years. As
212   Green, Palmquist and Schickler (2002) point out, southern whites, who were
213   once a key component of the Democratic coalition, have been moving into the
214   Republican camp since the 1950s. More recently, gender, marital status, sexual
215   orientation, and religious beliefs have emerged as important correlates of party
216   affiliation: members of traditional families and those with strong religious convic-
217   tions tend to be Republicans while singles, gays, and less religious voters tend to
218   be Democrats. The changing relationship between social groups and the parties
219   raises the question of whether membership in social groups has a direct impact
220   on party identification, as the social identity theory proposes, or whether partisan
221   differences between social groups are simply a result of the policy preferences of
222   group members. According to this ideological differences hypothesis, the reason
223   that some groups such as white evangelicals have become increasingly Republican
224   in recent years while other groups such as gays and lesbians have become increas-
225   ingly Democratic is because of the policy preferences of their members. As a first
226   test of the social identity and ideological differences hypotheses, . . . [w]e measured
227   the ideological orientations of respondents in the exit poll with the three-point
228   liberal-conservative identification question because this question was included in
229   all three versions of the exit poll questionnaire. The results show that, except for
230   African-Americans, the differences between liberals and conservatives within
231   each social group were much larger than the differences between social groups.
232   African-Americans, regardless of their ideological orientation, strongly favored
233   the Democratic party. Otherwise, across all social groups, liberals strongly
234   preferred the Democratic party and conservatives strongly preferred the
235   Republican party. While the large majority of Hispanics identified with the
236   Democratic party, the large majority of conservative Hispanics identified with
237   the Republican party. Jews overwhelmingly identified with the Democratic party
238   but conservative Jews overwhelmingly identified with the Republican party.
239   Wealthy liberals favored the Democrats while poor conservatives favored the
240   Republicans; conservative gays and lesbians preferred the Republican party by
241   a wide margin while liberal evangelicals (yes, there were some) preferred the
242   Democratic party by a wide margin. The results provide only limited support
243   for the social identity theory. It is true that the partisan orientations of certain
244   groups cannot be completely explained by their policy preferences. For African-
245   Americans, in particular, social identity and party identification seem to be
246   closely connected. African-Americans, regardless of ideology, tend to be
247   Democrats. For other groups, however, the connection between social identity
248   and party identification is much weaker or nonexistent. Even for members of
249   groups with very close ties to one party or the other, such as Jews or evangelical
250   Christians, ideology trumps social identity. The reason why most Jews identify
251   with the Democratic party is because of their liberal policy preferences, not

252 because of their social identity; the reason why most evangelical Christians
253 identify with the Republican party is because of their conservative policy prefer-
254 ences, not because of their social identity.
255
256 **Social Identity, Ideology, and Party Identification in 2004**
257
258   The major conclusion that emerges [from a logistic regression analysis with
259 party identification as the dependent variable] is that the impact of ideology on
260 party identification was much stronger than that of any of the social background
261 variables. . . . Many social characteristics including age, income, gender, marital
262 status, and church attendance had little or no impact on party identification after
263 controlling for ideology. In contrast, the estimated coefficient for the ideology
264 scale is highly statistically significant. . . . Even after controlling for social back-
265 ground characteristics, the probability of identifying with the Republican party
266 was 63 percentage points higher for a voter at the 75th percentile of the liberal
267 conservative scale than it was for a voter at the 25th percentile of the liberal-
268 conservative scale [consult original for statistical support].
269   According to Green, Palmquist and Schickler (2002) the questions most vot-
270 ers ask themselves in deciding which party to support are: "What kinds of social
271 groups come to mind as I think about Democrats, Republicans, and Independents?"
272 and "Which assemblage of groups (if any) best describes me?" Based on our
273 evidence, however, it appears that the questions most voters ask themselves in
274 deciding which party to support are actually: "What do Democrats and
275 Republicans stand for?" and "Which party's positions are closer to mine?"
276
277 **The Consequences of Ideological Realignment for Voting Behavior**
278
279   The growing consistency of ideology and party identification has important
280 consequences for voting behavior because voters whose party identification
281 and ideological orientation are consistent are much more loyal to their party
282 than voters whose party identification and ideological orientation are inconsis-
283 tent. In the 2004 presidential election, according to data from the national exit poll,
284 96 percent of liberal white Democrats voted for John Kerry compared with only
285 62 percent of conservative white Democrats. Similarly, 97 percent of conservative
286 white Republicans voted for George W. Bush compared with only 58 percent of
287 liberal white Republicans. . . . [V]oters' party affiliations are now more consistent
288 with their ideological orientations than in the past. . . . Because of this growing
289 consistency, the outlook . . . is for a continuation of high levels of partisan voting.
290

291 *Source:* Abramowitz, A. I., & Saunders, K. L. (2006). Exploring the bases of partisanship in
292 the American electorate: Social identity vs. ideology. *Political Research Quarterly, 59,*
293 175–187. Published by SAGE on behalf of the University of Utah.

294 *Note:* Consult original for references. This article has been edited for length.

ETHNOGRAPHY OF RACIAL IDENTITIES IN PARIS: PUBLIC INDICATORS OF SOCIAL HIERARCHY. A RESEARCH NOTE

Benjamin P. Bowser

Social Science Information, 46, 591–605

1   Inequalities have existed among the French since the inception of the Republic,
2   with racial differences subtly embedded in social-class differences (Kritzman,
3   1995; Philipson, 2000; Stovall and Van den Abbeele, 2003), although social-class
4   and regional inequalities have been very effectively reduced by the extensive
5   French social welfare system in an attempt to actualize the principle of universal
6   equality. But since the second World War France has incorporated large numbers
7   of Antilleans, Muslim and Arab North Africans, and Black Africans from former
8   French colonies. It has been suggested that new social divisions have resulted;
9   there are now those who are French by birth (in France) and those who are French
10 by immigration (Noiriel, 2006). Those who are French by acquisition are not
11 randomly distributed throughout French social classes. They cluster at the bottom,
12 and the second generation born and reared in France is disproportionately unem-
13 ployed. Many North African and African youth see no opportunities for upward
14 mobility or movement toward future equality in France, as they articulated in the
15 recent riots. This new form of inequality challenges the adequacy of not only
16 social-class and regional differences as the bases of French inequality, it also
17 challenges the adequacy of current government measures to reduce inequality.
18   More specifically, the emerging social division in France appears to be based
19 upon religious differences (Muslim versus Christian and Jew) and ethnic-ancestry
20 differences (African and Asian versus European). While these differences are not
21 new in the world community, they are new and emerging divisions in metro-
22 politan Europe. . . .
23   As yet, there is no way to directly measure the extent to which France is
24 becoming a multi-ethnic state or the extent of inequality by ethnic group differ-
25 ences. There are no official counts of the population by ethnic prescriptive status
26 or self-identification, and there are historic and principled reasons against ever
27 doing so (De Rudder, Poiret and Vouc'h, 2000). . . .
28   So there is no way to tell the extent to which income, education and employ-
29 ment vary, for example, in Paris by ethnic prescription or self-identity among the
30 French by birth and French by acquisition. Are some Parisians 'more equal' than
31 others based not only on social class but now ethnicity as well? Are social
32 inequalities in Paris and other cities increasing and moving further away from the
33 ideal of equality or are they in fact decreasing? For the moment there is no way

34   to answer these questions directly. What government does, attempts to do, and
35   what national ideology says are one thing; but how people express and experi-
36   ence social inequalities in public are something else. What exists officially or is
37   ideally desired may be very different from what actually exists. Fortunately there
38   are indirect ways to measure social differences in actuality that can give us a
39   sense of what we might find if they were measured directly.
40
41   **Method**
42
43   Based upon 5 months of participant observation in Paris during the winter
44   and spring of 2005, I was able to observe apparent expressions of social hierarchy
45   based upon social class *and* ethnicity, and to directly experience some of these
46   expressions. In doing so, I developed a qualitative method for exploring the
47   extent to which ethnic prescription and self-identity are new bases of social
48   inequality in Parisian public behavior (Lofland and Lofland, 1995). The theoreti-
49 · cal premise in this research is the following: variations in social status are evident
50   in social relations among diverse groups of people in public space.
51   My specific working hypothesis is: people who are perceived to be of French
52   European ancestry by skin color, dress and behavior are at the top of the hierarchy,
53   followed by Antilleans and Africans. Muslims and, in particular, women who wear
54   'le voile' (the headscarf) are at the bottom of social hierarchy in Parisian public space.
55   An objective of this research was to explore evidence of this emerging social
56   stratification by using qualitative methods and to point out how quantitative
57   methodology might be used to test the accuracy of this hypothesis.
58   There is no assumption here that public identity accurately represents actual
59   identity. Because of the complexity of presentation of self in public, it is impos-
60   sible to know precisely what is any one person's ethnic self-identify or their offi-
61   cial identity without interviewing them. For example, an 'Arab-appearing' young
62   person could be Spanish or Italian; a 'Black African' could be Antillean or
63   African-American; an apparent 'Parisian' could be from any place else in France,
64   Europe, the Middle East or North Africa. An apparent 'immigrant' may be second-
65   or third-generation French. Even orthodox Muslim attire is no foolproof cue for
66   immigrant status; the person in the attire could be a visitor from the Middle East,
67   another European country, the USA or someone who is French by birth and has
68   converted to Islam. Real social class is equally elusive; an individual dressed in
69   expensive cloth and who drives an expensive car may be only middle or working
70   class. Likewise, someone dressed casually and even in work clothes may be in
71   fact wealthy and from an aristocratic background. . . .
72   Regardless of who people are officially and in person, my hypothesis is that
73   there is now a hierarchy of public identities based upon perceived ethnicity and
74   Muslim affiliation. It is hypothesized that this hierarchy is acted out through social
75   interaction at outdoor markets, in stores, tobacco shops, on the streets, in restau-
76   rants and in other public spaces. With the central hypothesis of this research
77   being that *social divisions can be observed, measured and tested for in public if*

78   *they are expressed through recurring social behaviors,* instead of official social
79   statistics, which may or may not be precise, evidence of social differences based
80   upon ethnic appearances in France, and specifically in Paris, is visible in plain
81   view and verifiable. One can learn approximately to what extent this social phe-
82   nomenon exists. So, against the grain of the strong French ideological commit-
83   ment to equality and belief in individuality, evidence of the basic architecture of
84   the new social inequality in Parisian public space is clearly observable.
85
86   **Social Inequality Observed Through Deference**
87
88   Observing patterns of deference is one of the best ways to measure informal
89   and unconscious social hierarchy.
90   In Paris one of the visible evidences of hierarchy in inequality is how defer-
91   ence varies among social actors walking on busy commercial streets. Deference
92   is defined here by altering one's walking speed and course by turning left or right
93   for an oncoming walker; that is by stepping out of their path or slowing down to
94   let them by or speeding up to get out of their way. Deference can be mutual: each
95   approaching walker changes speed and course equally for the other. Deference
96   can also be unequal: one actor changes speed and course, while the other varies
97   less or not at all. The objective of this research was to see if a hierarchy exists
98   among those who give and receive deference to fellow-walkers by perceived
99   ethnicity and Muslim identity. The highest-status walkers give the least deference
100 and take the most; the lowest-status walkers give the most and receive the least.
101
102   *Setting*
103
104   A rich setting in which to observe variations in public deference is a crowded
105 thoroughfare such as the Boulevard Saint-Germain-des-Prés on the Left Bank of
106 Paris. Saint-Germain, like hundreds of similar streets throughout the world, has
107 an observable mix of people from all varieties of Parisian, French and foreign
108 social life. . . . There are casually dressed and well dressed shoppers; people
109 walking in groups, as couples and alone, of all different ages; some are Antilleans,
110 North Africans, African and orthodox Muslims. There are also tourists from all
111 over the world. One can select a person or a group that visibly reflects one or
112 another apparent racial and religious identity, follow them and carefully observe
113 to and from whom they give and receive deference and to what extent there is an
114 imbalance. By comparing patterns and rates of deference across groups, the
115 working hypotheses of this research can be illustrated and followed up for further
116 examination and testing by others.
117
118   *Observation*
119
120   This observer first followed a series of well-dressed couples of apparent
121 European ancestry who were at least in their mid-40s and who appeared materially

122 comfortable. They fit the fictional image of the affluent 'Parisian bourgeoisie.' On
123 block after block, younger couples, single men and women, children, apparent
124 Africans and Antilleans gave deference as they approached the Parisian couples,
125 who rarely reciprocated. Younger and casually dressed apparent French or non-
126 French couples alike would separate, passing them to the left and right or, in
127 giving deference, the younger non-bourgeois would collapse their ranks to pass
128 single file when there was not sufficient room on the sidewalk to pass two
129 abreast. Rarely did anyone try to cut between the Parisian couples.
130   There were occasions when the Parisian couples did give deference. It was
131 to other and apparently older Parisian men, women and couples who dressed and
132 carried themselves in the same way. Then there were rare occasions when some-
133 one would refuse to change their path or speed; the Parisian couples would have
134 to step around them, abruptly change their speed or stop outright at the last
135 second—giving some deference. There were other occasions when people would
136 walk toward them or change direction without looking where they were going
137 (something Parisians do rather a lot). The couples would have to stop or change
138 direction abruptly; these were not seen as instances of giving or receiving defer-
139 ence; they were simply avoiding collisions.
140   When one looks for similarly aged and dressed apparent French Antillean,
141 African and Muslim North African couples, one realizes how rare they are on
142 Saint-Germain-des-Prés. But when one does find and follow them, it is rare that
143 they receive any deference. These couples gave deference so often that they
144 ended up walking in single file and unable to casually converse with one another
145 as did the Parisian couples. . . . Couples of color provided no shield whatsoever
146 to me as an observer walking behind them. Unequal deference was not only
147 observable by apparent ethnic background, it was also evident by social class,
148 gender and age. I also followed and observed small groups of same-sex French-
149 speaking adults. The same deference that Parisian couples received was given to
150 same-sex groups of men and women dressed in business attire. In contrast,
151 French-speaking small groups of walkers who were casually dressed received less
152 deference than those in business attire. Only when similarly attired French-
153 speaking groups met one another was mutual deference given. If these groups left
154 enough space between them, individuals would dart through; but rarely were
155 those who took such liberty apparent Antillean, African or visibly North African,
156 i.e. people of color. Only groups of same-sex French-speaking young people gave
157 nearly as much deference as they received, especially younger women. They gave
158 deference generally to older people but, surprisingly, also to people of color. It
159 was also interesting to follow small groups of apparently Antillean, African and
160 North African young people; they gave deference far more often to people of
161 apparent European ancestry than they received in return.
162   It was primarily among individual walkers that deference was clearly con-
163 tested. Older and middle-aged apparent Parisian men and women gave mutual
164 deference to each other and expected to receive it from all others. . . . Apparent
165 Parisian men would refuse to turn even half way when passing others on a narrow

166   street. If you did not turn more than half way when passing them, you would
167   bump into them. When they were forced to stop abruptly or collided with some-
168   one who did not give way to them, they would become visibly annoyed and were
169   the only ones to utter words to themselves or to the violator loud enough for them
170   to hear. Apparent Parisian women were equally demanding of deference from
171   other classes of walkers. Their treatment of other walkers as invisible and there-
172   fore demanding total deference from them went way beyond gentility. . . . No
173   other groups of walkers, especially people of color, expected mutual deference
174   or walked as if others were invisible.

175   In fact, people of color, young casually dressed women, and especially women
176   in orthodox Islamic attire gave so much deference that it was difficult to follow
177   them. When they were approached by others, they stopped and started fre-
178   quently, slowed down, speeded up and would cut to the left and then to the right.
179   They deferred so often, it was like following someone through an obstacle course.
180
181   *Significance*
182
183   These patterns of deference were all followed without any evidence that the
184   social actors were in any way conscious of their varied and unspoken habits of
185   giving, receiving and expecting deference. What they did was quite normal.
186   Visible differences of race, age and social class (evidenced in dress and disposi-
187   tion) were played out in a very complex and dynamic choreography of varied
188   deference in public space. Apparent middle-aged well-dressed Parisians of appar-
189   ent European ancestry were at the top of the hierarchy; they gave the least defer-
190   ence and expected the most. Younger Parisians in casual attire had contested
191   patterns of deference, and people of color and young women were at the bottom
192   of the hierarchy; they gave the most deference and expected the least.
193
194   *Verification*
195
196   There is a way to determine whether my observations are correct. The con-
197   crete sidewalks of Saint-Germain, like those of many other cities, have horizontal
198   and vertical lines in them. An individual or group walking from one end of a
199   block for the most part walks in a straight line if they do not encounter walkers
200   coming in the opposite direction or across their path. When they do encounter
201   others and are on a collision course, an observer can measure the extent to which
202   one, the other or both walkers give deference by the extent to which they deviate
203   from the sidewalk-lines they were originally tracking. As a person walks they fol-
204   low a vertical course that approximates vertical lines in the sidewalk; deviations
205   from their course can be observed. In which case, an observer can count the
206   number of deviations made or not made relative to oncoming walkers from their
207   tracking lines as counts of received and given deference. You can manually plot
208   any walker's transit from one end of a city block on a graph and count the num-
209   ber of deferential deviations. . . . If the initial walker deviates measurably and the
210   other does not, the initial walker has given deference or visa versa. If both deviate

211   measurably, they have given mutual deference. By doing this experiment and
212   noting the observed social characteristics of the initial walker and those whom
213   they encounter, you can test the validity of the central hypothesis.
214

215   **Line-Jumping (*Resquiller*)**
216

217   Observing deference while walking on a busy street is not the only way to
218   measure social inequality in public. Another way is to closely observe the fine art
219   of 'line-jumping' in Paris. Parisians are for the most part very patient while waiting
220   in long lines at the central police station, City Hall, supermarket and for subway
221   and bus tickets, etc. But some practice to a fine art working their way into a long
222   line well ahead of others. The French have a word for this: *resquiller*. . . . To
223   closely watch who *resquilleurs* cut in front of provides another opportunity to
224   observe social inequality in Paris.
225   It is my observation that *resquilleurs* are more likely to cut in front of people
226   they perceive as having low status in French society, as is the case in any hierar-
227   chical society. . . . The lower a person's perceived social status, the more likely
228   they will be cut in front of. I observed that those who were visibly North African,
229   African and Antillean were more frequently cut in front of than the apparently
230   European French. I have stood in a number of lines and if I said nothing I believe
231   that I was mistaken for Antillean and was a particular mark for *resquilleurs*.
232   Whenever I challenged the *resquilleurs* in French, they were surprised but tried
233   to ignore me. Interestingly, if I challenged them in English, they were quick to
234   abandon their effort to stay in front of me. There were occasions when I was able
235   to ask a person of color if people jumped in front of them often. Their response
236   was that it was 'd'habitude'—it was a habit and expected.
237   This phenomenon could be tested by having apparent Black African,
238   Antillean and North Africans and European French keep journals of the number
239   of times they stand in line and then the number of times someone jumps in front
240   of them. After two weeks, one month or several, their journals could be com-
241   pared to see who was cut in front of more often, under what circumstances and
242   by whom.
243

244   **Counter-Crashing**
245

246   *Resquilleurs* are one thing, but there is another form of 'line-jumping'—in
247   circumstances where Parisians who are immediately behind you in line simply
248   ignore the fact that you are ahead of them. When it is your turn for service, they
249   speak up to get the server's attention and proceed as if you were not there. It is a
250   rare server who stops and tells them that it is not their turn. Most servers simply
251   wait on them and ignore your presence and position in line if you do not protest.
252   I would hypothesize that people of color experience 'counter-crashing' more
253   frequently than apparent European Parisians. Again, Parisians respond that they
254   do this to each other. But in months of observation, I saw only one apparent

255   European Parisian do this to another. Instead I saw this done frequently to people
256   of color, who, equally surprisingly, never protested.
257   It was not as if those who jumped in front of you made a conscious choice
258   to take advantage of you. As they became more and more impatient waiting in
259   line, you became more and more invisible. The lower your perceived social sta-
260   tus, the more quickly you become invisible. The higher-status person's time and
261   presence become vastly more important than yours. Those of higher status expect
262   to be served ahead of those of lower status, and you and the server are expected
263   to appreciate this fact. One incident underscores this dynamic. While waiting to
264   be served in a France Télécom (the French Telephone company) store, there was
265   no physical line to observe. As customers came into the store and stood waiting,
266   they noted who was there before them. As each person's turn came around, that
267   person had to speak up. A number of people had come in behind me and did not
268   know where I was in line. As the number of people who came into the store
269   increased and as the waiting-time grew, the group became more and more impa-
270   tient. The turn of each person ahead of me was begrudgingly respected. When my
271   turn came and I, a person of color, stepped up, pandemonium broke out. The
272   people who had come in after me and who did not know where I was in line
273   immediately rushed the three other servers in the store. They demanded to be
274   served at once despite the fact that these servers were busy with other customers.
275
276   **Service-Jumping**
277
278   A variation of counter-crashing which illustrates apparent social inequality in
279   Paris, service-jumping can happen in the middle of a purchase. You are in a store,
280   your turn comes and you are in the middle of being served. Some Parisians will
281   casually walk up to you and the server, ignore the fact that you are in the middle
282   of being served and request service. They will start by asking a question; once
283   they get the server's attention away from your transaction, they expect to keep the
284   server's attention until they have finished their transaction. Most servers seem to
285   understand this 'social trumping,' will stop serving you, help the other person and
286   then come back to you after the other person has been served. In Paris it was my
287   observation that those who trump others see themselves as more important; their
288   time and business are more important than some lesser person's. Furthermore the
289   server and the person trumped are expected to understand this. A variation of
290   service-jumping occurs when you are in the middle of paying for something at a
291   cash register and someone comes up and hands the cashier their money in the
292   middle of your transaction. They do not simply hand the cashier exact change to
293   be processed after you are finished. They need change, will ask questions and
294   even make another purchase. Again you are invisible because their time is more
295   important than yours, and it is understood that your turn continues after theirs.
296   Service-jumping is not some deviant one-time event nor does it happen to
297   everyone equally. Parisians do this frequently to people of color, businessmen do

298 this to women customers ahead of them and older Parisians do this to younger
299 people. It is accepted and expected behavior on the part of servers and customers
300 who trump and are trumped alike. To test the extent to which 'service-jumping'
301 is a Parisian social norm, I waited until it happened to me and intentionally pro-
302 tested the interruption of my turn. On the several times I challenged this practice,
303 both the server and persons who assumed that they would trump my turn were
304 shocked. The servers explained that Monsieur was only in a hurry, only asked a
305 question, only needed a moment and that they would quickly get back to me. The
306 trumpers were indignant that I would challenge their right to trump me. There was
307 no embarrassment whatsoever unless I protested in English.
308
309 **Significance and Verification**
310
311   There is a way to measure the extent to which line- and service-jumping and
312 counter-crashing occur and if it happens more or less often to people of color.
313 People of different apparent racial backgrounds could be recruited. Counter-
314 crashing and line- and service-jumping could be explained to them. Then they
315 could be asked to note the number of times it happened to them within a month
316 or more and what was the apparent ethnicity of those who did it to them. They
317 could also be asked to describe each incident. At the end of the observation
318 period, an investigator could record if one or the other group of participants
319 reported significantly more or fewer incidents. A more elaborate and objective
320 test would require recruiting test shoppers who were visibly Parisian, African,
321 Antillean and North African. They would be asked to shop in a variety of venues
322 and to have an observer follow and observe their interactions with servers and
323 other customers. Incidences of line- and service-jumping and counter-crashing
324 could even be video- and audiotaped for review.
325
326 **Qualitative Observational Techniques in Use**
327
328   These initial observations of ethnic and social-class discrimination in
329 Parisian public settings were made through qualitative observational research.
330 The strength of this technique is that it uncovers unknown behaviors and social
331 interactions; it generates insight about human behavior through systematic obser-
332 vation. The weakness of this approach is that there is no way to assess the validity
333 or accuracy of what is observed. In this study, observations were made of poten-
334 tial public demonstrations of systematic social inequality in Parisian life. But
335 suggestions were also offered about how the observations might be tested and put
336 through a process of quantitative verification.
337 _____

338 *Source:* Bowser, B. P. (2007). Ethnography of racial identities in Paris: Public indicators of
339 social hierarchy. A research note. *Social Science Information, 46,* 591–605.

340 *Note:* Consult original for references. This article has been edited for length.

THE DIGITAL IDENTITY DIVIDE: HOW TECHNOLOGY KNOWLEDGE IMPACTS COLLEGE STUDENTS

Joanna Goode

New Media & Society, 12, 492–513

1 **Introduction**
2
3   The ubiquitous nature of technology on university campuses is hard to deny.
4 Increasingly, students must navigate electronic library databases to find scholarly
5 journals and books. In the classroom, students are required to conduct research
6 using electronic resources, complete multimedia assignments, turn in assign-
7 ments via email and use specialized subject software to gain deeper academic
8 understandings.
9   Knowing how to utilize the technological ecosystem of university life is cer-
10 tainly critical for academic success. However, there are rarely explicit technology
11 prerequisites for college entrance, resulting in a range of student technology
12 knowledge among the student population. Too often, females, low-income stu-
13 dents and students of color are the ones most underprepared for the digital col-
14 lege environment (Farrell, 2005; Margolis and Fisher, 2001).
15   To shed light on the impact of the digital divide on higher education, this
16 article posits a sociocultural approach to studying the scope and nature of digital
17 inequalities. The article adopts the concept of *technology identity* as a framework
18 to explore how formative experiences and social context influence skills and
19 attitudes toward computing. A technology identity represents a blend of four
20 areas of an individual's belief system: beliefs about one's technology skills, about
21 opportunities and constraints to use technology, about the importance of technol-
22 ogy, and about one's own motivation to learn more about technology. Using
23 qualitative data collected from a mixed-methods study, this article considers the
24 complex ways that schools and universities perpetuate the digital divide.
25
26 **The Evolution of the Digital Divide**
27
28   *The Access Divide*
29
30   Scholarship around the digital divide originally considered the disparities in
31 access to and use of digital technology. [R]eports revealed that whites, males, the
32 wealthy, college educated, people under the age of 55 and those living in urban
33 communities were more likely to be users of new technologies (National
34 Telecommunications and Information Administration, 1998, 1999, 2000). [S]tudies

35 continue to show that gender, race, socioeconomic status, primary language,
36 geographical location, (dis)ability, educational level and generational character-
37 istics are associated with disparities in access to and use of technology. . . . These
38 surveys provide important information about the unequal distribution of resources
39 and knowledge, yet surveys alone cannot reveal the more nuanced causes and
40 effects of these inequalities.
41   Several studies have documented how the integration of technology across
42 subject areas varies across schools serving different student populations. . . .
43 Warschauer (2000) examined how technology initiatives were enacted in two
44 schools: a high-poverty school and an affluent school. Warschauer concluded
45 that 'One school was producing scholars and the other school was producing
46 workers. And the introduction of computers did absolutely nothing to change this
47 dynamic; in fact, it reinforced it' (Warschauer, 2000, p. 5).
48   Not only does technology integration across academic disciplines vary
49 according to socioeconomic status, but research examining which students
50 encounter rich computing learning experiences also exposes discrepancies in
51 access along lines of race and gender. . . . Researchers found that while the stu-
52 dents from primarily Latino and African American high-poverty high schools were
53 relegated to low-level vocational computer courses, the affluent school which
54 served the highest numbers of white students provided several college preparatory
55 computing courses. [S]tudies also suggest that home context trumps school expe-
56 riences in terms of building technology knowledge (Ching et al., 2005). Yet, low-
57 income households and people of color have less home internet access, which
58 hinders child engagement in computing experiences outside of school (Fox, 2007;
59 Pew Internet and American Life Project, 2007). Also, studies have documented
60 how computers are typically placed in boys' rooms, possibly accounting for some
61 of the gender digital divide (Margolis and Fisher, 2001). . . . Despite these impor-
62 tant research findings, it is still unclear how the sociocultural context of computing
63 at home and school shapes the knowledge and attitudes students develop around
64 technology. To shed light on these influences, it is necessary to go beyond access
65 and use characteristics to study the intricacies of the digital divide. . . . In recent
66 years, sociology and communication scholars have called for a more robust defini-
67 tion of the digital divide which moves away from a technological determinist
68 perspective and toward a framework that examines how the digital divide reflects
69 and reinforces society's social and economic inequities (Light, 2001; Mossberger
70 et al., 2003; Rodino-Colocino, 2006; Warschauer, 2003b). . . .
71
72 **Technology Identity as a Conceptual Framework**
73
74   The study presented in this article uses identity as a theoretical and method-
75 ological guide to examine the digital divide. This framework considers how
76 experiences lead to the construction of a technology identity and examines how
77 holding, or not holding, a technology identity impacts an individual's ongoing
78 endeavors. . . .

79   In his article 'Identity as an Analytic Lens for Research in Education,' James Gee
80   notes the analytical potential of identity and forwards a definition of identity as 'act-
81   ing and interacting as a "certain kind of person"' (Gee, 2000–1: 100). He suggests
82   that each individual has an affinity-identity which is formed as a result of participat-
83   ing in an affinity group, analogous to Wenger's (1998) community of practice. . . .
84   Viewing identity as a product of participation in communities can strengthen our
85   investigation of how past computing experiences influence individuals' relationships
86   with technology. These communities might revolve around technology, such as par-
87   ticipation in computer camp or a computer science course. . . .
88   Defining a technology identity, while difficult to capture, is an important
89   exercise for this conceptual shift in thinking about the digital divide. Martin's
90   (2000) exemplary examination into the mathematics identities of African
91   American students provides guidance in developing an analytical conception of
92   a technology identity along four aspects of one's belief system. Applied to a tech-
93   nology identity, this theoretical framework includes: beliefs about one's own
94   technology abilities; about the importance of technology; about participation
95   opportunities and constraints that exist; and one's sense of motivation to learn
96   more about technology. This study adopts these beliefs as the conceptual back-
97   bone of a technology identity.
98
99   **Measuring a Technology Identity**
100
101   This study implements the suggestions of Sfard and Prusak (2005) and uses
102   the collection of narratives as a methodological strategy for studying the digital
103   divide. To examine the development and influence of students' technology iden-
104   tities, students were asked to tell the story of their experiences with computers
105   and share the attitudes and beliefs they hold around technology. This study uses
106   narrative inquiry to investigate how holding a technology identity subtly influ-
107   ences academic and social life at the university setting.
108   The research reported in this article represents the qualitative portion of a
109   mixed-methods study conducted at an urban West Coast research university. . . . This
110   particular university was an ideal site as it attracts academically elite students
111   who typically have experienced a college preparatory curriculum in high
112   school. Additionally, the research site enrolls a high rate of low-income students,
113   with over one-third students receiving Pell Grants (Mortenson, 2004). Students
114   were solicited online through the official residential hall mailing list and through
115   residential hall floor meetings. Though it is difficult to know the exact participa-
116   tion rate due to incorrect or deleted emails, the minimum rate of participation is
117   24 percent of solicited residents, accounting for 513 students participating in the
118   survey portion of the study. Wave analysis and statistical distribution of the
119   disciplinary majors of the sample reveals that participants were representative of
120   the student population at the university. Following the administration of the
121   survey, three students with varying levels of technology knowledge served as
122   case studies based on their expressed interest in participating in follow-up

123   interviews noted in the survey portion of the study. The three students were
124   selected because they represented different points on the spectrum of techno-
125   logical fluency, cultural identity and experience. . . . The students were inter-
126   viewed for approximately one hour each using a semi-structured protocol. A
127   constant comparative method of analysis was used to draw patterns between the
128   experiences and attitudes described by the participants in the case studies (Glaser
129   and Strauss, 1967).

130

131   **Technobiographies**

132

133   *'. . . You always fall behind'—The Story of Lara*

134

135   Lara emigrated from Mexico when she was 16 and was academically suc-
136   cessful at her Los Angeles 'underperforming' high school. She had little comput-
137   ing experience at home or in high school, but her academic accomplishments
138   brought her to the university a few years later.
139   For financial reasons, after her first year of college Lara moved home with
140   her parents and two younger brothers in the eastern part of the city and com-
141   muted to campus. Her story of technology was short and incomplete. She noted
142   that her first interaction with a computer was with a donated used computer dur-
143   ing her sophomore year. However, nobody in her immediate family knew how to
144   use a computer. Desperate to learn about computers to keep up with school, Lara
145   learned about word processing from her cousins. But she received no computing
146   support at school. She stated, 'They didn't tell me how to use the internet.' . . .
147   This narrow use of computers can be explained when looking at the structural
148   constraints in Lara's school. According to Lara, the internet was not readily acces-
149   sible, textbooks were not available for all subjects, the science laboratory equip-
150   ment was inadequate and public data sources confirm that the teacher certification
151   level was well below the state average. Lara believed that her teachers did not
152   know much about computers. Eager to be successful in college, Lara enrolled in
153   a summer preparatory program for minority students at the university as well as
154   the freshmen orientation program before she began her first term at college.
155   Yet, Lara's low technology proficiency haunts her academic career. Among
156   her college peers, she ranks in the lowest quartile of knowledge and skills. From
157   enrollment in classes to library research to science homework, Lara has had
158   trouble adapting to the digital infrastructure of the university. One of her classes
159   recently held a library training session, and she was in disbelief that she had not
160   known about these resources earlier in her college career. . . . She held the uni-
161   versity responsible for these limitations in her university technology knowledge:

162

163   If they want to help the freshmen class, do so at orientation. We're paying $340
164   and all they do is talk to us, and we take nothing away. What's the point of the
165   computer labs when students don't know how to access them? We should learn
166   this instead of the dumb workshops we go through that we already know. . . . they

167   never told us how to drop a course or change classes on [university online
168   registration system]. They never told us. . . . I would also have them teach you to
169   use [the] library's database.
170
171   Lara recently switched from a science to a humanities major, claiming she
172   felt ill-equipped, compared to her peers, to complete her science assignments.
173   She struggled to use the specialized science software, and generally felt under-
174   prepared and uncomfortable with the competitive culture in the science learning
175   environment. Though it is difficult to claim that technology was the primary factor
176   in her decision, it certainly played a role. . . .
177   But despite her decision to switch majors, she continued to encounter tech-
178   nology obstacles outside of the classroom. She often failed to benefit from time-
179   saving and money-saving technology resources on campus. For example, during
180   an interview it was revealed that she was unaware that the university provides
181   free dial-up access to the internet and university intranet. Without the funds for
182   home online access, Lara had been commuting by bus to campus twice a week,
183   a three-hour round trip, to access the internet and library network from campus.
184   For Lara, this low level of technology knowledge did not translate into nega-
185   tive attitudes toward technology, however. She loves computers, recognizes their
186   potential benefits and expresses a desire to learn more about technology at col-
187   lege. It is the academic applications of technology which drives her desire to
188   learn more. Lara believes that it is important to know about technology in col-
189   lege, but acknowledged her location on the 'wrong side of the divide,' saying
190   'I think that computers are very important. Because they always have something
191   different each year, something different comes out, you always fall behind.' So far,
192   the attempt to try to keep up has been more a product of her agency than any
193   institutional effort to support her academic pursuits.
194   Lara's story illustrates how high schools fail to prepare students for the techno-
195   logical needs of college, and how the university neglects to support students' emerg-
196   ing technology needs. But universities also need to build in support networks to
197   proactively aid students like Lara. As she wisely, and bitterly, stated, 'During orienta-
198   tion they gave us a tour of campus so we'd know where all the buildings were. But
199   they didn't teach us about how to enroll in classes online. I could have just found
200   the buildings with a map—they should have taught us about the computers.'
201
202   *'It's just not such a big thing for me, I guess'—The Story of Jeff*
203
204   Jeff is a 5th year senior completing his final course requirements before his
205   graduation. Jeff is half Chinese and half Vietnamese; both of his parents were born
206   in the USA and met while at college. Jeff is an avid reader and into sports. The
207   history of Jeff and computing is extensive. He first used a computer around the
208   age of 11, and had two computers at home while growing up. As a student at a
209   Jesuit school in the San Francisco Bay Area, he began using computers in the
210   classroom during 7th grade. He reported quality learning conditions at his high
211   school, including new computers and internet access when needed. With these

212 conditions in place, Jeff used computers once a week in his academic classes,
213 and also learned how to use his high school library's electronic catalog.
214   Yet, Jeff attributed home as the primary place in which he learned about com-
215 puters. He had an old Apple computer, which he used for word processing, then a
216 newer internet-capable PC when he was older. But the learning component was also
217 impacted by his family. Though he did not understand his father's profession until
218 recently, his father is a programmer for Blue Shield. Jeff noted that his father did not
219 really teach him about computers, or ever discuss his job, but Jeff was aware that his
220 father's career involved technology. After Jeff took an introductory programming
221 course at college (which he did not enjoy), he finally comprehended the substance
222 of his father's career. His mother has also sought to learn more about computers.
223   Jeff's university experiences with technology have been generally positive.
224 Jeff has taken a physics class and biology class in which the teaching assistants
225 conducted data laboratories to teach students how to create Excel charts and
226 graphs for laboratory write-ups.
227   As a result of these extensive computing experiences, Jeff has a fairly extensive
228 knowledge about computers. Indeed, Jeff has high levels of technology skills, not-
229 ing, 'I try to figure things out on my own, when I got to college I wanted to build a
230 computer and see how it works, so I bought all the parts and put it together.'
231   Yet, Jeff's fluency with computers did not seem to signify any love of or addi-
232 tional interest in computers. He reported a neutral feeling toward the technology,
233 noting that 'There's nothing that I dislike about it, it's just not such a big thing for
234 me I guess. I can't really be more specific. I'm not like everyone else who says
235 computers are great.' . . . It seems that though Jeff expressed little interest in learn-
236 ing more about technology specifically, computing applications are seamlessly
237 woven through much of Jeff's social and academic endeavors.
238
239   *'I'm a technophile'—The Story of Scott*
240
241   The case study of Scott reveals a rich technobiography that is shaped by oppor-
242 tunity and larger social contexts. As a 5th year senior, Scott works as a residential
243 assistant. He is a white middle-class student who attended an affluent public high
244 school in the central valley of California. Like most students, Scott learned the most
245 about computers at home. His father worked as an electrical engineer and began
246 bringing computers home when Scott was a small child. He recalls begging to use
247 his father's first computer, and was consequently given the computer when his
248 father brought home a newer computer. Scott noted that 'From then on, when he
249 would upgrade I would get the old computer, or be able to use it more and I could
250 put games on that, and could do that. I don't know what got me into web pages,
251 but I guess it's because I was on the internet and thought, hey, I want to do this.'
252 During high school, his family had three computers, all connected to a high-speed
253 internet connection. Scott took a summer course in web design in middle school
254 and played video games with his friends throughout his childhood.
255   Despite few technology experiences at school, Scott ranked in the highest
256 quartile of technology knowledge and skills of the sample of students. In fact, his

257 rich digital knowledge led to a job working in the university's computer store. He
258 feels confident troubleshooting his own computer, and has used technology suc-
259 cessfully at college to enroll in classes and conduct research. . . . His knowledge
260 of computing accompanies a very positive attitude toward computers. As Scott
261 stated, 'I'm a technophile. I like having the latest gadgets.'
262   Scott not only knows about technology, but he also takes advantage of virtual
263 resources to save time and money:
264
265   I've been dealing a lot with eBay and Amazon and stuff like that. It's a goldmine.
266   You can sell a lot of things. . . . I've been able to sell stuff when I upgrade. I
267   bought a laptop, and they came out with better ones, and I sold my laptop and
268   made money. Technology-wise, I sell a lot online.
269
270   It is clear that Scott's fluency with technology provides academic and finan-
271 cial affordances which shape his scholarship, social life and career endeavors.
272 Beyond these benefits, Scott's relationship with technology is a defining charac-
273 teristic of his sense of self.
274

275 **Technology Identity and the Digital Divide**
276
277   [W]e can see a student's technology identity as being shaped by their beliefs
278 about one's ability to use technology, the essence of typical computer use in the
279 context of opportunities, [and] the level of importance attributed to technology
280 and motivation to learn more about computing. . . .
281   Lara's narrative of limited technology skills, academic obstacles associated
282 with technology, a view of technology as important and a desperate desire to
283 learn more about technology could be signified as a *not fluent, challenged,*
284 *important and eager* technology identity. Jeff, on the other hand, holds significant
285 knowledge about computing but takes for granted how technology supports his
286 academic and social life. Since he demonstrates only a lackluster attitude toward
287 computers, Jeff might be described as having a *fluent, productive, mildly impor-*
288 *tant and unexcited* technology identity. Lastly, Scott's extensive knowledge, aca-
289 demic and recreational activities and adoration toward computing might be
290 characterized as *highly fluent, saturated, important and infatuated.*
291

292   *Unequal Opportunities to Learn About Technology*
293

294   Unfortunately, this study shows that the precise opportunities needed to sup-
295 port the development of technology identity were largely unavailable for Lara at
296 school or at home. Her story is a typical one, as low-income Latino students are
297 significantly more likely to attend schools with these learning conditions
298 (Darling-Hammond, 2002; Fine, 2002; Kozol, 2005; Oakes, 2002).
299   On the other hand, Jeff and Scott both described ongoing technology access
300 at home and school, rich home learning experiences and knowledgeable fathers

301 and others to help them with their technology needs. They attended schools
302 primarily composed of middle-class and white students.
303
304   *Technology Identity and University Life*
305
306   Despite the under-preparedness of many students, it is clear that having
307 technology knowledge is implicitly required for college success and career
308 pathways. For Jeff and Scott, transitioning to the university's digital infrastructure
309 did not pose a problem and actually enhanced their academic careers. . . . For
310 Lara, her technology identity continued to cause academic and social obstacles,
311 even after she abandoned her science major. Technology knowledge serves as a
312 gatekeeper to college success.
313
314 **Conclusion**
315
316   This study demonstrates how holding a particular technology identity creates
317 both academic opportunities and obstacles for students. In these students' stories
318 are accounts of complex, daily interactions with technology which continually
319 inform and shape how the students view themselves as college students. . . .
320   An examination of the sociocultural forces on the development of a technology
321 identity deepens our understandings of how the digital divide is reproduced in edu-
322 cational institutions. The stories of Lara, Jeff and Scott illustrate how three students,
323 who were given vastly different learning experiences at home and school, develop
324 different relationships with technology. When each of these three students entered
325 college, they found their previous relationship with technology was reinforced by
326 the university—Lara continued to be offered no support or learning opportunities
327 and felt she was on the 'wrong side of the digital divide,' while Jeff and Scott con-
328 tinued to interact with technology in ways that positively impacted their studies.
329   The findings of this study suggest several new directions for future research
330 on the digital divide. First, examining individual attitudes and beliefs around
331 technology illuminates our understandings of how it impacts the lived experi-
332 ences of individuals and how these differences shape future opportunities.
333 Second, the intersection between cultural backgrounds, gender and technology
334 identity is ripe for investigation. . . .
335   In conclusion, this research supports moving away from a technological
336 determinist approach for studying the digital divide. The results of this study
337 underscore the role of the digital divide as an indicator of larger economic and
338 social inequalities found across the education system; thus, the digital divide
339 must be studied within this larger sociocultural context.
340 ───
341 *Source:* Goode, J. (2000). The digital identity divide: How technology knowledge impacts
342 college students. *New Media & Society, 12*, 492–513.
343 *Note:* Consult original for references. This article has been edited for length.

FITTING IN BUT GETTING FAT:
IDENTITY THREAT AND DIETARY CHOICES
AMONG U.S. IMMIGRANT GROUPS

Maya D. Guendelman, Sapna Cheryan, and Benoît Monin

Psychological Science, 22(7), 959–967

1   Obesity prevalence in the United States has risen to epidemic proportions
2   (Ogden, Yanovski, Carroll, & Flegal, 2007), and immigrants to the United States
3   and their children are one of the subgroups of Americans most highly affected by
4   this epidemic. Levels of obesity are considerably lower among immigrants newly
5   arrived to the United States, but after 15 years of residence, these levels approach
6   those of the overall U.S. population (Goel, McCarthy, Phillips, & Wee, 2004). In
7   addition, U.S.-born children of immigrants are as prone to obesity as children of
8   American-born parents are (Harris, Perreira, & Lee, 2009). One explanation for
9   the rise in obesity and related chronic diseases (e.g., diabetes, hypertension, car-
10 diovascular disease) among immigrants and their children is the adoption of a
11 less-healthy American diet of fast food, sweets, and soda (Kim, Kim, Juon, & Hill,
12 2000; Lv & Cason, 2004; Pan, Dixon, Himburg, & Huffman, 1999). The choice
13 to eat American foods is certainly, in part, due to their alluring convenience,
14 affordability, and ubiquity (Satia-Abouta, Patterson, Kristal, Teh, & Tu, 2002).
15 What people eat, however, is not only a matter of sustenance, but it also signals
16 their identity to others (Barthes, 1997; Levi-Strauss, 1997). In two experiments,
17 we investigated whether members of non-White immigrant groups choose and
18 consume American food as a way to convey that they belong in America.
19   A prominent concern for members of non-White immigrant groups is having
20 their American identity go unrecognized or questioned by fellow Americans
21 (Cheryan & Monin, 2005). According to research on social-identity threat
22 (Branscombe, Ellemers, Spears, & Doosje, 1999; Steele, Spencer, & Aronson,
23 2002), having one's membership in a social group doubted can be a threatening
24 experience that triggers behaviors designed to resolve that threat. One such strat-
25 egy is to engage in behaviors that prove one's group membership to other people
26 (Bosson, Vandello, Burnaford, Weaver, & Wasti, 2009; Cheryan & Monin, 2005;
27 Maass, Cadinu, Guarnieri, & Grasselli, 2003). In an effort to be considered more
28 American, members of non-White U.S. immigrant groups may distance them-
29 selves from behaviors associated with their ethnic identities in a manner similar
30 to the strategy observed in response to stereotype threat (e.g., African Americans
31 distancing themselves from the sport of basketball; Pronin, Steele, & Ross, 2004;
32 Steele & Aronson, 1995).

33   Individuals who attempt to prove their American identity can do so by
34   directly embracing behaviors associated with being American. For instance,
35   Asian Americans whose American identity was questioned (i.e., "Do you speak
36   English?") spent more time recalling American cultural knowledge than did Asian
37   Americans who were not similarly questioned (Cheryan & Monin, 2005). In con-
38   trast, White Americans, who fit the prototypical American image and therefore do
39   not need to prove they are American to other people (Devos & Banaji, 2005), did
40   not increase their efforts to recall American cultural knowledge.
41   Even behaviors that are potentially harmful to a person's health may be
42   invoked to establish his or her status as a group member. When African Americans
43   and Latinos were reminded of their racial-group membership, they reported more
44   health-fatalistic beliefs to better fit the norms of their racial group (Oyserman,
45   Fryberg, & Yoder, 2007). A longitudinal study on sorority members found that they
46   altered reports of binge eating behaviors over time to better fit in with fellow
47   sorority members (Crandall, 1988). . . . In the work reported here, we investi-
48   gated whether the motivation to convey an identity can also bring about actual
49   dietary decline.
50   Might attempts to prove one's belongingness in America result in the
51   selection of more-American foods over foods related to one's ethnic back-
52   ground? We investigated how threats to American identity affect food choices
53   among Asian Americans. Preliminary evidence for our hypothesis was obtained
54   by surveying Asian American and White American undergraduates ($N = 41$) to
55   investigate whether their food practices are a source of threat. Participants
56   were asked to list any "ethnic foods or food-related practices" they ate or per-
57   formed at home growing up that would have made them embarrassed if seen
58   by White Americans. Asian Americans were more likely than White Americans
59   (68% vs. 27%) to have had one or more actual experiences of embarrassment
60   due to their food-related practices while growing up. . . . Examples of embar-
61   rassing foods and practices listed by Asian Americans included "rice, and oxen
62   soup, and Chinese dumplings, and our use of chopsticks"; "eating all the parts
63   of animals (chicken feet, etc.)"; "eating fried tilapia (eyes and all)"; "no dessert,
64   pork head/butt, pig blood clots, chicken feet"; and "kimchi!" Most White
65   participants responded that they could not think of any examples or left the
66   section blank. . . .
67   Traditional ethnic diets are typically healthier than the prototypical American
68   diet (Nestle, 1994), yet the findings of our survey provide initial real-world evi-
69   dence suggesting that misgivings about one's traditional ethnic cooking are a part
70   of growing up for many Asian Americans. . . . Ethnic dietary practices may thus
71   serve as a reminder to Asian Americans that they are different from the proto-
72   typical American and could be a source of threat to their American identity. We
73   investigated directly whether such threats cause Asian Americans to change their
74   espoused food preferences and actual food choices. Experiment 1 examined
75   whether Asian Americans report favorite foods that are more prototypically

76   American than their usual food choices when faced with a threat to their
77   American identity. Experiment 2 investigated the influence of identity threat on
78   actual food choices and how healthy those foods are. . . .
79
80   **Experiment 1: Identity Threat and Espoused**
81   **Preferences for American Foods**
82
83   Experiment 1 investigated whether Asian Americans whose identity as
84   Americans is threatened would change a seemingly stable fact about themselves—
85   their favorite food—to appear more American. On the basis of our previous find-
86   ing that White Americans did not feel a need to assert their American identity
87   when it was questioned (Cheryan & Monin, 2005), we hypothesized that White
88   Americans' reported favorite foods would not differ in response to threats to their
89   Americanness. Including White American participants in this study also enabled
90   us to rule out the possibility that Asian Americans' preference for American food
91   when threatened did not result simply from activating the concept "American"
92   (if this were the case, the same response would have been elicited from White
93   Americans as well).
94
95   *Method*
96
97   **Participants.** Sixty-four participants recruited on the Stanford University
98   campus were paid $5 to participate in the experiment. Three who identified
99   themselves as neither Asian American nor White American and eight who were
100   not United States or Canadian citizens were eliminated, leaving 53 partici-
101   pants (27 women, 26 men; mean age = 23.3 years). Twenty-four of the 53 were
102   Asian American (15 Chinese/Taiwanese Americans, 4 Korean Americans,
103   3 Vietnamese Americans, 1 Indonesian American, and 1 unidentified), and
104   29 were White American.
105
106   **Procedure.** Participants were randomly assigned to one of two conditions. In the
107   experimental condition, the American identity of participants in the two groups
108   was threatened by a White American experimenter, who approached participants
109   and asked them whether they spoke English (see Cheryan & Monin, 2005). In the
110   control condition, the experimenter did not ask this question. Participants were
111   then asked to write down their favorite food. . . .
112
113   **Rating Foods.** Favorite foods were rated in two ways. First, a separate sample
114   ($N = 31$; 17 women, 13 men, 1 unidentified; 17 Asian Americans, 14 White
115   Americans) rated how American each food was on a scale from 1 (*not at all*) to 5
116   (*very much*); results were based on averaging across raters. Second, three coders
117   (2 Asian American, 1 White American) blind to hypothesis categorized partici-
118   pants' favorite foods as American, Asian, or neither. . . .

119   *Results and Discussion [Note: consult original for*
120   *supporting statistical tests]*
121
122   Using the scale ratings of how American each food was, a 2 (ethnicity:
123   Asian vs. American) × 2 (condition: experimental vs. control) analysis of vari-
124   ance (ANOVA) revealed no main effects but the predicted interaction. Asian
125   Americans who felt their identity was threatened listed favorite foods that were
126   more prototypically American than did Asian Americans whose identity was not
127   threatened. In contrast, White Americans' favorite foods did not differ between
128   conditions. Seen another way, in the control condition, the food preferences of
129   Asian Americans looked less prototypically American than the food preferences
130   of White Americans; however, in the experimental condition, Asian Americans'
131   food preferences looked as American as those of White Americans. The cate-
132   gory coding revealed that a significantly greater percentage of threatened than
133   nonthreatened Asian Americans (75.0% vs. 25.0%) listed an American food as
134   their favorite. In contrast, the percentage of White Americans listing an
135   American food did not differ between conditions (experimental: 85.7%; con-
136   trol: 80.0%). We also investigated whether the shift toward American foods
137   corresponded to a shift away from Asian foods, similar to the distancing effect
138   found in response to stereotype threat (Steele & Aronson, 1995). Threatened
139   Asian Americans were significantly less likely to list an Asian food as their
140   favorite (25.0%) than were nonthreatened Asian Americans (66.7%). Asian
141   Americans, but not White Americans, altered their food preferences to assert a
142   threatened American identity.
143
144   **Experiment 2: Eating to Assert an American Identity**
145
146   Does the effort to assert an American identity also explain the actual food
147   choices of Asian Americans? This is an important question because an affirmative
148   answer would demonstrate that Asian Americans go as far as altering their diet
149   and potentially compromising their health in response to identity-based threats.
150   We hypothesized that threats to their American identity cause Asian Americans
151   to choose more prototypical American foods as a way to prove their Americanness,
152   and this leads them to consume less-healthy foods. We also investigated an alter-
153   native causal path: that identity threat increases the desire for unhealthy foods,
154   and this in turn causes selection of American foods.
155
156   *Method*
157
158   **Participants.** Fifty-five U.S.-born Asian Americans were recruited through the
159   subject pool at the University of Washington. Participation in the experiment was
160   open only to students who were both U.S.-born and self-identified as Asian
161   American, without their knowledge of this racial restriction. Three vegetarian

162   participants and one other participant who encountered technical difficulties
163   were eliminated. The final sample consisted of 51 participants (28 women, 23 men;
164   mean age = 19.4 years), among whom were 15 Chinese/Taiwanese Americans,
165   13 Southeast Asian (i.e., Vietnamese, Thai, Cambodian, Filipino, Indonesian)
166   Americans, 11 Korean Americans, 3 Japanese Americans, 2 South Asian
167   Americans, and 7 participants of mixed or unidentified Asian ethnicities.
168
169   **Food Web Site and Pretest.** Participants were shown a fake food-delivery Web
170   site. . . . Clicking on the American or Asian links brought up restaurants with a list
171   of foods and corresponding prices. The mean price was the same for both the
172   American and the Asian menu items. An initial list of prototypical American and
173   Asian dishes was generated by culling online menus of 10 midpriced American
174   restaurants . . . and 10 midpriced Asian restaurants . . . in Seattle. For the Asian
175   dishes, we sampled two restaurants each from five of the six ethnic Asian catego-
176   ries (Japanese, Chinese, Vietnamese, Thai, and Korean) that represented the most
177   common Asian cuisines found in Seattle. . . . Thirty-three dishes that were easy to
178   procure and occurred repeatedly on at least three American menus or on both
179   ethnic Asian menus in each category were then given to a separate sample of
180   27 Asian American students (18 women, 9 men), who rated the dishes for how
181   Asian and how American they were on a scale from 1 (*not at all*) to 5 (*very much*).
182   The foods included on the fake food-delivery Web site were the 13 dishes rated
183   by the separate sample as the most American—bacon, lettuce, and tomato sand-
184   wich, chicken tenders, Cobb salad, fish and chips, fried chicken, grilled cheese
185   sandwich, grilled chicken club salad, hot dog, hamburger, macaroni and cheese,
186   pepperoni pizza, Philly cheesesteak sandwich, and submarine sandwich—and
187   the 13 dishes rated as the most Asian—beef yakisoba (noodles), bibimbap (rice
188   with vegetables and meat), chicken katsu (fried chicken), chicken teriyaki, com
189   tom xaorau (prawns and vegetables), kalbi (ribs), lad na (wide noodles), pad thai,
190   pho (noodle soup), pork banh mi (Vietnamese sandwich), sushi plate, tempura
191   udon (noodle soup), and Thai curry with chicken.
192
193   **Nutrition Information.** Calories, fat, and saturated fat for a single serving of each
194   dish were obtained using Nutritionist Pro software (http://www.nutritionistpro
195   .com/). Information was available in Nutritionist Pro for 15 of the 26 dishes, and
196   information for the remaining 11 dishes was obtained by entering the dish's
197   ingredients into the software. . . . Consistent with observed differences between
198   the healthiness of prototypical American foods and the healthiness of prototypical
199   Asian foods (e.g., Franzen & Smith, 2009; Kudo, Falciglia, & Couch, 2000),
200   data showed that, on average, the 13 American foods were higher than the 13 Asian
201   foods in calories (649.63 vs. 507.57), fat (32.59 g vs. 20.55 g), and saturated
202   fat (11.87 g vs. 7.00 g). All of these effects were sizeable, even if these dif-
203   ferences were not statistically significant, presumably because of the small
204   sample of foods.

205 **Procedure.** Participants were randomly assigned to one of two conditions. On
206 participants' arrival, the experimenter told those in the identity-threat condition,
207 "Actually, you have to be an American to be in this study" (this procedure was
208 also used in Cheryan & Monin, 2005). All participants told the experimenter that
209 they were American, at which point the experimenter invited them in. In the
210 control condition, the experimenter simply invited them in. Participants were told
211 that the purpose of the study was to investigate "how appetite affects cognitive
212 processing" and that they would be ordering food for a second session.
213 Participants saw the food delivery Web site and were told to select a dish from
214 either the American or Asian restaurants because the experimenters had accounts
215 there. The Web site recorded how long participants spent on each menu and their
216 food choice. . . .
217
218   *Results and Discussion [Note: consult original for*
219   *supporting statistical tests]*
220
221 **Choice of Food.** As predicted, a 2 (between subjects: identity threat condition vs.
222 control condition) × 2 (within subjects: Americanness of the food vs. Asianness of
223 the food) ANOVA on average pretest ratings of the foods chosen in the main
224 experiment revealed no main effects but a significant interaction. Participants in
225 the identity-threat condition chose dishes that had been rated as more American
226 than dishes chosen by control participants and less Asian than control partici-
227 pants' dishes. Consistent with this result, the choices of the majority of threat-
228 ened participants were dishes from the American menu (58.1%); in contrast,
229 the majority of participants in the control condition chose foods from the Asian
230 menu (70.0%).
231
232 **Healthiness of Food Choice.** Compared with participants in the control condi-
233 tion, participants in the identity-threat condition ordered and ate dishes with an
234 additional 182 calories; an additional 12 g of fat; and an additional 7 g of
235 saturated fat. . . .
236
237 **General Discussion**
238
239   In two experiments, we tested an identity-based explanation for the situa-
240 tional adoption of an American diet by Asian Americans. When faced with a
241 threat to their American identity, Asian Americans altered both their food prefer-
242 ences (Experiment 1) and their actual food choices (Experiment 2) to be more
243 prototypically American—and, as a consequence, less healthy (Experiment 2)—
244 than did Asian American participants who were not confronted with a threat to
245 their American identity. The same pattern was not observed among White
246 Americans (Experiment 1), who do not have to contend with similar everyday
247 threats to their American identity (Cheryan & Monin, 2005).

248   Subtle challenges to American identity can lead to increased consumption
249 of American foods over traditional ethnic foods. Trading a traditional diet for a
250 prototypical American diet may thus provide a way, albeit a potentially harmful
251 one (Nestle, 1994), for individuals to prove their American identity to others
252 who might doubt it. . . . Our research thus contributes a possible identity-based
253 psychological explanation for dietary decline, which to date has been under-
254 stood primarily as a socioeconomic, cultural, and structural phenomenon
255 (Satia, 2010).

256 _____

257 *Source:* Guendelman, M. D., Cheryan, S., & Monin, B. (2011). Fitting in but getting fat:
258 Identity threat and dietary choices among U.S. immigrant groups. *Psychological Science,*
259 *22*(7), 959–967. Published by SAGE on behalf of the Association for Psychological Science.

260 *Note:* Consult original for references. This article has been edited for length.

ADDICTS' NARRATIVES OF RECOVERY FROM DRUG USE: CONSTRUCTING A NON-ADDICT IDENTITY

James McIntosh and Neil McKeganey

Social Science & Medicine, 50, 1501–1510

1 **Introduction**
2
3   In the minds of many people addiction to illegal drugs is a one way road
4 leading inevitably to destitution and ultimately to the death of those who become
5 addicts. This image, however, could hardly be further from the truth. While it is
6 certainly the case that individuals addicted to illegal drugs are at risk of a range
7 of adverse outcomes, it is not the case that all drug users become addicts or that
8 there is no road back from such addiction. Many addicts do eventually recover
9 (Waldorf, 1983; Prins, 1994). However, the process through which such recovery
10 comes about remains far from clear. We know relatively little, for example, about
11 the contribution of treatment interventions in facilitating such recovery; what
12 works, for whom and under what circumstances are questions that are a long way
13 from being resolved. It is certainly the case that many addicts recover only on the
14 basis of lengthy and extensive contact with drug treatment agencies. On the other
15 hand, research has shown that it is not at all uncommon for individuals to over-
16 come their dependence upon illegal drugs without any recourse to treatment
17 (Klingemann, 1994).
18   Almost all of the terms one might employ in any discussion of recovery
19 from dependent drug use are subject to conflicting interpretations; for exam-
20 ple, 'addiction,' 'dependence,' 'recovery' and 'behaviour change' are all
21 contested concepts. . . . However, our interest in this paper is not in adding
22 to, or attempting to resolve, these complex definitional and ontological dis-
23 putes but, instead, in examining addicts' own accounts, or narratives, of their
24 recovery. We are particularly interested in the way in which such narratives
25 may be used by addicts as an integral part of the process of coming off illegal
26 drugs; specifically, by helping them to construct a non-addict identity for
27 themselves. However, as a prelude to looking at addicts' narratives of recov-
28 ery, it will be useful to review some of the ways in which the process of
29 recovery from dependent drug use has been portrayed by addictions research-
30 ers and practitioners.

31   **Recovery From Addiction**
32
33   One of the most widely cited descriptions of the recovery from dependent
34   drug use is the maturing out of addiction thesis articulated by Charles Winick
35   (1962). According to Winick, for the majority of addicts, addiction is a self-limiting
36   process in which up to two thirds of addicts 'mature out' of their addiction by the
37   time they reach their mid thirties. Although the maturing out thesis has been
38   widely quoted in the addiction literature, there have been very few attempts to
39   set out in any precise way what the constituents of the maturing out process might
40   be. . . . Waldorf (1983) has identified five routes out of addiction in addition to
41   maturing out; drift; retirement; religious or political conversion; becoming alco-
42   holic or mentally ill; and situational change. . . .
43   In conceptualising the process of recovery from dependent drug use many
44   researchers have used the notion of a series of stages through which the indi-
45   vidual may pass on the road to recovery. For instance, Prochaska et al. (1992)
46   have developed a five stage model of recovery in which the individual pro-
47   gresses from a stage of "precontemplation," before the user has considered
48   stopping, to "contemplation," when she or he begins to think about stopping,
49   to "preparation," in which the decision to stop occurs and efforts are made to
50   prepare for stopping, to "action" in which specific steps are taken to reduce
51   drug use and finally to "maintenance," in which non-using behaviour is con-
52   solidated and the individual is now defined as an ex-addict. While there is
53   disagreement among addictions researchers as to the number and nature of the
54   stages through which an individual may pass in the course of his or her recov-
55   ery, one element about which there is considerable agreement is the impor-
56   tance of an identifiable 'turning point' in the individual's drug using career; a
57   point at which the decision to give up drugs is taken and/or consolidated
58   (Simpson et al., 1986; Shaffer and Jones, 1989; Prins, 1994). Such turning
59   points have been described by some researchers as constituting a 'rock bottom'
60   experience (e.g., Maddux and Desmond, 1980; Shaffer and Jones,
61   1989). . . . Whatever terminology is used, the suggestion is that the individual
62   has reached a point in his or her drug using career beyond which she or he is
63   not prepared to go. For many authors, such turning points are an essential step
64   on the road to recovery from addiction (Bess et al., 1972; Brill, 1972). Moreover,
65   according to the literature, this turning point is usually accompanied by some
66   experience or event which serves to stimulate or trigger the decision. These
67   triggers can be either positive—e.g. securing a job, starting a new relationship
68   or the birth of a child—or negative—e.g. a sudden deterioration in health, an
69   adverse drug effect, being faced with the prospect of going to prison or the
70   death of a partner or close friend (Waldorf and Biernacki, 1981; Stimson and
71   Oppenheiner, 1982; Stall and Biernacki, 1986). . . .
72   In a different context, Bury (1982) and Williams (1984), have shown how
73   arthritis sufferers seek to reconstruct their identity by providing a narrative of their

74   illness, its possible causes and its impact upon their lives and sense of self. In
75   much the same way, we seek to show in this paper that the narratives which our
76   interviewees provided of their recovery from dependent drug use can be seen as
77   being part of the process by which they sought to construct a non-addict identity
78   for themselves.
79
80   **Sample and Methods**
81
82   The aim of the research on which this paper is based was to collect detailed
83   information from drug users themselves on their experience of coming off ille-
84   gal drugs (McKeganey and McIntosh, in press; McIntosh and McKeganey, in
85   press). We deliberately selected our sample on the basis of addicts' own defini-
86   tions of whether they had given up rather than using a more objectively defined
87   measure such as no illegal drug use for at least a six or twelve month period
88   backed up by regular urine testing. The reason for this was that our interest was
89   not in objectively defining an ex-addict group but, rather, in exploring
90   individuals' own sense of the recovery process. In consequence, some of the
91   individuals interviewed in this research had (according to their own
92   accounts) ceased their illegal drug use entirely, others were confining their drug
93   use to cannabis, while still others were receiving methadone on a regular
94   basis. . . . What we sought to do was not to critically assess individuals'
95   accounts of their recovery experience in order to produce a genuine ex-addict
96   group, but rather to look at the process of coming off drugs from the perspective
97   of the drug users themselves. Our question was not 'have they genuinely man-
98   aged to become ex-addicts' but 'what is the nature of the individuals' accounts
99   of their recovery and in what ways might the recounting of those narratives be
100 part of the recovery process?' . . .
101   In total, interviews were carried out with 70 recovering addicts. They were
102 recruited from across Scotland by a variety of means. These included snowball
103 sampling, the follow up of ex-clients of drug services, and newspaper advertise-
104 ments. The average age of the interviewees was 29.5 (range 20.2 to 45.3), the
105 average length of drug use was 9.3 yr (range 2 to 20 yr) and 52% of the sample
106 was female. Heroin had been the drug of choice of 60% of interviewees and the
107 average length of time for which the members of our sample had ceased using
108 their drug of choice was 4.3 yr (range 7 mo to 12 yr). The interviews followed a
109 semi-structured format in which respondents were encouraged to describe, in
110 their own terms, how they had come off drugs. Interviews lasted between thirty
111 minutes and two hours and were audio-taped. . . .
112
113 **Constructing a Non-addict Identity**
114
115   There were three key areas in which the recovering addicts' narratives could
116 be seen to be doing the work of constructing a new, non-addict identity for the

117   individual; firstly, in relation to their reinterpretation of aspects of their drug using
118   lifestyle; secondly, in relation to the reconstruction of the individual's sense of
119   self; and thirdly in relation to the provision of convincing explanations for their
120   recovery. We look at each of these in turn.
121
122   *Re-interpreting the Addict Lifestyle*
123
124   In his classic book "The Outsiders" Howard Becker (1963) was able to
125   show that an important part of the process of acquiring an identity as a drug user
126   involved the individual in learning to interpret the experience of using marijuana
127   and in developing favourable attitudes towards it. For our interviewees this pro-
128   cess was put into reverse to the extent that an important part of their attempt to
129   fashion a non-addict identity involved the individual in re-interpreting various
130   elements of his or her drug use in a negative light. . . .
131
132   That's the problem with drugs. You take them at the beginning and they make
133   you feel great. You know, for you, they just make you feel like an empty per-
134   son. At the beginning you feel like the best there is and then in the end you
135   take them to feel the best you possibly can. The way you and I are sitting now,
136   a lot of people take drugs every morning just to feel the way you and I do now
137   which is completely normal. Not to get stoned, not intoxicated, just normal.
138   (Jimmy)
139
140   . . . In re-interpreting their experience of using drugs, the recovering addicts
141   in our sample would often emphasise the fact that, by the latter stages of their
142   drug career, the drugs had long since ceased to induce any kind of pleasurable
143   effect. . . . By describing the effects of drug use in these terms, our interviewees
144   could be seen to be underlining the fact that, for them, illegal drugs had lost
145   much of their previous power and mystique. . . .
146
147   I have gained a lot of self-respect for myself as a straight person and a lot of
148   confidence for myself. And all the self-respect and confidence I had as a user was
149   just all false, it wasn't real. I like myself as a straight person better that I did when
150   I was a user, but I thought I liked myself as a user, but I like myself better as a
151   straight person. (Helen)
152
153   In this extract the individual contrasts the sense of confidence which she felt
154   when she was using illegal drugs with that which she now feels as someone who
155   has stopped using them. Drawing a distinction between the synthetic confidence
156   associated with her drug use—"it was just all false"—and the authentic confi-
157   dence associated with her recovery can be seen as an important part of the indi-
158   vidual's attempt at reconstructing herself as someone who was moving away from
159   her previous life as a drug addict. . . .

160   *Reconstructing the Sense of Self*
161
162   The addicts' narratives of recovery would often involve differentiating
163 between the following images of the self:
164
165   1. The individual's sense of self before drugs became a central part of their life.
166   2. The individual's sense of the person they had become as a result of their
167   drug use.
168   3. The individual's sense of the person they aspired to be.
169
170   The recovering addicts' sense of self while they were using drugs was fre-
171 quently contrasted with the sort of person they believed themselves to have been
172 before taking up drugs and with the sort of person they aspired to be in the future.
173 In other words, a distinction was made between the sort of person that addiction
174 had made them and the person they believed themselves to be 'at heart.' . . .
175
176   I was really sick of life revolving around drugs and sick of the things I would do
177   to get drugs and just sick of the drugs being the main thing in my life. Drugs came
178   before anything, they came before myself, the house, my family. I hated the folks
179   I was associating with and the lifestyle. . . . I hated the lying, the cheating and the
180   sleeping with folk I didn't like just because they had drugs on them. I just hated
181   having no self-respect. I really hated myself. . . . Whereas in actual fact I should
182   have been thinking what was I going to get my child for her breakfast, her lunch,
183   her tea, what's she doing, who's she playing with? (Angela)
184
185   This sense of a disjunction between the individual's understanding of the
186 person they had become as a result of their drug use and the person they felt
187 themselves to be "at heart" was further illustrated by interviewees through the
188 process of recounting, in a highly critical way, the various deeds which they had
189 carried out in support of their drug habit. For Mary it was having to prostitute
190 herself that emphasised how low she had sunk.
191
192   Basically I couldn't live with it. I didn't work the streets for a long time. I worked
193   the streets for 6 weeks but that was long enough for me to feel really sh***y about
194   myself. Basically I would have done anything for the money and that was just
195   pure degrading myself. . . . That was my lowest point. . . . (Mary)
196
197   In the last two extracts, the recounting of negative actions is combined with
198 an evaluative judgement on the part of the individual. In Angela's case this is
199 seen in her comments about how much she hated the drug centredness of the
200 junkie lifestyle, while with Mary it is reflected in her comments about how
201 degraded she felt at the realisation that she would have been prepared to do
202 anything to obtain the money to support her habit. These evaluative judgements

203   were an important part of the individual's narrative of recovery in that, not only
204   did they show the individual's capacity to reflect upon some of the most painful
205   aspects of their life as an addict but, more importantly, they also enabled them
206   to demonstrate that they were no longer the same person they had been when
207   they were using drugs. Another important part of the addicts' attempts to con-
208   struct a non-addict identity for themselves through their narratives of recovery
209   involved differentiating between their sense of who they were "at heart" and
210   the image of themselves which they saw reflected back in the reactions of oth-
211   ers around them:

212
213   I think the main thing that got me off was basically seeing my children growing
214   up, seeing the hurt in my ex-wife's eyes. I never even realised what I had done
215   'till I saw the hurt in her eyes. . . . I would take every penny so I could score drugs
216   and leave her with practically nothing. Her and my child. (Glen)

217
218   . . . Many of our addicts referred to their belief that illegal drugs had prevented
219   them from expressing what they felt was their true sense of self. . . . However,
220   the individuals' efforts at constructing non-addict identities for themselves
221   entailed more than their capacity to reflect back upon their lives as drug users in
222   a critical way. An equally important aspect of their narratives of recovery involved
223   presenting the future as an opportunity for them to reclaim control over their lives
224   and to fulfill the potential they felt they had had prior to becoming involved with
225   drugs. . . .

226
227   I didn't really have any wild dreams, just hope for the future, but the more
228   straight you get the more your imagination returns to what you wanted when you
229   were a child; . . . my memory started coming back and it was just all unfolding
230   in front of me. I teach aerobics now and I go to college. A year ago I'd never have
231   seen me this far down the line. (Betty)

232
233   . . . In sum, then, not only had the recovering addict's drug using past to be
234   rejected, their future also had to be re-designed in order to enable them to give
235   expression to their true self. . . .

236
237   *Providing Explanations for Recovery*

238
239   . . . Earlier in the paper, we noted that many of the existing models of recov-
240   ery from drug addiction emphasise the importance of particular turning points
241   such as "rock bottom experiences" or "existential crises." Many of our recovering
242   addicts' narratives gave similar emphasis to such key moments. In the case of one
243   of our interviewees, the key moment was the point at which she realised that she
244   might have to have her leg amputated as a result of accumulated injection related
245   abscesses: "The doctor told me straight, you've not got a chance in hell, stop this.
246   If you don't you're going to have to get your leg amputated and eventually it will
247   be death" (Fay).

248   For another interviewee it was an impending court appearance and the pros-
249   pect of a long custodial sentence that acted as a trigger to coming off. . . . However,
250   the events which precipitated the decision to give up drugs were by no means
251   always negative. For example [there can be] the positive impact of starting a new
252   relationship. . . . The birth of a child was another of the positive experiences that
253   were cited by our recovering addicts as having led to the decision to cease or
254   fundamentally change their drug use.
255

256   **Summary and Implications**

257

258   The starting point for this paper was Biernacki and Waldorf's claim that an
259   important part of the process of recovery from dependent drug use is the indi-
260   vidual's ability to construct a non-addict identity for him- or herself. However, the
261   sociological literature on identity had also suggested that narratives of recovery
262   were likely to form an important part of the process of constructing and/or recon-
263   structing this sense of self. Accordingly, our aim in this paper has been to explore
264   the ways in which identity reconstruction work can be observed as occurring
265   within addicts' narratives of recovery. From the analysis of our data, there would
266   appear to be three key areas in which addicts' narratives can be seen to be
267   doing the work of constructing a non-addict identity; firstly, in relation to their
268   reinterpretation of aspects of the addict life-style; secondly, in relation to
269   their reinterpretation of their sense of self; and, thirdly, in relation to the provision
270   of convincing explanations for their recovery. . . .
271   The addicts also sought to reinforce their claim to having renewed their
272   identity by providing, in their narratives, explanations for why their recovery had
273   come about. Often individuals would use some variant of the rock-bottom type
274   experience in accounting for their decision to reduce or to cease their drug use.
275   While such accounts correspond closely with descriptions of the recovery pro-
276   cess in the addictions literature this may well result from the fact that, in many
277   cases, the addicts' accounts of their recovery may have been constructed in
278   interaction with representatives of drug treatment agencies.
279   We believe the key policy implication arising from this work has to do with
280   the issue of identity. If it is the case that an important part of the process of over-
281   coming dependence upon illegal drugs is the capacity on the part of the recover-
282   ing addict to construct or reconstruct a non-addict identity for themselves and,
283   further, if one of the means through which this is achieved is through the process
284   of providing a narrative of their recovery, there may be a need to ensure that drug
285   agency staff are able to address issues of identity and narrative construction in
286   their work with clients.
287

---

288   *Source:* McIntosh, J., & McKeganey, N. (2000). Addicts' narratives of recovery from drug
289   use: Constructing a non-addict identity. *Social Science & Medicine, 50,* 1501–1510. Reprinted
290   with permission from Elsevier.

291   *Note:* Consult original for references. This article has been edited for length.

UNASSAILABLE MOTHERHOOD, AMBIVALENT DOMESTICITY: THE CONSTRUCTION OF MATERNAL IDENTITY IN *LADIES' HOME JOURNAL* IN 1946

Sarah Burke Odland

Journal of Communication Inquiry, 34, 61–84

1 On July 24, 1959, Vice President Richard Nixon and Soviet Premier Nikita
2 Krushchev engaged in an impromptu debate at the opening of the American
3 National Exhibition in Moscow. An exercise in cold war propaganda, the exhibi-
4 tion showcased a full-scale model of a suburban ranch-style house filled with
5 labor-saving appliances (Kushner, 2002). Nixon informed Krushchev that
6 American supremacy in the cold war did not rest on bombs or missiles but on the
7 ideal of the suburban home, filled with modern appliances. Nixon explained,

9   To us, diversity, the right to choose . . . is the most important thing. . . . We have
10   many different manufacturers and many different kinds of washing machines so
11   that the housewives have a choice. . . . What we want to do is make easier the
12   life of our housewives. ("The Two Worlds," 1959)

14   In emphasizing women's role within the home, Nixon invoked the dominant
15 image of postwar family life: male breadwinners supporting female housewives
16 in affluent suburban homes (May, 1999/1998; Meyerowitz, 2004).
17   Nearly half a century later, images of postwar women tending to family and
18 home remain part of the American cultural consciousness. . . . However, over the
19 past 15 years, historians of women's history have begun to question the accuracy
20 of these representations, arguing that such one-dimensional portrayals efface the
21 complexity of the past by neglecting to consider the countless women who lived
22 outside the boundaries of White, middleclass suburban life (see, e.g., Feldstein,
23 1994; Garrison, 1994; Hartmann, 1994; Meyerowitz, 1994).
24   These challenges to conventional interpretations of postwar culture have
25 sparked a historiographical debate, at the center of which is Betty Friedan and
26 her critique of suburban domesticity in *The Feminine Mystique*. . . . Friedan's
27 description of suburban housewives' disillusionment has been challenged on
28 multiple fronts. For example, bell hooks (1984) charges that by making the
29 plight of upper-middle-class White women synonymous with the plight of all
30 American women, Friedan "deflected attention away from her classism, her
31 racism, her sexist attitudes toward the masses of American women" (p. 3).

32   Meyerowitz (1994) believes that this perspective is incomplete and that
33   Friedan's emphasis on the domestic subordination constitutes "only one piece
34   of the postwar puzzle" (p. 231). . . .
35   It is within this contested historical space—between the traditional view of
36   suburban and quiescent housewives and the revisionist approach that argues for
37   complexity and contradiction in the lives of women—that I have chosen to situate
38   my study. . . . I examine how *Ladies' Home Journal,* the top-selling women's
39   magazine of the time, participated in the discursive construction of maternal
40   identity. . . . Most work on postwar women has subsumed motherhood within the
41   broader concept of domesticity (Friedan, 1997/1963; Meyerowitz, 1994; Walker,
42   2000). However, altering the analytical lens through which scholars have tradi-
43   tionally examined discursive constructions of postwar female identity reveals that
44   *Ladies' Home Journal*'s ideological treatment of motherhood differed in signifi-
45   cant ways from its treatment of domesticity.
46
47   **Women in the Postwar Era**
48
49   Responding to the industrial demands of the war, women joined the labor
50   force in unprecedented numbers between 1941 and 1945, as more than 6 million
51   women filled a manpower void created by a rejuvenated economy and the depar-
52   ture of young men to the battlefront (Evans, 1989). Concerned that women would
53   want to retain their high-paying industrial jobs after the war, the federal govern-
54   ment, in coordination with various media outlets and advertising agencies, con-
55   sistently reassured the public that women would return to their traditional roles
56   once the war was over (Evans, 1989; Hartmann, 1982; Honey, 1984). . . . Postwar
57   demographic data indicates that millions of women voluntarily left their jobs, and
58   marriage and birth rates skyrocketed (Evans, 1989; May, 1999/1988). Motherhood
59   took on increased importance during this period (Coontz, 1992; May, 1999/1988).
60   Concerned with the need to restore the nation's feelings of security and safety,
61   experts infused motherhood with a sense of national purpose. Psychologists and
62   sociologists directed women to rear responsible, patriotic children who would
63   become future scientists and defeat the Russians in the cold war (May,
64   1999/1988).
65   Yet, revisionist historians argued that [this] tells only part of the postwar
66   story (Meyerowitz, 1994). For example, Chafe's (1992) examination of the
67   postwar period reveals that contrary to the standard historical accounts, many
68   women expressed the desire to continue working in paid employment after
69   the war. . . .
70   The contradictory developments of the postwar period produced a "strange
71   paradox" for women (Chafe, 1992). On the one hand, women had been exposed
72   to new opportunities in the public sphere, yet on the other, traditional ideas about
73   a woman's proper place persisted and became even more entrenched in some
74   instances. . . .

75   **Identity, Motherhood, and Women's Magazines**
76
77   The postwar confusion and discontent about women's roles suggest that the
78   concept of gender identity, far from being essential or fixed, is a construct shaped
79   by social and historical circumstance.
80   The media, of course, play a key, albeit complex role in the construction of
81   gender identity. . . . Women's magazines, in particular, have been shown to have
82   a significant impact in shaping women's identities within established codes of
83   normative femininity (Ferguson, 1983; McCracken, 1993). . . . However, it would
84   be a mistake to view women's magazines as all powerful in the construction of a
85   discrete female identity. While McCracken (1993) and Ferguson (1983) ascribe
86   ideological influence to women's magazines, they do not view this influence as
87   absolute. . . .
88   As this review of literature demonstrates, significant scholarship has been devoted
89   to the analysis of the construction of femininity in women's magazines. . . . What
90   differentiates my study from previous studies is that I draw a clear distinction
91   between motherhood and domesticity. In the analysis that follows, I focus on
92   representations of motherhood to demonstrate that while *Ladies' Home Journal*
93   provided a complicated—even ambivalent—portrayal of domesticity, the maga-
94   zine regarded maternal identity as an unassailable ideological position.
95
96   **Protocols for Analysis**
97
98   My study examines the 12 issues of *Ladies' Home Journal* from 1946, a year
99   which marked an important turning point in U.S. history (Graebner, 1990).
100 Graebner has characterized the 1940s as being divided into two half decades: the
101 first half was public, nationalistic, and committed to production and to the new
102 roles for women it required; the second half was private, familial, and committed
103 to consumption and the consequent return to traditional gender roles. As the top-
104 selling women's magazine in 1946, with a circulation of more than 4 million
105 readers (N. W. Ayer & Son's Directory, 1946), *Ladies' Home Journal* focused on
106 issues related to home and family. . . . *Ladies' Home Journal* targeted a female,
107 White, and middle-class audience (Walker, 2000). . . .
108   [M]y study examines both the editorial and advertising content of *Ladies'*
109 *Home Journal,* drawing on McCracken's (1993) contention that "advertising and
110 editorial material, are, on a practical level, inseparable in women's magazines"
111 (p. 3). In disentangling motherhood from domesticity, I define motherhood as it
112 relates to activities involving the care of children—both physical and emotional—
113 and I define domesticity as it relates to the physical location of women within the
114 home, tending to the daily chores of managing a household, excluding the care
115 of children. Through the use of two distinct analytical terms, we are able to see
116 how it is possible for a woman to be a mother without being domestic (e.g., a
117 mother who engages in full-time paid employment outside the home) and for a

118   woman to be domestic without being a mother (e.g., a woman who stays at
119   home, does not engage in paid employment, and does not have children). To this
120   end, I developed a set of criteria to identify text and visual images that made
121   explicit reference to motherhood. The criteria include the following:
122

123   • references to the word *mother* or *mom,*
124   • images depicting a woman and child together,
125   • the hailing of *you* in advertisements for children's products in which the
126   implied *you* is the mother of the child (e.g., "your care, your wisdom, the
127   way you feed your children"),
128   • advertisements for children's products in which no person is hailed, but
129   because the advertisement features children's products and *Ladies' Home*
130   *Journal* appeals to a female audience, it can be assumed that the advertise-
131   ment's target is mothers.
132

133   Using these criteria, I included 23 pieces of editorial material (nonfiction
134   articles, short stories, biographical profiles, cartoons, letters to the editor) and
135   10 advertisements that made reference to motherhood in my textual analysis.
136   From my analysis, six major themes emerged. The first four themes address
137   the particular construction of maternal identity that emerged from the pages of
138   the magazine, identifying the specific criteria required to achieve the proper
139   performance of postwar motherhood. These themes include the emphasis on
140   mothers' patriotic duty to raise productive citizens, the location of White middle-
141   class mothers within the home, the ethic of maternal self-sacrifice and hands-on
142   child rearing, and the critical role of the expert in the lives of postwar mothers.
143   The fifth theme explores *Ladies' Home Journal*'s inclusion of challenges to the
144   ideology of domesticity, while the sixth theme addresses the magazine's position-
145   ing of postwar motherhood as an unassailable ideological position.
146

147   **Motherhood and the Nation/State**
148

149   The lingering effects of World War II permeated the 1946 issues of *Ladies'*
150   *Home Journal.* . . . Returning servicemen populated advertisements throughout
151   the magazine. An Ivory Soap advertisement depicted a father meeting his young
152   child for the first time (Ivory soap advertisement, 1946, January, p. 19), while an
153   ad for Gayla bobby pin showed a young woman dancing and kissing a service-
154   man as the copy read, "Back home for good means a lot of romancing. Gayla
155   Hold-Bobs keep your hair-do entrancing" (Gayla Hold Bobs advertisement, 1946,
156   January, p. 13). Anxiety about the devastation of the war, the use of the atomic
157   bomb, and the onset of the cold war were palpable in the pages of the magazine.
158   A lengthy article entitled "What Is Civilization?" stood out amid editorial and
159   advertisement copy dominated by issues of home, children, and beauty. The
160   article, written by Will Durant (1946), Pulitzer Prize winning philosopher, writer,

161   and historian, questioned whether "civilization will survive the partnership of
162   science with modern warfare." Durant was optimistic. Viewing family as the
163   "nucleus of civilization," he called for "order in the relations of the sexes" and
164   encouraged men and women to adhere to their traditional roles within the home.
165   Contending that a "civilization may will its own decay by allowing its birth rate
166   to fall to a point where its population no longer suffices to meet the tests of war,"
167   Durant (1946) explicitly linked women's role as mothers to the health of civiliza-
168   tion (pp. 23, 107). . . .
169   In an impassioned letter to the editor, Elizabeth Look, a reader from Mosinee,
170   Wisconsin, argued that no career should be considered more valuable than
171   women's role as mother. "If it were not for fine, brave mothers, who would train
172   each new generation—mold the youth of our land into useful, worthy citizens?"
173   A "good mother," she explained, not only "sees that her youngsters are properly
174   fed and clothed" but also instills "character-building qualities—teaching the val-
175   ues of the basic virtues and the importance of being a good son or daughter, a
176   loyal citizen, a follower of Christ" (Look, 1946, p. 10). . . . In a time of insecurity
177   and anxiety, the successful performance of motherhood—continued reproduc-
178   tion, the instruction of proper social values, and the purchase of nutritious food—
179   helped to ensure the future success of democratic civilization.
180
181   **Motherhood and the White, Middle-Class, Domestic Ideal**
182
183   The editorial and advertising content of the *Ladies' Home Journal* was
184   dominated by images of mothers dutifully attending to the needs of their chil-
185   dren within the confines of suburban homes. Shielding their families from the
186   turmoil of the outside world, mothers created a haven of calm and comfort,
187   governing their children's lives with benevolence and compassion. As author
188   Marceline Cox (1946b) explained in her monthly column, "The highest goal a
189   woman can reach is having those who belong in her home believe it is the best
190   place on earth" (p. 126). Yet, this vision of domestic bliss was not all inclusive;
191   it was limited to White, middle-class women. Women of color rarely appeared
192   in the pages of the magazine, and when they did, they were depicted exclusively
193   as domestics employed by White families. The middle-class lifestyle was pre-
194   sented as normative. Mothers tended to the home, while fathers pursued well-
195   paying jobs to support the financial needs of the family. While the White,
196   middle-class mother of *Ladies' Home Journal* was firmly entrenched in the
197   home, her activities within the domestic realm varied, although all her activities
198   supported her ultimate role as caregiver to her children. . . . The kitchen, how-
199   ever, proved to the most popular domain of the postwar mother. It was here,
200   surrounded by the latest in time-saving appliances, that mothers, clad in dress,
201   apron, and high heels, were shown smiling, fulfilled in their role as nurturer. An
202   advertisement for Youngstown Kitchens presented the kitchen as a source of
203   pride, as something to be desired. The copy read, "For years you've always

204 dreamed of a beautiful new kitchen . . . spotlessly white . . . carefully planned . . .
205 a pleasure to work in because every kitchen task is easier" (Youngstown Kitchens
206 advertisement, 1946, p. 89).
207
208 **Responsibilities of Self-Sacrificing Motherhood**
209
210   The practice of permissive childrearing also became central to the proper
211 performance of motherhood in the pages of *Ladies' Home Journal.* In the postwar
212 period, permissive childrearing, which urged mothers to avoid setting strict rules
213 and boundaries for fear of stifling children's development, replaced the scientific
214 child rearing and regimented routines of an earlier generation (Evans, 1989). The
215 editorial and advertising content of *Ladies' Home Journal* reflected this shift,
216 emphasizing the principles of maternal self-sacrifice and hands-on mothering by
217 encouraging mothers to follow the inclinations, moods, and needs of the child.
218 In the pages of *Ladies' Home Journal,* the good mother was depicted as deeply
219 invested in all aspects of a child's life, lovingly anticipating and meeting her
220 child's every need. . . .
221   The principle of maternal selflessness also surfaced in advertising, which
222 depicted mothers as dutifully attending to their children's every need. An ad for
223 Lipton soup encouraged mothers to prepare a "wonderful" and "surprise"
224 home-from-school lunch that was "sure to make children's faces light up"
225 (Lipton Noodle Soup advertisement, 1946, p. 68). . . . In an ad for Gold Label
226 molasses, mothers were instructed to protect their families from the effects of
227 wartime rationing. The ad showed a young girl enjoying a stack of pancakes as
228 the copy read, "She's not worrying about the shortage of sugar and syrup. Why
229 let shortages keep your family from enjoying pancakes and waffles? Pour on
230 molasses" (Gold Label Molasses advertisement, 1946, p. 63). The message was
231 clear: No matter how serious or trivial a child's need, a mother's work was
232 never done. Her commitment to the hands-on, self-sacrificing performance
233 must be unwavering. . . .
234
235 **The Rise of the Expert and the Decline of Maternal Subjectivity**
236
237   The fourth and final component of the proper performance of postwar moth-
238 erhood involved mothers' reliance on childrearing experts to guide them in their
239 daily interactions with their children. . . . In the pages of *Ladies' Home Journal,*
240 Dr. Herman Bundesen, a physician with the Chicago Board of Health, fulfilled
241 this role, lending his expertise to a monthly column on pediatric medical
242 issues. . . . In an article about the prevention and treatment of burns, Bundesen
243 wrote, "Every year thousands of children are painfully burned, and many die as
244 a result in accidents that should not and need not have happened; . . . usually
245 someone's ignorance or thoughtlessness is to blame." The "someone"
246 Dr. Bundesen referred to was not gender neutral; he understood child safety to be

247   a mother's domain. Making this link explicit, he continued, "Burns don't often
248   happen to children of mothers who were aware of the hazard themselves and
249   instructed their children and other members of the household accordingly"
250   (Bundesen, 1946a, p. 95). The implication was clear: Bad mothers who were
251   "ignorant" and "thoughtless" would be held responsible for their child's suffering
252   and scarring.
253   The theme of mother blaming was ubiquitous in Bundesen's columns. In an
254   article on asthma, Bundesen (1946b) argued that unless a mother has "helped the
255   doctor search relentlessly for the cause" of the asthma, "the child's suffering . . . may
256   be her own fault" (p. 162). The death of a child from pneumonia was also blamed
257   on a mother's inattentive care because, as Bundesen (1946c) explained, "children
258   do not die of pneumonia any more—*unless mothers fail to recognize the signs*
259   *and act promptly to get medical science on the job*" (p. 196).
260   If Bundesen demeaned mothers' efforts to care for their children, a series of
261   Johnson's Baby Lotion advertisements (1946) stripped the postwar mother of her
262   subjectivity altogether (April, p. 201; June, p. 196; October, p. 228). The ads
263   showed a giant male infant towering over his miniature mother, who looked up
264   at the child with a mixture of apprehension, curiosity, and helplessness. In one of
265   the most troubling advertisements, the miniature mother stood against a height
266   chart, as the giant infant crouches down and asked, "Think you measure up,
267   Mom?" The ad went on to stage a mock conversation between the giant infant
268   and the miniature mother. Displeased with his mother for not using Johnson's
269   Baby Oil, the infant informed his mother, "Now, I've trimmed you down to my
270   size, Mom—still think you measure up as a mother?" The mother, plagued by
271   guilt for having failed to properly perform her maternal duties responded, "I feel
272   about so-o-o big! I'd completely forgotten what it's like to be a baby, wriggling
273   around and twisting all day."
274   Whether taking direction from paternalistic experts or giant infants, mothers
275   were stripped of their subjectivity as the proper performance of motherhood,
276   increasingly controlled by a masculinist scientific discourse, was dictated at an
277   "increasing distance from women and children themselves" (Ehrenreich &
278   English, 1978, p. 184).
279
280   **Dissonance With Prevailing Norms of Domesticity**
281
282   As the preceding sections demonstrate, the pages of *Ladies' Home Journal*
283   provided a limited and quite specific portrayal of motherhood. However, when it
284   came to the issue of domesticity, the magazine's portrayal was not monolith; the
285   magazine included several moments of resistance to dominant ideologies of
286   domesticity that assumed a woman's place—whether she was a mother or not—
287   was in the home. . . . An example of *Ladies' Home Journal* willingness to chal-
288   lenge dominant ideas of domesticity can be found in a cartoon from the August
289   issue. The cartoon showed two women sitting at a table having a conversation,

290   with one remarking to the other, "We're just an old-fashioned couple. My hus-
291   band works; I stay home" (Old-fashioned couple cartoon, 1946, p. 28). The
292   implication was that by adhering to traditional gender roles, the couple had failed
293   to keep pace with societal changes. *Ladies' Home Journal* included a more sub-
294   stantial discussion of and challenge to prevailing norms of domesticity in two
295   articles entitled, "Meet Three Career Girls" and "Profiles of Success." "Meet Three
296   Career Girls" featured three recent college graduates who had recently moved to
297   New York City to find employment. The magazine presented the idea of working
298   in the city as an exciting adventure for young women, full of fun and opportunity
299   (Hoffman, 1946, January, p. 109). The second article, "Profiles of Success," . . . pro-
300   filed careers in merchandizing, advertising, fashion designing, business, and
301   journalism, [and] provided an in-depth discussion of what it took for women to
302   succeed in the professional world. . . .
303   A handful of advertisements also featured working women, although the
304   overwhelming majority of these advertisements highlighted women in tradition-
305   ally feminine occupations, including secretary, model, nurse, and ballerina. For
306   example, Ivory Soap included testimonials from working models, discussing how
307   Ivory Soap provided them with flawless complexions (Ivory Soap advertisement,
308   1946, February, p. 89, April, p. 16, June, p. 163, August, p. 198). . . . However, it
309   is important to note that not all of *Ladies' Home Journal*'s advertisements featured
310   working women in traditional female professions. The ads for Avon Cosmetics are
311   unique in challenging his trend. The Avon ads celebrated women of achievement,
312   including photographer Margaret Bourke-White and anthropologist Margaret
313   Mead. As all these examples illustrate, *Ladies' Home Journal* supplied moments
314   of resistance that challenged the traditional ideology of domesticity. . . .
315
316   **Motherhood as Unassailable Ideological Position**
317
318   Despite *Ladies' Home Journal*'s willingness to accommodate challenges to
319   dominant ideas about domesticity, the magazine proved virtually intractable in its
320   narrow construction of motherhood. On this issue, there was little room for ambi-
321   guity: Motherhood was a woman's highest and most important calling, and its
322   proper performance involved women selflessly attending to the needs of their
323   children within the confines of the home.
324   The idea that motherhood should be located exclusively within the home
325   was important to *Ladies' Home Journal;* the magazine made clear its opposition
326   to women combining paid employment and motherhood, vigorously contrasting
327   depictions of mothers' happy existence within the home to the negative conse-
328   quences of mothers' presence in the marketplace. The assumption was that a
329   woman's employment interfered with her primary responsibility to be a doting
330   and attentive mother. As an illustration, "Profiles of Success," which had provided
331   the strongest endorsement for women's entry into the labor force, referred to
332   motherhood as the "Achilles' heel" of the career woman, arguing that professional

333 women were unable to devote the necessary time to their children. . . . The con-
334 clusion? A woman may pursue employment before she had children, but once
335 she became a mother, she would achieve the "deepest satisfactions" and "best
336 results" by abandoning her career and committing herself fully to her children.
337   The magazine also explored the incompatibility of employment and mother-
338 hood in a fictional piece, "Prelude to Happiness," about a young woman who
339 decided to give up her job after she became pregnant. Describing pregnancy as
340 the "most sentimental period of her life," she explained that employment was no
341 longer possible because her "mind stopped working" and that she preferred to
342 spend her time organizing baby clothes and preparing for her role as a mother
343 (Alzamora, 1946, p. 99). . . .
344   In an effort to protect their reproductive capacities, Ladies' Home Journal
345 made clear that White, middle-class women had to learn to substitute the ambi-
346 tion of the workplace for the happiness and contentment of the home; . . . this
347 meant that women's employment outside of the home was tolerated before she
348 had children (although the magazine's embrace of this was lukewarm at best),
349 but once a woman became a mother, the magazine proved unyielding in its
350 conviction that motherhood was a woman's primary responsibility and that this
351 responsibility was fundamentally incompatible with her participation in the
352 public sphere.
353
354 **Conclusion**
355
356   The year 1946 marked a unique moment in the country's understanding of
357 and tolerance for shifting gender roles. In the transition from wartime to peace-
358 time, as millions of women relinquished—often reluctantly—their factory jobs to
359 return to their domestic responsibilities, the nation faced new questions about the
360 role of women. . . . In the pages of Ladies' Home Journal, however, this cultural
361 confusion and discontent found limited expression, extending only to the maga-
362 zine's discussion of domesticity; portrayals of motherhood failed to reflect any of
363 the societal tensions surrounding gender roles. By separating the concept of
364 motherhood from domesticity, and therefore altering the analytical lens through
365 which scholars have traditionally examined discursive constructions of postwar
366 female identity in women's magazines, this study finds that while Ladies' Home
367 Journal did not require domesticity of all women, it did require domesticity of all
368 mothers.
369   In the pages of Ladies' Home Journal in 1946, the magazine portrayed moth-
370 erhood as an unassailable ideological position, the feminine ideal. The magazine
371 made clear that before a woman became a mother, participation in paid labor
372 was acceptable—even celebrated in some instances—but once she took on the
373 role of mother, she was expected to abandon her career and return to the
374 home. . . . The result was a quite specific and narrow portrayal of motherhood
375 that involved White, middle-class women tending to their children through the

376 performance of selfless, hands-on mothering in the confines of their suburban
377 homes. Yet, in presenting only one vision of the postwar mother in 1946, *Ladies'*
378 *Home Journal* failed to reflect the realities of countless mothers who lived outside
379 this narrow frame.
380   While an audience reception analysis is outside the scope of this study, we
381 can safely assume that readers of *Ladies' Home Journal* in 1946 would have had
382 a varied reaction to the magazine, accepting dominant or preferred readings in
383 certain instances and resisting or reading messages oppositionally in other
384 instances (Hall, 1980). However, to ascribe no ideological influence to *Ladies'*
385 *Home Journal* is to adopt a naïve and uncritical view of women's magazines and
386 their ability to shape cultural understandings of gender identity. In its nearly
387 unequivocal treatment of maternal identity, and in its position as the top-selling
388 women's magazine of the period, *Ladies' Home Journal* undoubtedly influenced
389 many women's perceptions about what constituted the appropriate performance
390 of motherhood in the immediate postwar period.
391 _____

392 *Source:* Odland, S. B. (2010). Unassailable motherhood, ambivalent domesticity: The
393 construction of maternal identity in *Ladies' Home Journal* in 1946. *Journal of Communication*
394 *Inquiry, 34,* 61–84.
395 *Note:* Consult original for references. This article has been edited for length.

SMOKING IDENTITIES AND BEHAVIOR: EVIDENCE OF DISCREPANCIES, ISSUES FOR MEASUREMENT AND INTERVENTION

S. Lee Ridner, Kandi L. Walker, Joy L. Hart,
and John A. Myers

Western Journal of Nursing Research, 32(4), 434–446

1   In the transition from high school to college, many young adults move from the
2   watchful eyes of parents to making decisions themselves. Many times these deci-
3   sions include experimenting with behaviors (e.g., smoking) that were not present
4   or permissible while at home. Although smoking rates among college students
5   have declined from those in 2000, recent data show that 16% of college students
6   are current smokers (e.g., at least once in the past 30 days; American College
7   Health Association [ACHA], 2009). Furthermore, during the college years, occa-
8   sional smokers (e.g., at least once in the past 30 days but not on a daily basis) are
9   quite typical (Centers for Disease Control and Prevention [CDC], 1997). Although
10 older adults are more likely to be daily smokers, younger adults are more likely
11 to be occasional smokers (Biener & Albers, 2004). Thus, if intervention methods
12 are successful, these occasional smokers may discontinue tobacco use rather
13 than escalate to daily cigarette use as they age.
14   The examination of smoking behaviors has routinely attempted to quantita-
15 tively link smoking behavior to an operational definition. Youth-oriented national
16 surveys routinely collect data concerning experimentation with smoking or ever
17 having puffed or tried a cigarette and current or past-30-day use (CDC, 2008;
18 Johnston, O'Malley, Bachman, & Schulenberg, 2009). The National Health
19 Interview Survey (NHIS) and National Health and Nutrition Examination Survey
20 (NHANES) determine whether participants have become established smokers by
21 smoking at least 100 lifetime cigarettes and whether they smoke some days or
22 everyday (CDC, 2009a, 2009b). Smoking some days is synonymous with occa-
23 sional smoking. One problem with occasional smoking is that it may be defined
24 using a number of different terms. When smoking is situational (e.g., with
25 friends), the term *social smoking* is often used (Gilpin, White, & Pierce, 2005;
26 Moran, Wechsler, & Rigotti, 2004), indicating that such smokers routinely smoke
27 when others are present rather than when they are alone. At other times, occa-
28 sional smoking is defined by the frequency of the behavior during the past month.
29 Occasional smoking has been defined as smoking every week but not every day
30 (Hines, Fretz, & Nollen, 1998), 1 day per week or less (Spencer, 1999), and

31 between 4 and 20 days in the past month (Turner, Veldhuis, & Mermelstein,
32 2005). Another problem with occasional (and social) smoking is that large por-
33 tions of these smokers have no intention of quitting, believe they have already
34 quit, or do not perceive themselves as smokers (Koontz et al., 2004; Morley, Hall,
35 Hausdorf, & Owen, 2006; Waters, Harris, Hall, Nazir, & Waigandt, 2006).
36 Other researchers have explored identity issues associated with smoking.
37 Collins, Maguire, and O'Dell (2002) pointed out that research has largely failed
38 to examine how smokers describe or categorize their smoking. . . . In a recent
39 study using focus groups, Walker, Ridner, and Hahn (2007) found a variety of
40 smoking definitions used by university students. Describing smoking status as
41 "ambiguously defined," these researchers noted that many self-labeled nonsmok-
42 ers discussed their smoking habits (e.g., they smoked when they were feeling
43 stressed, others were smoking, they were drinking); thus, these social or occa-
44 sional smokers saw themselves as nonsmokers.
45 Despite emerging evidence of discrepancies between smoking behavior
46 and smoking identities, researchers and health care providers tend to use estab-
47 lished category systems for smokers. These systems may fail to uncover actual
48 smoking behavior, which increases risks for individuals and decreases the effec-
49 tiveness of smoking prevention and cessation efforts. Thus, it is vital to explore
50 smoking identities, especially in college students who may not yet have become
51 regular, lifelong smokers. The purpose of this study was to examine smoking
52 identity and smoking behavior among college students. The specific aim was to
53 explore the relationship between smoking identity and number of days smoked
54 in the past month.
55
56 **Method**
57
58 The data were obtained during a campuswide health assessment at a large
59 southeastern university conducted during the Spring 2008 semester. . . . A ran-
60 dom sample of 4,000 full-time students 18 to 24 years of age was obtained from
61 the Registrar's Office. The 4,000 students received an email inviting them to
62 participate in the study. Participation was voluntary and anonymous. If they
63 agreed, a link embedded in the invitation directed participants to a secure
64 Internet server where they completed the online survey. . . . Three email remind-
65 ers were sent within 2 weeks of the invitation to participate. Participants complet-
66 ing the survey entered a lottery to win prizes ranging from $10 to a bicycle worth
67 $500. . . . The response rate was 18.5% ($N = 741$).
68
69 *Measures*
70
71 **Instrument.** The National College Health Assessment (NCHA) was the instrument
72 used for data collection (ACHA, 2005). The NCHA survey was developed and
73 piloted in 1998 for the purpose of assessing behaviors associated with the leading

74   causes of morbidity and mortality. . . . Construct validity and reliability were
75   demonstrated by comparing the survey to the National College Health Risk
76   Behavior Survey (CDC, 1997), the Harvard School of Public Health College Alcohol
77   Study (Wechsler, Lee, Kuo, & Lee, 1999), and the U.S. Department of Justice National
78   College Women Sexual Victimization Study (Fisher, Cullen, & Turner, 2000).
79
80   **Empirically Defined Smoking Status.** In addition to demographic information
81   (i.e., age, sex, ethnicity, employment), the NCHA collects data about smoking
82   status. An ordinal measure of smoking status was used. Participants respond to the
83   question "Within the last 30 days, on how many days did you use cigarettes?" The
84   eight ordinal responses available are *never used, have used but not in the last*
85   *30 days, 1–2 days, 3–5 days, 6–9 days, 10–19 days, 20–29 days,* and *all 30 days.*
86   In addition, a dichotomous form of the variable was constructed; where individu-
87   als who smoked 1 to 30 days were defined as a "current smoker" and individuals
88   who never smoked or did not smoke in the past 30 days were defined as "not a
89   current smoker" using the CDC (2008) classification. . . .
90
91   **Self-Described Smoking Identity.** In this study, the NCHA was modified to mea-
92   sure an individual's self-described smoking identity. . . . Participants responded to
93   the question "Which of the following best describes you?" Response choices
94   were *nonsmoker, smoker, occasional smoker,* and *social smoker.* No definitions
95   of the smoking behaviors associated with these terms were provided so that par-
96   ticipants could select the one that they saw as best representing their identity. . . .
97
98   *Analysis*
99
100   Initially a nonstratified descriptive analysis was performed of participant
101   demographics as well as individuals' self-described smoking identity and actual
102   smoking rate. Smoking rates were then stratified by gender, age, ethnicity, resi-
103   dence (e.g., lived with parents, lived on campus), hours worked per week, Greek
104   affiliation (i.e., membership in a social fraternity or sorority), and self-described
105   smoking identity. Differences in smoking rates among these groups were tested
106   for using traditional chi-square techniques. The relationship between an individ-
107   ual's self-described smoking identity and frequency of smoking was evaluated
108   graphically and by calculating the correlation between the two variables, thus
109   establishing whether there were four distinct self-described smoking identity cat-
110   egories. For example, whether individuals who self-described as a social or an
111   occasional smoker could be classified in one category was examined.
112
113   **Results** [*Note: Consult original for supporting statistics*]
114
115   [T]he sample was primarily female, on average 20 years of age, and pre-
116   dominantly White. A majority lived off-campus, worked less than 20 hours
117   per week, and were not affiliated with a Greek organization. Although 80.9%

118 of participants considered themselves as nonsmokers, 17.9% of the total
119 sample reported that they had smoked in the past 30 days (classified as cur-
120 rent smokers in the study). These results are consistent with national statistics
121 for these variables.
122   There were no differences in smoking rates between males and females,
123 individuals younger than 21 years of age and individuals older than 21 years of
124 age, Whites and non-Whites, individuals who lived off-campus and on-campus,
125 individuals who worked and did not work, and Greeks and non-Greeks.
126 However, there was a significant difference in smoking rate based on how indi-
127 viduals described themselves; not surprisingly, individuals who self-described as
128 nonsmokers had the lowest current smoking rate (4.6%), when compared to
129 individuals who self-described as smokers (97.5%).
130   There was a positive correlation between self-described smoking identity
131 (e.g., smoker, social smoker, occasional smoker, and nonsmoker) and the number
132 of days smoked in the past 30 days. That is, self-described smokers have the high-
133 est smoking frequency followed by social smokers, occasional smokers, and
134 nonsmokers. In addition, these data suggest that there may only be three distinct
135 classes of individuals, not four: (a) smokers, (b) social or occasional smokers, and
136 (c) nonsmokers. Smokers had higher smoking frequencies than social smokers,
137 occasional smokers, and nonsmokers. Although social smokers were not signifi-
138 cantly different from occasional smokers, they were significantly different from
139 nonsmokers. Furthermore, nonsmokers were significantly different from occa-
140 sional smokers. . . .
141
142 **Discussion**
143
144   Our data show that smoking identity and smoking behaviors remain a con-
145 cern in college-age students. Although a number of differences have been noted
146 between college students who smoke daily, occasionally, and not at all, little
147 research examines the smoker's identity (Hines et al., 1998; Kenford et al., 2005;
148 Moran et al., 2004; Ridner, 2005). Developing a better understanding of how
149 college smokers see themselves is essential as researchers develop prevention
150 and/or cessation activities targeting this group of smokers.
151   This study shows the importance of selecting appropriate language when
152 assessing smoking behaviors among the college-age group. Assessing current
153 smoking status (i.e., number of cigarettes or days smoked in the past 30 days) may
154 be appropriate to identify at-risk behaviors. However, health care providers rely-
155 ing solely on that measure may miss an opportunity to provide smoking preven-
156 tion interventions to a number of people who are "at risk" for adopting smoking
157 and who see themselves as nonsmokers. . . .
158   Campus health providers are encouraged to view smoking status as the "fifth
159 vital sign" and stamp patient encounter forms with a current, former, or never
160 smoker descriptor (Fiore et al., 1995). This strategy has been recommended
161 because it increases the number of smokers receiving cessation counseling from

162   providers. However, recent findings have led to calls for health centers on cam-
163   puses to use a more time-anchored (e.g., past 30 days) quantitative approach on
164   patient health forms (Levinson et al., 2007). The current study demonstrates
165   that when using that approach, college students who have not smoked in the past
166   30 days yet consider themselves smokers may be missed. Other widely accepted
167   recommendations include having clinicians ask "Do you smoke?" (Fiore et al.,
168   2000; Fiore et al., 2008). . . . Perhaps a better way to obtain the needed informa-
169   tion is to ask a series of questions: "Do you ever smoke cigarettes?" "Are you
170   considering starting smoking?" and "How many cigarettes have you smoked in
171   the last 30 days?"
172   Despite providers' best efforts, it is likely that a number of occasional or
173   social smokers will be classified as nonsmokers. That may be because they do not
174   see themselves as smokers, or as Morley and colleagues (2006) found, they think
175   they have already quit.
176   This study has a number of limitations. The data were collected as part of a
177   campus wide health assessment and the analysis was secondary. As a result, for
178   example, smoking frequency was collected on an ordinal scale and such mea-
179   sures as mean number of days in which an individual smoked could not be cal-
180   culated. Smoking identity and smoking behaviors are not static and thus these
181   measures will change over time. The cross-sectional nature of the data collected
182   does not allow for longitudinal investigations that may provide more information.
183   In addition, data were collected via self-reports and as a result rely on partici-
184   pants' truthfully answering survey items; when examining smoking status, the
185   reliability of answers may be threatened. Finally, the population sampled may be
186   a limitation. The sample was predominately educated Caucasian women from a
187   tobacco-producing state; therefore, generalizing results to other populations may
188   be difficult. In addition, a response rate of 18.5% limits the generalizability of our
189   results, although the response rate is consistent with similar studies using Internet-
190   based survey administration in college students.
191   _____

192   *Source:* Ridner, S. L., Walker, K. L., Hart, J. L., & Myers, J. A. (2010). Smoking identities and
193   behavior: Evidence of discrepancies, issues for measurement and intervention. *Western*
194   *Journal of Nursing Research, 32,* 434–446.

195   *Note:* Consult original for references. This article has been edited for length.

GANG-RELATED GUN VIOLENCE:
SOCIALIZATION, IDENTITY, AND SELF

Paul B. Stretesky and Mark R. Pogrebin

Journal of Contemporary Ethnography, 36, 85–113

1 This study considers how gangs promote violence and gun use. We argue that
2 socialization is important because it helps to shape a gang member's identity
3 and sense of self. Moreover, guns often help gang members project their violent
4 identities. . . .
5
6 **Gangs and Violence**
7
8   Research suggests that gang members are more likely than non-gang mem-
9 bers to engage in crime—especially violent crime (Gordon et al. 2004). . . . Do
10 gangs attract individuals who are predisposed to violence or do they create vio-
11 lent individuals? The debate in the literature about these explanations of gang
12 violence is rather extensive.
13   Thornberry et al. (1993) point out that there are three perspectives that
14 inform the debate concerning the relationship between gangs and violence. First,
15 the selection perspective argues that gang members are individuals who are
16 delinquent and violent prior to joining the gang. The second perspective is known
17 as the social facilitation perspective. This perspective argues that gang members
18 are no different from non-gang members until they enter the gang. Therefore, the
19 gang serves a normative function. . . .
20   The enhancement perspective is the third explanation for the relationship
21 between gangs and crime (Thornberry et al. 1993). The enhancement perspective
22 proposes that new gang members are recruited from a pool of individuals who
23 show propensity to engage in crime and violence, but their level of violence inten-
24 sifies once they enter the gang because the gang provides a structure that encour-
25 ages crime and violence (see also Decker and Van Winkle 1996). . . . [I]t still
26 leaves open the question about why gang members increase their violent behavior
27 after they join a gang. It is for that reason that we focus our research on the con-
28 cept of socialization as a mechanism that leads to gang-related gun violence.
29
30 **Gang Socialization**
31
32   Research on gang socialization—the process of learning the appropriate
33 values and norms of the gang culture to which one belongs—suggests that group

34 processes are highly important (Sirpal 1997, Vigil 1988, Miller and Brunson
35 2000). . . . Vigil (1988, 63) has found that gangs help to socialize "members to
36 internalize and adhere to alternative norms and modes of behavior and play a
37 significant role in helping . . . youth acquire a sense of importance, self-esteem,
38 and identity." One way to attain status is to develop a reputation for being violent
39 (Anderson 1999). . . .
40   The reasons individuals join gangs are diverse (Decker and Van Winkle
41 1996). According to Decker and Van Winkle (1996), the most important instru-
42 mental reason for joining a gang is protection. In addition to instrumental con-
43 cerns, a large portion of all gang members indicate that their gang fulfills a variety
44 of more typical adolescent needs—especially companionship and support, which
45 tend to be more expressive in nature. . . . Even though there is a good deal of
46 research examining the important relationship between violence and status
47 within the gang as it relates to socialization, little is known about the specific
48 ways that status impacts gang violence.
49   Socialization into the gang is bound up in issues of identity and self. Identity,
50 according to Stone (1962), is the perceived social location of the person. Image,
51 status, and a host of other factors that affect identity are mostly created by group
52 perceptions of who we are and how we define ourselves. . . .
53   Moore (1978, 60) has suggested that "the gang represents a means to what
54 is an expressive, rather than an instrumental, goal: the acting out of a male role
55 of competence and of 'being in command' of things." The findings of Decker and
56 Van Winkle (1996) and Moore suggest that although instrumental reasons for
57 joining a gang are important, once a member joins a gang they largely see the
58 gang as an important primary group that is central to their lives and heavily influ-
59 ences their identity and personality. . . . It is this expressive reason for remaining
60 in a gang that may help to explain gang crime and violence, especially as it
61 relates to socialization.
62   Guns also play an important role in many gangs and are often reported to be
63 owned for instrumental reasons (Decker and Van Winkle 1996). Gang members
64 who perceive a threat from rival gangs are believed to carry guns to protect them-
65 selves and their neighborhoods (Decker and Van Winkle 1996; Horowitz 1983;
66 Lizotte et al. 1994; Wright and Rossi 1986). . . . However, the reason that gang
67 members carry guns is still unclear. . . . Given the importance of guns to a gang
68 member's identity, it is interesting to note that little research exists that examines
69 the relationship between guns and gangs in terms of identity formation.
70
71 **Methods**
72
73   The interviews in this study of twenty-two gang members were taken from a
74 larger qualitative study of seventy-five Colorado prison inmates who used a fire-
75 arm in the commission of their most recent offense. Inmates were asked general
76 questions about their families, schools, peer groups, neighborhoods, prior contact

77   with the criminal justice system, and experiences with firearms. They were also
78   asked a series of questions surrounding the circumstances that led up to the
79   crime for which they were currently incarcerated. It was from this vantage point
80   that we began to see the importance of gang socialization, self, and identity as
81   important aspects of violence and gun use.
82   Inmates we interviewed were located in eleven different correctional facili-
83   ties scattered throughout Colorado and were randomly selected by means of a
84   simple random sample from a list of all inmates incarcerated for a violent crime
85   in which a firearm was involved. . . .
86   During the interview process, we made every effort to ensure that inmates
87   understood that our conversations were both voluntary and confidential. We told
88   each inmate that only we would be able to identify their answers and that any
89   information they provided to us would be used only for research-related pur-
90   poses. Moreover, we informed inmates that if they were uncomfortable with any
91   of the topics of discussion, they could simply tell us that they felt uncomfortable
92   and we would proceed to other topics of interest. . . . Again, we are confident in
93   the validity of our data because inmates often gave answers that closely matched
94   available information recorded in their official inmate files.
95   All interviews were conducted in the prison in private conference rooms,
96   vacant staff offices, and empty visitation rooms. Each interview was tape-
97   recorded with the subjects' consent and lasted between 60 and 120 minutes. A
98   semistructured format was used that relied on sequential probes to pursue leads
99   provided by the inmates. This technique allowed subjects to identify and elabo-
100   rate important domains they perceived to characterize their life histories.
101   Generally, these included their gang experience, engagement in violent encoun-
102   ters throughout their life, and their involvement with a firearm in those situations.
103   The interview tapes were transcribed for qualitative data analysis, which
104   involves scanning and identifying general statements about relationships among
105   categories of observations. We looked for explanations concerning gang mem-
106   bers' perceptions about how they learned to become gang members and their
107   perceptions of the importance of guns in that process. Thus, we used an inductive-
108   methods approach where the inmates' responses directed our empirical general-
109   izations and conclusions. . . .
110   It is important to point out that although we would have preferred to conduct
111   and establish a long-term relationship with our subjects and observe their behavior
112   as they went about their daily lives, such an approach is, unfortunately, highly
113   unrealistic in the case of the most violent gang members. . . . Given the fact that
114   intensive interviews are often part of participant observation, we argue that they
115   are sufficient to draw conclusions regarding gang socialization and the creation
116   of a gang identity among the gang members in our sample—those who find
117   themselves incarcerated for violent crimes.
118   One potential methodological issue that could be interpreted as cause for
119   concern has to do with the generalizability of our sample. The gang members we

120 talked with were probably more highly integrated into their gang than the typical
121 gang member. We believe this because our subjects were incarcerated for gang-
122 related violence, which we interpreted as a sign of high commitment to their
123 group. Thus, we should expect that our subjects' gang experiences are quite dif-
124 ferent from gang members in general who have not displayed similar levels of
125 violence. Such selection bias might be problematic if the purpose of the study is
126 to generalize our findings to all gang members. The purpose of this research,
127 however, is more modest in nature. We are interested in the experiences of vio-
128 lent gang members in our sample precisely because they are likely to be the most
129 committed to the gang and because that commitment is likely to be translated
130 into gang-related gun violence.
131
132 **Findings**
133
134   *Gang Socialization, Self, and Identity*
135
136   Goffman (1959) argues that as individuals we are often "taken in by our own
137 act" and therefore begin to feel like the person we are portraying. . . . Related to
138 the current study, the socialization process of becoming a gang member required
139 a change in the subject's self-perception. That is, who did our gang members
140 become as compared with who they once were? . . . Most inmates we inter-
141 viewed appeared to indicate that their socialization into the gang began at a
142 relatively young age:
143
144   At about fifteen, I started getting affiliated with the Crips. I knew all these guys,
145   grew up with them and they were there. . . . I mean, it was like an influence at
146   that age. I met this dude named Benzo from Los Angeles at that time. He was a
147   Crip and he showed me a big wad of money. He said, "Hey man, you want some
148   of this?" "Like yeh! G****mn straight. You know I want some of that." He
149   showed me how to sell crack, and so at fifteen, I went from being scared of the
150   police and respecting them to hustling and selling crack. Now I'm affiliated with
151   the Crips; I mean it was just unbelievable.
152
153   Another inmate tells of his orientation in becoming a member of a gang:
154
155   I started gang banging when I was ten. I got into a gang when I was thirteen.
156   I started just hanging around them, just basically idolizing them. I was basically
157   looking for a role model for my generation and ethnic background; the main
158   focus for us is the popularity that they got. That's who the kids looked up to. They
159   had status, better clothes, better lifestyle.
160
161   Violent behavior appeared to play an important role in this transformation of
162 identity and self. Most gang members noted that they engaged in violent behavior
163 more frequently once they joined the gang.

164   At an early age, it was encouraged that I showed my loyalty and do a drive
165   by . . . anybody they (gangster disciples) deemed to be a rival of the gang. I was
166   going on fourteen. At first, I was scared to and then they sent me out with one
167   person and I seen him do it. I saw him shoot the guy. . . . So, in the middle of a
168   gang fight I get pulled aside and get handed a pistol and he said, "It's your turn
169   to prove yourself." So I turned around and shot and hit one of the guys (rival gang
170   members). After that, it just got more easier.
171
172   A further illustration of situated identity and transformation of self is related
173   by another inmate, who expresses the person he became through the use of
174   violence and gun possession. Retrospectively, he indicates disbelief in what he
175   had become.
176
177   As a gang banger, you have no remorse, so basically, they're natural-born killers.
178   They are killers from the start. When I first shot my gun for the first time at some-
179   body, I felt bad. It was like, I can't believe I did this. But I looked at my friend
180   and he didn't care at all. Most gang bangers can't have a conscience. You can't
181   have remorse. You can't have any values.
182
183   The situations [they find] themselves in, in this case collective gang violence,
184   together with becoming a person who is willing to use violence to maintain
185   membership in the gang, is indicative of a transformed identity. . . .
186
187   *Commitment to the Gang*
188
189   . . . Commitment to the gang also serves individual needs for its members.
190   We found that gang identification and loyalty to the group was a high priority for
191   our subjects. This loyalty to the gang was extreme. Our subjects reported that they
192   were willing to risk being killed and were committed to taking the life of a rival
193   gang member if the situation called for such action.
194
195   What I might do for my friends [gang peers] you might not do. You've got people
196   out their taking bullets for their friends and killing people. But I'm sure not one
197   of you would be willing to go to that extreme.
198
199   Another inmate tells us about his high degree of identity for his gang:
200
201   If you're not a gang member, you're not on my level . . . most of my life revolves
202   around gangs and gang violence. I don't know anything else but gang violence.
203   I was born into it, so it's my life.
204
205   The notion of the gang as the most important primary group in a member's
206   life was consistently expressed by our study subjects. Our subjects often stated
207   that they were willing to kill or be killed for the gang in order to sustain their
208   self-perception as a loyal gang member. This extreme degree of group affiliation

209   is similar to that of armed services activities during wartime. . . . The following
210   gang member points to the important role his gang played for him in providing
211   physical safety as well as an assurance of understanding.
212
213   That's how it is in the hood, selling dope, gang bangin', everybody wants a piece
214   of you. All the rival gang members, all the cops, everybody. The only ones on
215   your side are the gang members you hang with.
216
217   For this particular member, his gang peers are the only people he perceives
218   will aid him from threatening others. The world appears full of conflicting situa-
219   tions, and although his gang affiliation is largely responsible for all the groups that
220   are out to harm him in some way, he nevertheless believes his fellow gang mem-
221   bers are the only persons on whom he can depend. . . .
222
223   *Masculinity, Reputation, and Respect*
224
225   For those gang members we interviewed, socialization into the gang and
226   commitment to the gang appear to be central to the notion of masculinity. . . .
227
228   **Masculinity.** "Every man [in a gang] is treated as a man until proven different. We
229   see you as a man before anything." This comment by a gang member infers that
230   masculinity is a highly valued attribute in his gang. The idea of manhood and its
231   personal meanings for each interviewed prisoner was a subject consistently
232   repeated by all participants. It usually was brought up in the context of physical
233   violence. . . .
234
235   Even if you weren't in one [gang], you got people that are going to push the issue.
236   We decide what we want to do; I ain't no punk, I ain't no busta. But it comes
237   down to pride. It's foolish pride, but a man is going to be a man, and a boy knows
238   he's going to come into his manhood by standing his ground.
239
240   Establishing a reputation coincides with becoming a man, entering the realm
241   of violence, being a stand-up guy who is willing to prove his courage as a true
242   gang member. . . . After eight years in the gang, the following participant was
243   owed money for selling someone dope. After a few weeks of being put off by the
244   debtor, he had to take some action to appease his gang peers who were pressur-
245   ing him to retaliate.
246
247   I joined the gang when I was eleven years old. So now that I'm in the gang for
248   eight years, people are asking, "What are you going to do? You got to make a
249   name for yourself." So we went over there [victim's residence] and they were all
250   standing outside and I just shot him.
251
252   A sense of bravado, when displayed, played a utilitarian role in conflicting
253   situations where a gang member attempts to get others to comply with his

254 demands by instilling fear instead of actually utilizing violent means. . . . Again,
255 the importance of firearms in this situation is critical.
256
257   The intimidation factor with a gun is amazing. Everybody knows what a gun can
258   do. If you have a certain type of personality, that only increases their fear of you.
259   When it came to certain individuals who I felt were a threat, I would lift my shirt
260   up so they would know I had one on me.
261
262   The image of toughness fits well under masculinity and bravado as an attri-
263 bute positively perceived by gang members we interviewed. Its importance lies
264 in projecting an image via reputation that conveys a definition of who the collec-
265 tive group is and what physical force they are willing to use when necessary.
266
267   Everybody wants to fight for the power, for the next man to fear him. It's all about
268   actually killing the mother f***ers and how many mother f***ers you can kill.
269   Drive-by shootings is old school. . . .
270
271 **Reputation.** On a collective group level, developing and maintaining the gang's
272 reputation of being a dangerous group to deal with, especially from other groups
273 or individuals who posed a threat to their drug operations, was important. . . . Guns
274 often played an important role in the development and maintenance of reputa-
275 tion, though they were rarely utilized in conflicting situations:
276
277   We had guns to fend off jackers, but we never had to use them, 'cause people
278   knew we were straps. People knew our clique, they are not going to be stupid.
279   We've gotten into a few arguments, but it never came to a gun battle. Even when
280   we were gang bangin,' we didn't use guns, we only fought off the Bloods.
281
282 **Respect.** According to the gang members we talked to, disrespect, or rejection of
283 self-professed identity claims by others, often was the cause of violence. The fol-
284 lowing inmate relates his view on this subject in general terms.
285
286   Violence starts to escalate once you start to disrespect me. Once you start to
287   second guess my manhood, I'll f*** you up. You start coming at me with threats,
288   then I feel offended. Once I feel offended, I react violently. That's how I was
289   taught to react.
290
291   When being confronted by gang rivals who have been perceived as insulting
292 an opposing gang member, the definition of street norms calls for an exaggerated
293 response. That is, the disrespectful words must be countered with serious physical
294 force to justify the disrespected individual's maintenance of self (or manhood).
295
296   So, as we were fighting, they started saying that this was their neighborhood and
297   started throwing their gang signs. To me, to let somebody do that to me is disre-
298   spect. So I told them where I was from.

299   The notion of disrespect is analogous to an attack on the self. Because many
300   of the inmates in our sample reported that masculinity is an important attribute
301   of the self, they believed any disrespect was a direct threat to their masculinity.
302   For those brought up in impoverished high-crime communities, as these study
303   population participants were, there are limited alternatives to such conflicting
304   situations (Anderson 1999). . . .
305
306   *Gangs and Guns*
307
308   Our analysis of the interview data dichotomized those gun-using encounters
309   as expressions of either power or protection, based on each participant's per-
310   ceived definition of the situation. Carrying a firearm elicits various feelings of
311   power: "When I have a gun, I feel like I'm on top of it, like I'm Superman or
312   something. You got to let them know." The actual use of a firearm is described in
313   a situation that most lethally expressed the power of guns in an attempt to injure
314   those belonging to rival gangs.
315
316   When I was younger, we used to do drive-bys. It didn't matter who you were. We
317   didn't go after a specific person. We went after a specific group. Whoever is
318   standing at a particular house or wherever you may be, and you're grouped up
319   and have the wrong color on; just because you were in a rival gang. You didn't
320   have to do anything to us to come get you, it was a spontaneous reaction.
321
322   Our findings showed that in the vast majority of gang member–related shoot-
323   ings, most of these violent gun-using situations involved individuals as opposed
324   to large numbers of gangs confronting each other with firearms. Yet, we were told
325   that in gang representation, either on an individual basis or in a small group,
326   whether it be in a protective or retaliatory mode, gang members needed to dis-
327   play a power position to those confronting them to maintain their reputations,
328   and guns were important in that respect.
329   The issues surrounding gun possession often have to do with interpersonal
330   conflict as opposed to collective gang situations. The fear of being physically
331   harmed within their residential environment, coupled with the relative ease in
332   which a person can attain a firearm, has resulted in a proliferation of weapons in
333   the community. . . .
334   Individually or collectively, rival gang members constantly pose a physi-
335   cal threat according to the next inmate. He also discusses the need for protec-
336   tion and how drug sales caused him to be a target for those who would try
337   and rob him.
338
339   I carried a gun because I knew what I was doing, especially since I was in a gang.
340   Other gangs are gonna try and come after us. So I used it [the gun] against those
341   gangs and to make sure that my investments in the drugs was protected. I don't
342   want nobody to take money from me.

343   For our prisoner/gang member study population, the descriptive attributes
344   they related all played an important role in shaping their individual gang identity.
345

346   **Discussion and Conclusion**
347

348   Gangs not only fulfill specific needs for individuals that other groups in dis-
349   advantaged neighborhoods may fail to provide, but as our interviews suggest,
350   they are also important primary groups into which individuals become social-
351   ized. It is not surprising, then, that self-concept and identity are closely tied to
352   gang membership. Guns are also important in this regard. We propose that for the
353   gang members in our sample, gang-related gun violence can be understood in
354   terms of self and identity that are created through the process of socialization and
355   are heavily rooted in notions of masculinity. . . . We believe that the conse-
356   quences of our findings regarding gang violence and guns are important for
357   public policy for three reasons.
358   First, because our sample only consisted of those gang members who com-
359   mitted the most severe forms of violence (i.e., they were incarcerated for rela-
360   tively long periods of time for their gun-related violence), there may be some
361   interest in targeting individuals like the ones in our sample early in their criminal
362   careers to "diminish the pool of chronic gang offenders."
363   Second, our research suggests that policies aimed at reducing gang violence
364   should take gang socialization into account. Simply reducing gun availability
365   through law enforcement crackdowns on violent gang members is probably not
366   sufficient (see Piehl, Kennedy, Braga 2000). . . .
367   Third, it is not clear from our research whether simply eliminating or reduc-
368   ing access to guns can reduce gun-related gang violence. . . . [O]ur interviews
369   suggest that there is little reason to believe that gang members would be any less
370   likely to look to gangs as a source of status and protection and may use other
371   weapons—though arguably less lethal than guns—to aid in transformations of
372   identity and preserve a sense of self. Thus, although reduction strategies may
373   prevent gang-related violence in the short-term, there is little evidence that this
374   intervention strategy will have long-term effects because it does not adequately
375   deal with gang culture and processes of gang socialization.
376

---

377   *Source:* Stretesky, P. B., & Pogrebin, M. R. (2007). Gang-related gun violence: Socialization,
378   identity, and self. *Journal of Contemporary Ethnography, 36,* 85–113.
379   *Note:* Consult original for references. This article has been edited for length.

INDEX

ABOUT THE AUTHOR

Donileen R. Loseke is a professor and graduate director in the Department of Sociology at the University of South Florida. She received her BA and MA in psychology (California State University, Dominguez Hills) and her PhD in sociology (University of California, Santa Barbara). Her books include *The Battered Woman and Shelters,* which won the Charles Horton Cooley Award from the Society for the Study of Symbolic Interaction, and *Thinking About Social Problems.* She also is the editor of *Current Controversies on Family Violence* (with Richard Gelles) and *Social Problems: Constructionist Readings* (with Joel Best). Numerous journal articles and book chapters report the findings of her empirical research projects, which have been on a variety of topics (including evaluation research, social problems, criminal justice, social service provision, occupations, emotion, identity, and narrative) and have used a variety of data generation techniques (including field experiment, written survey, in-depth interview, ethnography, and document analysis). She has been the editor of the *Journal of Contemporary Ethnography* and an advisory editor for *Social Problems.* Currently she is an editorial board member of *Social Psychology Quarterly,* an advisory editor for *The Sociological Quarterly,* and an associate editor of *Symbolic Interaction* and *Journal of Contemporary Ethnography.*

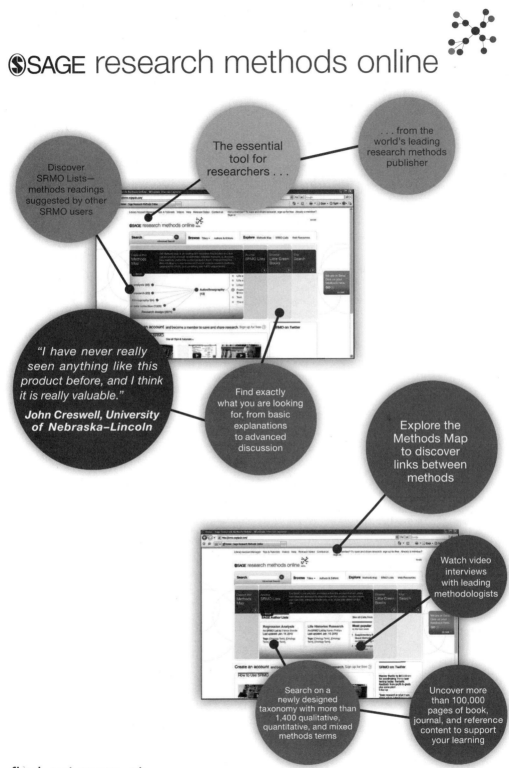

⑤SAGE research methods online

The essential tool for researchers . . .

. . . from the world's leading research methods publisher

Discover SRMO Lists— methods readings suggested by other SRMO users

"I have never really seen anything like this product before, and I think it is really valuable."

John Creswell, University of Nebraska–Lincoln

Find exactly what you are looking for, from basic explanations to advanced discussion

Explore the Methods Map to discover links between methods

Watch video interviews with leading methodologists

Search on a newly designed taxonomy with more than 1,400 qualitative, quantitative, and mixed methods terms

Uncover more than 100,000 pages of book, journal, and reference content to support your learning

find out more at
www.srmo.sagepub.com